The Great British Railway Station
KING'S CROSS

King's Cross was not particularly pretty in places, but it was the spiritual home of some of the finest locomotives ever seen in Britain. Sir Nigel Gresley was responsible for many of them and 60007 carried his name. The A4 is at Platform 4 on 29 June 1961 waiting to leave with the 5.35pm to Newcastle. Photograph L Nicolson, transporttreasury.co.uk

Paul Anderson

IRWELL PRESS

Copyright IRWELL PRESS LIMITED

ISBN 978-1-911262-01-5

Dedication
by Paul Anderson

Although I dedicated my first book to my father in 1973 I would like to do the same with this one as it was he who first took me to the end of Platform 10 in 1958 and introduced me to the wonderful world that was Kings Cross.

First published in the United Kingdom in 1990
This enlarged and expanded edition 2016 published
by Irwell Press Limited, 59A, High Street, Clophill,
Bedfordshire MK45 4BE
Printed by Ackcent Media, UK

CONTENTS

Acknowledgements

The Railway Correspondence and Travel Society *Locomotives of the LNER* 'Green Guides' were, as usual, an invaluable source of information on locomotives and their exploits. Paul Anderson would like to thank Frank King for his valuable contributions concerning shed allocations of both steam and diesel locomotives. Thanks also to Paul Roberts for numerous items of background information, Mike Webster for details of buses and trams and Pip Bloor for King's Cross shed allocations. Brian Bailey provided much useful advice, as too did Dave Rollins.

Note. Irwell Press first published *Great British Railway Station King's Cross* in 1990, before 'the biggest urban renewal project in Western Europe' got under way and 'The Cross' metamorphosed into the restored and enhanced modern wonder of today. The seediness, the littered grimy streets and 'Norf London' working class air has utterly vanished which is in a way a shame but the old place has gained, well, take a look round Cubitt's stolid building, once mirrored but now conjoined by the Gothic pile across the road and judge for yourself what it might have gained.

That 'biggest urban renewal project in Western Europe' back in 1990 I and many others saw as a dire threat, with proposals to demolish the Great Northern Hotel and other outlandish mortifications but in the end it has all gone rather well and the stations, King's Cross and St Pancras are happily safe as long as there is a London – remember, for many years both lived under the threat of annihilation. Their fate could so easily have been that of Euston, just up the road.

I wrote the book as a sort of lament for the Kings Cross and the 'Caley' (the Caledonian Road) of my parents' lives and my early childhood and in the 1980s the place had changed little from the 1930s; I remember shrapnel holes from German bombs but these had somehow disappeared by the 1970s. Then they cleaned the buildings(!) and it was change all the way. There is now barely even a whiff of the tuber and its times, the steam lorries, coal dust and barking steam locomotives but instead a modern shimmering magnificence attracts praise from every corner. Who (certainly not me) could possibly have thought that one day the dear old Cross *would attract tourists?* It would have been laughable.

The book has long been out of print and we are constantly asked about it. Now Paul Anderson has nobly taken up the task of updating and expanding it, though the 'body' text of each chapter remains much as the original. He is one of the best writers on railway matters that I know of and I cannot imagine 'my' book being in better hands.
Chris Hawkins, 2016

Although the aspect of King's Cross most seen by the public is simple and symmetrical, stern even, it is unmistakable and now applauded. It should be remembered that like most early termini the offices and facilities were alongside the departure platform rather than across the head of the tracks, so the façade is just a way of finishing off the twin train sheds. The huge semi-circular openings and projecting buttresses break up what is basically a screen wall, but the Italianate clock tower makes the station distinctive, despite its shortcomings. As a consequence of road alterations made in connection with the building of St Pancras, an open space was created in front of King's Cross and this became occupied by all manner of makeshift buildings, often bemoaned and generally known as the 'native village'. It could be said that this squalor was fitting, as the area was hardly salubrious before the Great Northern arrived. Goods Manager J Medcalf summed up the situation as follows: 'The Great Northern had got hold of the waste, howling wilderness for their London terminus and soon a clean sweep in a very complete sense was made and the plain straightforward solid brickwork of the station arose to dominate King's Cross'. The place was a meeting of several roads by 1850, coming together just to the east of the station where Maiden Lane, later York Road and now York Way, became John Street and met Grays Inn Road at a crude 'circus'. The obelisk here was used as a datum reference for driving the Great Northern tunnels. King's Cross remained a poor district and during the 1930s families still lived in verminous single rooms in the surrounding streets and malnourished urchins, frequently bare-footed, abounded in the footways and courtyards. After the Second World War the area remained far from well-off, but neither the neighbourhood nor 'native village' are apparent in this atmospheric view. Floodlights show off the frontage as never before, the well-lit concourse looks inviting and an oil lamp is hooked jauntily round the timber frame in the foreground, presumably there for some minor road works. For those seeking even brighter lights there is a poster for 4s 6d evening excursions to Southend Illuminations from Liverpool Street on Saturdays, Sundays and Thursdays and Fenchurch Street on Saturdays and Thursdays. There is also a poster for the London Hippodrome announcing that Jack Hylton is presenting Arthur Askey, Sally Ann Howes and Noele Gordon in 'Bet Your Life'. This production and the dates of the Southend excursions reveal the year to be 1952.

1. A Howling Waste

Judged by many the greatest of London's stations, King's Cross has been perhaps the most enduring of the great termini. This despite a mean clutter of buildings jumbled unthinkingly at its feet, two World Wars and successive attempts at reconstruction. All this has now culminated in a wondrous transition, a successful fusion of new with the old and much to be welcomed – for decades after the War until the 1990s all manner of schemes threatened to wreck this gem-like corner of London for ever. King's Cross then and even more so

now, might possibly be the best known station in Britain. Of all our country's great stations it is possibly the most likely to spring to the lips even of the uninitiated. Of the four Monopoly stations it is the first to be recalled and King's Cross is possibly alone (though Euston might press it close here) in the public mind as firstly a railway station and only secondly a district. Its austere façade (it is difficult to be wholly original in describing King's Cross, but that is the term which leaps immediately to mind, amongst a variety of observers)

is the perfect foil to the dreaming Gothic of St Pancras. And herein lies some hope for the verdict our descendants may give upon some less admirable post-war contrasts; the shock tends to lessen over the generations. Both buildings were denigrated over periods but are now artistically unassailable.

An obscure district, King's Cross had already been made unlovely by the sprawling effects of industry and urbanisation, even as the 1850s dawned. The Imperial Gas Works was already open and dismal courts huddled close

Platform Perceptions

The usual smoke haze hangs above the two engines on pilot duties, probably N2s, which have brought in empty stock for the expresses loading at Platforms 7 and 8. That on the right at 8 has King's Cross-Edinburgh carriage boards. It is obviously holiday time judging by the number of suitcases and other luggage, while a fair amount of light clothing points to the summer season. Having said that, a coat, tie and trilby or flat cap were still obligatory for many men, summer holidays or not! The transition from carmine and cream to lined maroon coaches suggests 1956-58. A trolley with a tea urn a short distance along the platform is no doubt doing reasonable business but there are only a couple of porters in evidence. It seems likely that most people were quite happy to carry their own cases on this festive occasion. There are also plenty of people waiting on Platform 10 to the right, this being the original departure platform and the only one for a few years. Until renumbering during the 1970s there never was a Platform 9, a hint of the confusing arrangements which grew up piecemeal over a long period as traffic increased. At one time this view would have revealed a series of carriage sidings, each of them numbered, but in 1926 a very narrow island accommodating Platforms 7 and 8 was constructed. With crowds like this it was a dangerous place, so during 1938 No.9 carriage road was abolished so that the island could be widened in the form visible here.

The entrance to King's Cross Platform 10 during the early 1950s, although the precise date of the photograph is unknown. On the extreme right there are some Gresley coaches in 'blood and custard' while flags and shields adorn the footbridge and roof girders, obviously for a special event or occasion. This platform provided the gateway to far off places for many travellers, but it was also a special place for enthusiasts as the far end of it was the best place to watch the comings and goings, both main line and suburban. As can be seen, there is no engine release road for No.10, so when a train was nearing departure time it was often the case that an N2 would be simmering at the inner end and an A4 building up steam out in the open.

about. An obelisk marked the centre of an important conjunction of roads, the original 'King's Cross' and the Regents Canal lay close by. So, the parishes of St Pancras and St Mary Islington were areas of contrast, the first ugly stirrings of industry amidst fields already plundered for brick workings. Kilns dotted the place and housing was growing up on the roads leading into the open country of Hornsey and the wilderness beyond. A plan exists at the Public Record Office, signed by Joseph Cubitt (son of Sir William Cubitt, knighted in 1851) labelled 'GNR King's Cross Passenger station and line extending to junction with main line at Copenhagen Tunnel 1852'. It shows crowded courts on the station site, the Fever Hospital (originally established safely beyond the outskirts of the capital, now uncomfortably close) and the Great Northern main line. In the middle of brickfields, this is pencilled on Cubitt's plan as 'already open'. The site of King's Cross yard and depot and later, 'Top Shed' were similarly dismal fields. The final link, delving under the Regents Canal, with all its complications, is shown making a junction with the existing line a few yards from the southern portal of Copenhagen Tunnel (scene long after of *The Ladykillers*) and a little east of the tile and brick making village of Belle Isle. The deviation limits of the approved route ran close to the margins of the village; it lay on the east side of Maiden Lane (later to form York Road then York Way) and the line at first crossed this thoroughfare, to land awkwardly in the middle of damp and open brick fields. It is nice to imagine that these inauspicious beginnings were owed in some small part to the Directors' desire to benefit from the Great Exhibition traffic of 1851; business would flow from this (and, with luck, honours and emoluments for the Directors) and the Engineer was whipped ever on through 1849 and 1850. The *London Temporary Passenger Station* opened amidst the Belle Isle brickfields on August 7th 1850, a few days late; on 6th June 1850 a Report had been received from Joseph Cubitt the Engineer ... *upon the apprehended delay in opening the line London-Peterborough till*

Top right. The Suburban Station could be found just beyond Platform 10 but it was a very different world to the main part of King's Cross. Platforms 11-13 had an overall roof and a proper concourse, both of which are seen here during LNER days. It is 1934, confirmation being a poster for the 'Scarborough Flier' announcing the summer departure time of 11.50am and a journey time of 4 hours 10 minutes, which applied during that year. Most available surfaces are occupied by advertisements, timetables and other information. The LNER has large posters for 'Summer Penny a Mile Return Tickets' and 'Night Travel Tickets to the North of England at Half Fares' while Bovril Sandwiches, Whitbread's Bottled Beers and inevitably Stephens Ink and Mazawattee Tea are recommended. Events at the Empire Stadium Wembley and Alexandra Palace are announced while 'Heat Lightning' and 'Cupid on the Beach' feature at the Euston Cinema. The W H Smith bookstall is selling Spanish, French, Russian and German phrase books. There is obviously a Refreshment Room in this part of the terminus, but travellers are also advised that the Restaurant and Grill Room on platform 10 does Breakfast from 6.30am, Table D' Hote and A la Carte Luncheons as well as Suppers until 10pm. The scene is completed in the lower right corner by a chocolate machine and one of those wonderful contraptions where we'd use a pointer to spell out their name and punch it on a metal strip. This part of the once sprawling Suburban Station still exists and though it is now devoid of clutter and a lot more accessible, there is still a separate feel to the place.

When the Metropolitan Railway opened between Paddington and Farringdon Street on 10 January 1863, subterranean single track connections were put in from the Great Northern. The Up line was on the York Road side of the terminus and known as the East Branch while the Down line on the west side was called the Hotel Curve as it almost passed beneath a corner of the Great Northern Hotel. A service known as the 'Suburban & City' from stations in growing residential areas to Farringdon commenced on 1 October 1863. This was extended to Moorgate Street and through Snow Hill Tunnel to the London Chatham & Dover Railway on 1 January 1866. Before long the Metropolitan tracks were unable to cope with the volume of traffic so the Metropolitan City Widened Lines were completed between King's Cross and Moorgate on 17 February 1868. At first, trains from the City calling at King's Cross had to reverse into the main station, but a platform opened at the top of the Hotel Curve gradient on 1 February 1878. By 1893 no less than 98 passenger trains and around 75 goods workings came up from the Widened Lines to the GN every weekday. Eventually trams, buses, trolleybuses and tubes became alternatives, although plenty of journeys were still being made on 'The Drain' sixty years later. On 26 March 1959 N2 69535 draws into the Widened Lines platform at King's Cross with the 2.54pm from Moorgate to Hatfield. Having just lifted its eight coaches up the notorious 1 in 43 gradient, the loco has dragged plenty of smoke out of Hotel Curve tunnel treating passengers standing on timber planking to that distinctive aroma and masking the dreaming spires of St Pancras. To the left, passengers make their way along the island platform built in 1924 on the site of the engine yard. Despite the rising pall behind the smoke was rarely all that bad in the cab of an N1 or N2. The tanks worked chimney first; the main problem with being bunker first uphill was the water level. By contrast, Hornsey men always had their J50 0-6-0Ts bunker first because of smoke, but they had inferior coal to deal with! There were two sets of runaway trap points here that discouraged any backing down. Photograph Brian Stephenson.

The East Branch to the Metropolitan Railway originally left the main line just south of Gasworks Tunnel then veered eastwards to enter a cut and cover tunnel under York Road. Having briefly broken the surface between a varnish works and some terraced houses, the line then joined the Metropolitan near that company's King's Cross station. The East Branch also opened for passenger services to Farringdon Street on 1 October 1863 and during 1866 a platform was provided near York Road. Construction of the second Gasworks Tunnel to the east of the first meant that the East Branch had to be realigned and a new station built. This is the one seen in this photograph and it probably came into use on 4 March 1878 at the same time as the new tunnel. The portal of this can just be made out behind the cab of the J50 to the left of this view. Although the number of this 0-6-0T cannot be made out, its contribution to the general smoke haze is quite clear. Help in this respect is being provided by L1 67749 shunting a six-wheel parcels coach. Another L1 can be seen in the distant North Spur to the right of the signal box steps. A London Transport RT is making its way along York Road beyond the gap in the station roof. This photograph was taken in 1960 and steam had not long to go at King's Cross. Diesel multiple units and diesel-hauled suburban trains were working to Moorgate by this time. Services were withdrawn on 5 November 1976, Hotel Curve and York Road platforms closing at the same time. Photograph A H Lucas, transporttreasury.co.uk

Moods

A3 60064 TAGALIE leaves Platform 8 with the 3.50pm to Leeds and York on 11 August 1953. This was a Doncaster engine at the time, but it went new to the Scottish Area as A1 2563 WILLIAM WHITELAW in August 1924 and spent the next quarter of a century based at Haymarket, Aberdeen, Eastfield, St Margarets, Dundee then Haymarket again. It was no stranger to King's Cross as Haymarket used it on the non-stop Flying Scotsman from May 1928. Strong Union pressure resulted in four right-hand drive A3s being exchanged for four left-hand drive engines from the Eastern Region and this one moved south during July 1950. 60064 was withdrawn from Grantham in September 1961. Photograph Brian Bailey.

In the depths of winter, when commuting was done almost entirely in the dark, L1 67745 waits at Platform 6 with the 6.25pm for Baldock on 11 January 1952. These tanks were also used on trains to Cambridge and Huntingdon. From September 1960 67745 had just over a year at King's Cross, then the same at Colwick before withdrawal in December 1962. Photograph Brian Morrison.

King's Cross Top Shed maintained its Pacifics in immaculate condition, in most cases almost to the very end of steam at the London end of the GN main line in summer 1963. With the sound of its chime whistle echoing round the terminus and a perfect white exhaust, A4 60032 GANNET leaves Platform 7 with the non-stop 'Elizabethan' to Edinburgh Waverley on a beautiful summer morning in the late 1950s. The engine had been at King's Cross since June 1950 and stayed until the shed closed exactly thirteen years later.

Above. The Elizabethan brought Haymarket A4s to King's Cross, on this occasion 60011 EMPIRE OF INDIA. When it was completed at Doncaster Works as 4490 in June 1937, this engine was actually allocated to King's Cross for the new Coronation streamlined service, but was transferred to Edinburgh in March 1938 and stayed there until June 1962. Like Top Shed, Haymarket turned out its first rank Pacifics with a gleaming finish. The departure is in glorious sunshine, which highlights the pile of coal carefully packed in the tender for the 393 miles of firing ahead.

Left. Then came the rain. The driver of A4 60029 WOODCOCK is in thoughtful mood as he waits for time with a York express on 3 April 1961. In their macs, nothing is going to stop the platform enders venturing into the open by the loco. Apart from a mere nine months further north, WOODCOCK was a King's Cross loco from when it was completed in summer 1937 to the closure of Top Shed 26 years later. Photograph David Knapman.

10

A3 60109 HERMIT, in this case with both a Kylchap blast pipe and 'blinkers', is ready to back out of Platform 7 on 3 April 1961. There are puddles galore and plenty of reflections to contemplate during the wait for the road to Top Shed where HERMIT had been based since spring 1959. Photograph David Knapman.

Forget the rain! Mam and Dad have succumbed and brought the offspring down the platform to see the engines. Beyond HERMIT, lurking under the train shed in Platform 5 is 60110 ROBERT THE DEVIL which had been a King's Cross resident since June 1957. Photograph David Knapman.

Clutter Corner

Famous expresses for the North and Scotland departed from Platform 10, yet this elevated status did not prevent it collecting all manner of official paraphernalia which made it look far from smart, unlike the trains. This view was taken on 15 July 1942 at the height of the war, but that was no excuse for the outbreak of signs, most of which are pointing to places elsewhere. People do need directions and information, but three large signs for the Tea Room within feet of each other seems somewhat excessive. Having arrived at this particular place of refreshment, the potential customer is reminded of two other outlets for food and drink further down the platform. The wartime signs are of interest. There is one with an S and arrow above the kiosk pointing to the air raid shelter and another outside showing the way to the Forces Free Baggage Room. Of the advertisements, the one outside is surely the most responsible 'If you MUST travel take Bovril sandwiches with you'. Inside, did the billposter have a wry smile when he put the one for throat pastilles next to that for 'Craven A', although the irony would probably not have been apparent in those days!

Although not exactly cluttered, this part of King's Cross certainly looked aesthetically untidy when the photograph was taken. It was not the fault of the LNER but a contribution from the Luftwaffe in 1941 and the story is told in Chapter 8. The temporary canopies were fabricated out of any bits of metal that were going spare while the bracing above was to help stabilise the arcade between the train sheds, this having lost three roof girders on the west side. Happily, the substantial thickness of brickwork put up in the 1850s coped perfectly well with the uneven forces.

This proliferation of advertisements above the concourse at the head of Platforms 6 to 10 was typical of the period up to and during the Second World War. The photograph was taken on 8 August 1940 and the clock tower of St Pancras can just be seen peering through the open space where there was once a window. There is a wide range of advertisements and slogans including Allenburys Diet 'To sleep better', Andrews Liver Salt 'I must have left it behind', Craven A 'They never vary' and Bovril 'Everybody needs the beef'. There is one for St Margaret hosiery, jerseys and underwear, this being the trademark of the large Corah factory in Leicester, and another showing the most hideous concrete building and urging people to 'Book to Welwyn Garden City, just minutes from King's Cross'.

the middle of August and upon the very great importance of steps being taken to ensure it being opened by the 1ˢᵗ August.

On Thursday 27ᵗʰ September 1849 Joseph Cubitt had reported his attempts to accelerate the rate of progress of the works between London and Peterborough. His efforts were rewarded; on 6ᵗʰ December 1849 the Board resolved that *he be appointed Architect for the London Temporary Passenger Station and permanent Goods Station, upon condition that his terms are satisfactory to the Station Committee, it being the opinion of the Board that from the extent of the works he ought to charge less than Mr Goddard.* On Thursday 18ᵗʰ July 1850 Cubitt was pleased to report to his Board that *the London to Peterborough portion of main line will be ready for the inspection of the Directors on the 27ᵗʰ July and be opened to the Public on Wednesday 7ᵗʰ August next.* This was indeed the opening date of the Great Northern main line, into what was recorded as its 'Temporary Pasfenger station at King's Crofs', frequently referred to in the literature as 'Maiden Lane'. Cubitt cut it fine, or his confidence was rewarded; there appears to be no mention of official Government approval for the works, though he records 'Peterborough to

Wennington – he presumably means Werrington – sanctioned for the public by the Railway Commissioners on 7ᵗʰ August 1850.

The Directors were concerned principally with costs and rates; dull fare, and there is no account of celebratory fanfares for the opening of the new route. On 6ᵗʰ June 1850 the Board is worrying itself about appointments for the new undertaking. 'Clerks and Guards' it declared, 'should not exceed 30 years of age'. Earlier, in February, it had been resolved 'that the Executive Committee do reconsider the question of the proposed widening of Maiden Lane with a view to avoid too great an outlay.' This is almost the only reference in these earliest years to Maiden Lane, now York Way; the new line was pushed across it to its lacklustre termination. This 'Temporary Passenger Station', whatever its precise location, at least had a roof (it afterwards apparently served as a potato warehouse) though it appears not to have given every satisfaction. On Thursday 24ᵗʰ October 1850 Lewis Cubitt* attended the Board 'and explained his plans for the roofing for the new station at King's Cross, which he proposes, instead of that now in use at the Temporary Passenger

Station, in consequence of it not being considered safe. Resolved, that his plans be approved and accepted'.

The Directors were much more concerned with revenue, and in particular that accruing from the Great Exhibition and as Joseph Cubitt prepared to delve and tunnel his great venture under the Regents Canal (the contractors, John and William Jay, were employing upwards of a thousand men) above ground the General Manager proposed the following Exhibition arrangements 'for the month of September:'

York. Up Train Monday and Saturday as at present, at 9.45am.

Sheffield. None.

Leeds and Wakefield. Up Train on Monday, Wednesday and Saturday.

Lincoln and Doncaster. Up Train on Monday and Saturday.

Peterborough and the Royston and Hitchin Districts. One train a week, say Thursday and back on that day or any other Exhibition day.

Down Trains Mondays, Thursdays and Saturdays to Leeds etc and the two days named above, to York, Doncaster and Lincoln, in order to balance the Scotch Fish Trains which run daily from York (excepts

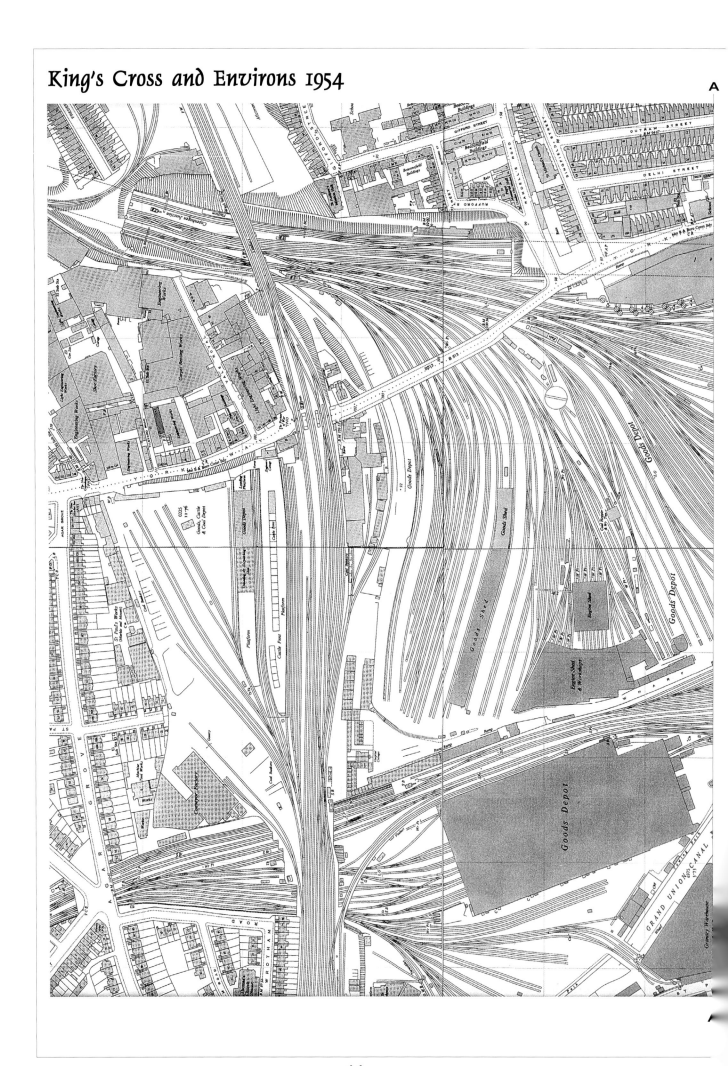

A

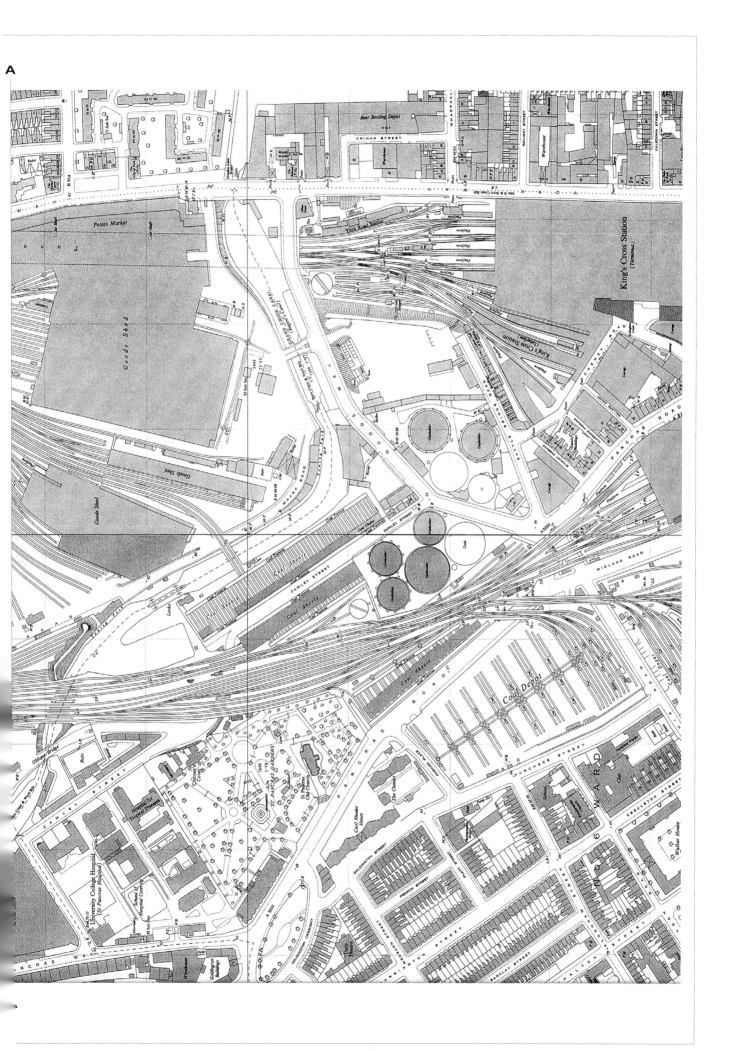

King's Cross and Environs 1871

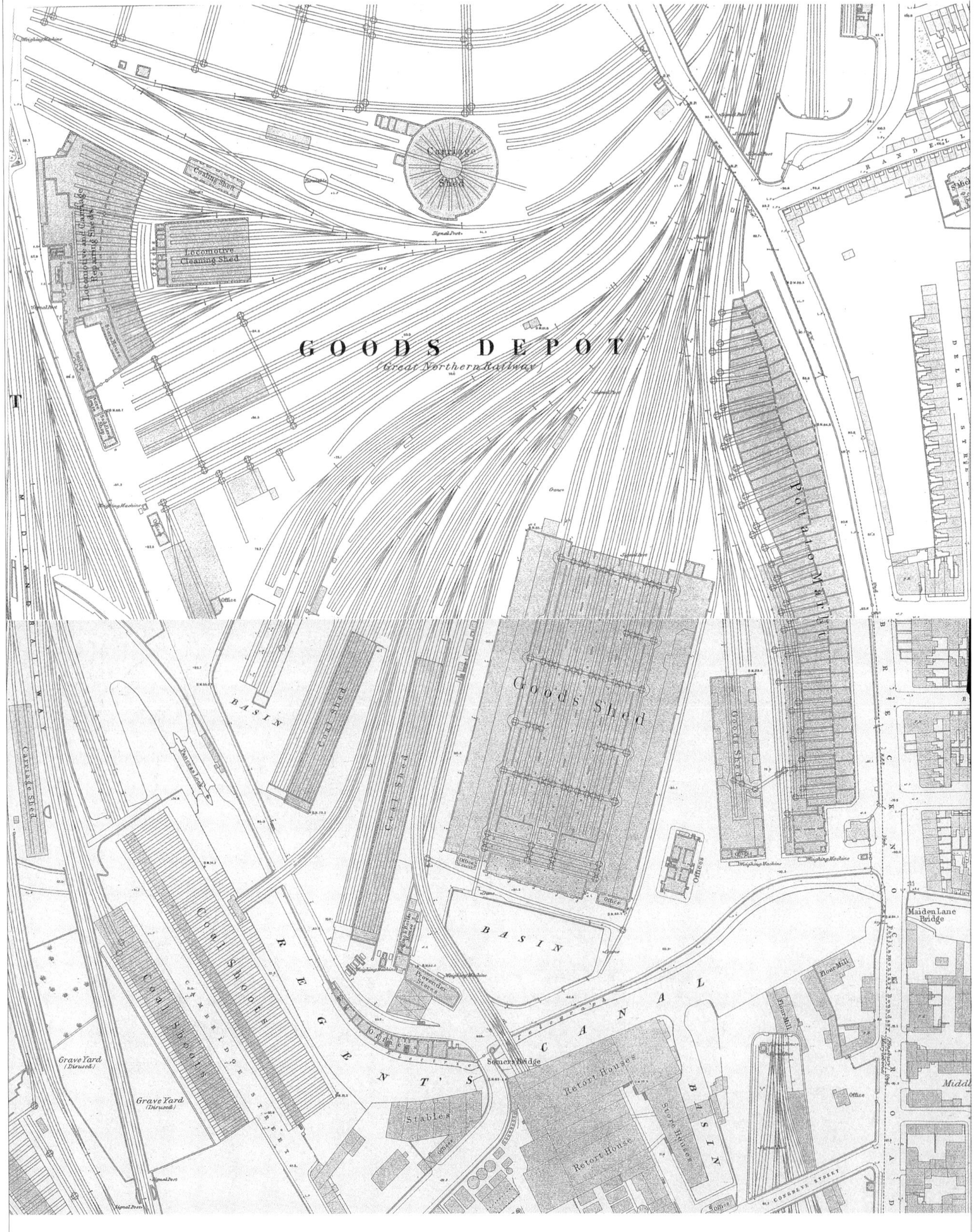

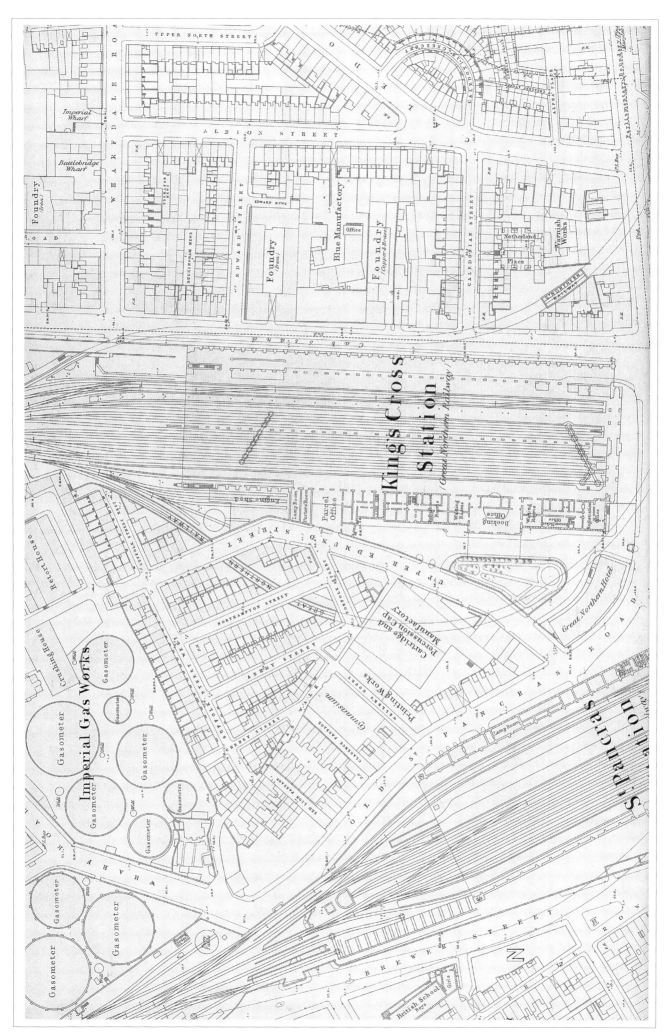

UPPER NORTH STREET

ALBION STREET

WHARFDALE ROAD

Imperial Wharf

Battlebridge Wharf

Foundry (Iron)

ROAD

EDWARD STREET

EDWARD MEWS

Foundry (Iron)

Blue Manufactory

Office

Foundry (Copper & Brass)

CALEDONIAN STREET

Netherland Place

Varnish Works

N. ROAD

CRESCENT

RAILWAY

King's Cross Station
(Great Northern Railway)

Engine Shed

Lamp Room
Porters Room

Parcel Office

Booking Office

Waiting Rooms

Waiting Rooms

Secondclass Office

Registration Office

Great Northern Hotel

RAILWAY

SUFFOLK STREET

RailWAY

Retort House

Crushing House

Imperial Gas Works

Gasometer

Gasometer

Gasometer

Gasometer

Gasometer

Gasometer

Gasometer

Gasometer

Gasometer

Well

Well

Well

Well

WHARF ROAD

Pure Fields

NORTHERN

NORTHAMPTON STREET

GREAT

NORFOLK STREET

ASHBY STREET

UPPER EDMUND STREET

Cartridge and Percussion Cap Manufactory

Printing Works

Gymnasium

WILLIER'S COURT

CLARENCE PASSAGE

CHENEY STREET

RED LION PASSAGE

ST. PANCRAS ROAD

Lamp Room

St. Pancras Station

BREWER STREET

BRITISH SCHOOL
Girls

N

CALEDONIAN ROAD

17

Climb to the Northern Heights

The King's Cross approach where the fan of tracks from York Road, the main station and the suburban platforms converged on Gasworks Tunnel was a smoky place. It was more or less a hollow, hemmed in by slightly rising ground, the train sheds, other tall buildings and the tunnel portals. Stationary locos adding to the haze on 3 June 1957 included an N2 to the left of the signal box, a B1 at Platform 10 and another B1 together with W1 4-6-4 60700 in the loco yard to the right. L1 67784 leaves Platform 12 in the Suburban Station with a local train including an articulated set. Despite their small wheels the L1s had a fair turn of speed occasionally. Unfortunately this engine was only in service for just over twelve years, starting off at Neasden for suburban services out of Marylebone and finishing off at Colwick for trips to the likes of Pinxton and Derby Friargate. Photograph Peter Groom.

It was an uphill slog out of King's Cross, around 1½ miles at mainly 1 in 105 to 1 in 107 through the tunnels and past Belle Isle with a dip under Regents Canal just inside Gasworks Tunnel to start with. Having put a fair amount of the climb behind it, A1 60122 CURLEW emerges from Copenhagen Tunnel and hammers up the remainder of Holloway bank with the 6.18pm to Leeds, Bradford and Hull on 11 May 1954. The engine was only about 5½ years old at the time and had been allocated new to King's Cross in December 1948 but a drastic reorganisation in September 1951 resulted in A4s being concentrated at Top Shed and A1s moving north, this one to Grantham. After a couple of years there, another move saw the Pacific at Copley Hill and it was based at this Leeds shed when the photograph was taken. Another change of mind by BR meant that the reverse happened with CURLEW returning to Grantham in August 1955 and King's Cross in September 1957. With years of work still in it, the loco was withdrawn from Doncaster at the end of 1962 after just fourteen years service. Photograph Brian Morrison.

A lofty perch at the top of the western train shed reveals a fine prospect of the immediate vicinity of King's Cross as well as the edge of the Northern Heights greeting travellers heading north to places from Alexandra Palace to Aberdeen. It is June 1947 and an express leaves Platform 10, an N2 is ready to remove empty stock from Platform 7 and other engines wait in the North Spur and Centre Spur ready for their next pilot duties. King's Cross signal box has been there for just fifteen years but it is totally blackened with soot. Some signals are fixed to overhead gantries while others are on steel supports, the reason for this arrangement being revealed in Chapter 7. The engine yard is on the left, Gasworks Tunnel straight ahead and York Road station on the right. Above the tunnel portals Goods Way runs alongside the Regents Canal and connects York Road with the confusing assemblage of buildings which make up King's Cross Goods Depot. In the distance the edifice later known as the Ebonite tower stands darkly on the skyline while immediately behind it and only just visible is the grand tower of Caledonian Road Market.

Sundays) I propose to run daily from King's Cross to York etc at 9.15pm. No Exhibition passengers to be carried Up or Down by ordinary trains.
(sgd) Seymour Clarke

Attention turns more and more to the new 'Permanent King's Cross' through the latter part of 1851 and into the following year. Sir William Cubitt 'requested to the Board' on 27th January 1852, *on the state of station buildings ... to the effect that work is now progressing satisfactorily and that no fears need be entertained either of its strength or safety.'*

On Tuesday 30th March after application from the Post Office a letter box 'free of cost and at no expense to the company' was approved for King's Cross. Opening of the station was not now far off though once again the Board Minutes are strangely indifferent to this

great event. 'Mr Joseph Cubitt and Mr Lewis Cubitt' on Tuesday 4th May 1852 were ...*authorised to come to terms with Mr Jay the Contractor for the station work at King's Cross in order to gain time for the necessary excavations and cellarage.*

On 17th August the General Manager ...*gave particulars of the arrangements he recommended for working trains into and out of the Permanent Passenger Station at King's Cross and suggesting that passengers be allowed to alight at the Ticket Platform near the Holloway Road and that two cottages for the principal ticket collectors be erected there. Approved.*

Joseph Cubitt wrote on 28th September: *I am proceeding with the completion of the works. I expect another month will bring most of them to conclusion. The wet weather and the unfavourable nature of the material have caused slips both of cuttings and embankments at various*

points but more particularly at Spittlegate near Grantham, at which place the embankment has caused a good deal of trouble. It is however, now, I believe, effectively cured... The works of the London Station are likely to be sufficiently completed to be able to open in a fortnight from this time: a great deal of wet weather and considerable difficulty in getting men are the reasons urged from time to time by Mr Jay for greater progress not having been made.
(sgd) Joseph Cubitt

Even the new 'permanent' station failed to evince comment in the Board Minutes – on 12th October 1852 a letter from the Secretary of the Railway Department, Board of Trade 'conveying the sanction of that Board to the new portion of line and Passenger Station at King's Cross being opened for Public traffic', was simply 'noted', and the Directors moved

Above. On the morning of 27 August 1951, A3 60065 KNIGHT OF THISTLE reaches the summit of Holloway Bank and approaches Finsbury Park station. Although in need of some attention here, the engine had to be in first rate condition for a debut some 23 years earlier. Completed by North British in August 1924 as 2564, the loco was allocated to the Scottish Area and worked from Haymarket shed. On 1 May 1928 the non-stop 'Flying Scotsman; began running between King's Cross and Edinburgh Waverley with Top Shed providing the motive power at first. As soon as corridor tenders became available Haymarket used their own Pacifics, this being one of the first two. During July 1950 60065 moved south to King's Cross then on to Grantham in September 1951. It was withdrawn from New England in June 1964. Photograph BKB Green.

Left. Although it was a stiff climb out of King's Cross, no such effort was required from B1 61223 as it descended Holloway Bank with an excursion from Cambridge to King's Cross on 17 May 1961. The engine must have been borrowed for the occasion as it was based at Lincoln at the time. When new from North British in August 1947, this was one of the B1s sent to Gorton for services over the Great Central Woodhead route across the Pennines. With the completion of electrification between Manchester London Road and Sheffield Victoria in September 1954 numerous steam locomotives were displaced and this one went to East Anglia, spending time at Cambridge, Norwich and Yarmouth South Town before moving to Lincoln in March 1960. It was withdrawn from Immingham in January 1966. Photograph Brian Morrison.

Great Northern Engines

When King's Cross opened the Great Northern already had around two hundred engines and many of those used on passenger traffic were 2-2-2s. Benjamin Cubitt, the Chief Engineer's brother, became responsible for ordering locomotives in 1846 and the first fifty were well-tried stock pattern 5ft 6in 'Singles' from the Manchester firm of Sharp Brothers from 1847. Cubitt died in 1848 and Edward Bury was in charge until 1850 when Archibald Sturrock took up office. By then the Great Northern system extended for over 140 miles and it was worked by a motley collection of 0-4-0s, 0-4-2s, 2-2-2s and 2-4-0s from a variety of makers. Sturrock was committed to introducing a degree of standardisation but there is also evidence that the quest for fast running had begun. No.215 was a 4-2-2 delivered in August 1853 and there were claims that it reached 75mph. The engine was also said to have covered the 31 miles from Hitchin to Holloway Ticket Platform in 28 minutes, 'frightening the fireman' in the process! Although the East Coast main line had been noted for speed already, the Railway Races to Edinburgh, then Aberdeen during the last two decades of the nineteenth century really brought it to the forefront of public attention. This was during the tenure of Patrick Stirling as Great Northern Locomotive Superintendent and the period when the lure of life on the footplate began. Certain locomotives were designed for fast running and here is one of them in the original engine yard at King's Cross with the wall of the Suburban Station in the background. Stirling 8ft Single 1007 of 1895 was one of the final batch of six which brought the total number of these beautiful 4-2-2s to 53. Their decline came from the relentless trend towards much heavier trains made up of larger bogie coaches often with dining cars. 1007 was condemned in January 1913 and the last Stirling Single was withdrawn during 1916.

on to tickets, rates, conveyances and solicitors.

'The Great Station' opened on 14th October 1852 and was rightly regarded as architecturally startling, a pair of yawning train sheds bound at first by giant 'laminated timbers', not the girders familiar to the last few generations. Its frontage now ranks foremost amongst the remaining Great British Stations and it survived periodic rebuilding proposals from the turn of the century onwards, sometimes by a whisker. In *Notable Railway Stations No.6*, in a turn of the century *Railway Magazine* account heavily redolent of the official Great Northern view, the station was said to occupy a site that was 'little more than a gigantic dustyard'. Long years of smoke nuisance and other complaints made a snipe at the local authority (what there was of it) irresistible: 'The London County Council was yet in the Womb of Time and even its unlucky predecessor, the Metropolitan Board of

Works, had still to be born'. The dismal air of the place prior to the arrival of the Great Northern had lingered long in the corporate memory of the company and J Medcalf (GN Out Door Goods Manager) recalled it in some style: 'A long battalion of rag sorters and cinder sifters ... the dull heavy thuds of the North London carpet beaters ... the stray cats with wicked propensities ... snapping at a dead sparrow or fighting fiercely with each other over the latest sample of fish bone.' The Great Northern had 'got hold ... of this howling waste ... and soon made a clean sweep ... the plain straightforward solid brickwork of the station arose to dominate King's Cross'. Here an element of inferiority complex begins to creep in... *according to all precedent we ought to bring in something about the style of architecture but we can't. The broad sweep of the frontage and the fine proportions of the two main arcades are undeniable but the clock tower and one or two other features*

are not what the dramatic critic would call 'convincing'. The stately Grecian columns of Euston and the ornate Gothic of St Pancras seem to call across 'what do you call yourself?' and King's Cross can only reply 'we don't know but we are a bit railway station and we are filling the part all the time.

King's Cross then, was for much of its time an unregarded building, almost an embarrassment to the Great Northern (which would explain in parts its recurring proposals to build upon the area of the frontage) and indeed it settled very quickly into the long banality that is at the heart of every station; Joseph Cubitt occupied the autumn of 1852 with various land purchases for 'King's Cross Goods' and on 20th October 1852 a cash bag containing more than £60 disappeared overnight from an unlocked drawer at the station. £14 10s 4d was lost forever but £48 in cheques and bank notes turned up in the post on the 27th. It might even have been posted from the new letter box...

*Lewis Cubitt designed the station itself, Joseph and his father William were responsible for the engineering of the line. Whilst of the same family, Jackson notes in 'London's Termini', 'they were not directly related'.

Below. During 1863 Sturrock converted eleven 'Sharpie' 2-2-2s to well tanks with condensing gear for use on the Metropolitan Railway and in 1865 the first of twenty specially designed 0-4-2WTs appeared, these having been described as the first purpose-built London suburban engines. Stirling built 0-4-2s with tanks at the back and eventually 0-4-4Ts, some of which survived as LNER G1s and G2s. Ivatt introduced 4-4-2Ts and 0-6-2Ts to cope with increasing traffic and these became the well known C12s and N1s. When Gresley took office there was no immediate need for further engines for local traffic but eventually he decided to design a more powerful version of the Ivatt 0-6-2Ts and the result was a class of loco which became as much a part of the King's Cross scene as Gasworks Tunnel. N2 1742, resplendent in its Great Northern livery at Top Shed, became LNER 4742 and BR 69521 in due course. Various changes occurred over the years and the Ramsbottom safety valves and Westinghouse feed water pump in front of the side tank would not be seen in later years. 69521 left King's Cross in July 1959 and was withdrawn from New England during June 1961.

Above. When Patrick Stirling took up office in 1866 he decided that more powerful locos were needed for a range of duties to cope with increasing traffic. Among them were 2-4-0s for secondary passenger, fast parcels and special goods work. Several were built in 1867-71 but the design was modified during 1874 and no less than 117 appeared over the next 21 years. Most were built at Doncaster, but fifteen were ordered from Kitson of Leeds, including 708 (it went into traffic during February 1884) here in King's Cross original engine yard with the Metropolitan City Widened Lines station in the background. The clean lines of the Stirling design is enhanced by the polished brass safety valve cover and the GN livery of grass green with darker green edging together with black and white lining. These engines worked all over the system and appeared on light expresses when Singles were not available as well as piloting Singles or new 4-4-0s on heavier trains from the turn of the century. They were regular performers on King's Cross-Cambridge services, but by the end of the First World War had all moved away from London and pursued a gentlemanly retirement on locals around Lincoln, Grantham and Boston. As LNER Class E1 there were heavy withdrawals in 1923-24, but this one did not quite make it to Grouping.

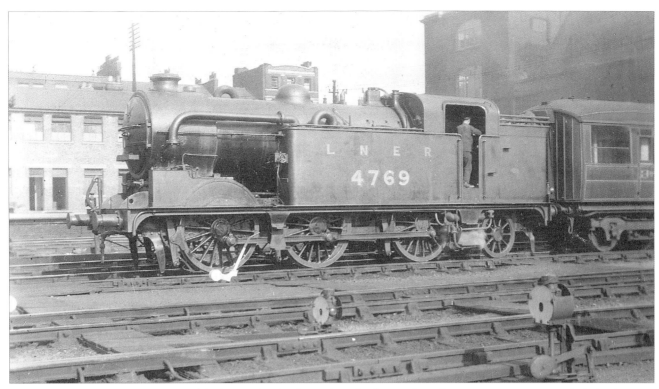

It was inevitable that the LNER would adopt a simpler livery for suburban tank engines. 4769 on empty stock duties in 1932 is in all over black with red lining, although eventually the latter was omitted. The Great Northern constructed ten of these 0-6-2Ts itself at Doncaster Works but a substantial order for fifty was placed with North British. This was the last but one of the engines built in Glasgow and it was delivered to King's Cross as 1769 in April 1921. Note the bunker footholds and cab roof handrail for the fireman to reach the coal. The N2s had considerable advantages over their predecessors and most had regular crews who became proud of them. Their inner suburban work involved trips to High Barnet, Alexandra Palace, Hertford North, Hatfield and Welwyn Garden City from King's Cross and Moorgate, invariably working chimney first out of London. As 69548, this engine was at King's Cross until December 1958 when it made a very unusual move to Bury St Edmunds for three months. After a period at Hitchin the loco was condemned in July 1959.

Another 47 N2s were built for the LNER, unevenly divided between Doncaster Works (6), Yorkshire Engine Co (9), Beyer Peacock (12) and Hawthorn Leslie (20). Some of these were intended for service in Scotland but 69572, at King's Cross shed in March 1956 was supplied by Hawthorn Leslie for use in the London area and delivered in November 1928 as 2666. These engines had to be driven hard from the suburban platforms at King's Cross to the first call at Finsbury Park as a start-to-stop time of just five minutes was allowed for the 2½ miles, which was on rising gradients and included Gasworks and Copenhagen Tunnels. From 1925, locos working over the Metropolitan City Widened Lines were fitted with trip cocks for activating the vacuum brakes should a red light be passed and the one on the right side of 69572 can be seen below the footsteps just in front of the middle driving wheel. Because of weight restrictions, N2s were not allowed to work from Farringdon to Ludgate Hill and beyond. This engine was at King's Cross until October 1957 when there was a move to Hornsey, but from November 1959 it was back at Top Shed until withdrawal in February 1961.

Arrivals

Even when it became clear that their Pacifics were doomed, Top Shed continued to maintain them in superb condition. In spring 1961 A3 60109 HERMIT has arrived with a morning train from Leeds and its condition is a tribute to the everyday quality of the cleaning gang. The engine had gone to Leeds the previous day with the Yorkshire Pullman (its reversed headboard sits above the buffer beam) and even after two lengthy trips it still looked good. Built as 4478 in July 1923, this was one of the first four A1s to move to the Great Central section as a result of A4s taking over many East Coast duties. It went to Gorton in March 1939 but was transferred to King's Cross at the end of 1942, the first of four stays there. During its second session at Top Shed HERMIT was in charge of the Yorkshire Pullman on 5 July 1948, the day it was permanently re-introduced following its suspension during World War Two and the acute coal shortage which followed. The engine was withdrawn from King's Cross in December 1962. Photograph Brian Bailey.

Two A3s in their final form with double chimneys and trough smoke deflectors at Platforms 1 and 2 in 1961. The furthest one prefers to remain anonymous, but nearest the camera is 60103 VICTOR WILD. This engine was new in March 1923 with its Great Northern number 1474 as it was ordered by that company from its Doncaster Works but delivered to the LNER. It became 4474 the following year. Like many of these Pacifics it had a relatively stable allocation at first but tended to move from shed to shed once the A4s arrived. This one was at King's Cross from new to January 1937 when it went to Doncaster for a couple of years. 4474 was transferred to Gorton on the former Great Central system in February 1939 and remained there until the winter of 1942, apart from four months at Leicester G C towards the end of 1939. It was back at King's Cross from November 1942 to September 1951 then spent the rest of its days at Grantham until withdrawal in June 1963. Photograph Brian Bailey.

An appropriate juxtaposition of two very different types of engine which were characteristic of King's Cross for over a quarter of a century. A4 60032 GANNET is backing out of Platform 1 past an N2 at Platform 2. Most of the Top Shed 0-6-2Ts were outshopped in fully lined black livery befitting their role on passenger trains to and from quite well-heeled suburbs. Most of them were also kept in clean condition which was also an asset during their high profile pilot duties around the terminus. Photograph D Clayton.

Some of the King's Cross Pacifics did look rather woebegone right at the end, though certainly no less impressive. On 2 December 1962 60030 GOLDEN FLEECE has arrived at Platform 2 with an express from the north. The engine was withdrawn at the end of the month with just over a quarter of a century of superb service to its credit. This A4 emerged from Doncaster Works as 4495 GREAT SNIPE in August 1937 but was renamed GOLDEN FLEECE the following month as it was one of the streamlined Pacifics selected for the new West Riding Limited, their names relating to the Yorkshire woollen industry. It hauled a press trip on 23 September 1937 to demonstrate the luxury of the train, although not its speed. During 1939 the engine was on the West Riding Limited for fourteen consecutive weeks with only three days off. Altogether, 4495 did 258 runs on the train and brought the last Up working into King's Cross on 31 August 1939. During early BR days 60030 was one of the A4s based at Grantham for working the Flying Scotsman non-stop to Newcastle and was maintained to a very high standard for this purpose. The layer of grime seen here in 1962 is therefore somewhat deceptive! Photograph Brian Stephenson.

A Morning Spotting

Although the end of Platform 10 was the usual place to congregate with notepads and Ian Allan *abcs*, a spot near the signal box on Platform 6 offered a good vantage point as well. This visit was probably during the summer of 1961. B1 61283 was actually at King's Cross shed from May to October 1957 but then moved to Cambridge and it had probably brought a train in from there on this occasion. It finished its career at Norwich then Stratford. Photograph JT Bassindale, courtesy Laurence Brownhill.

A J50 on shunt duty ambles past towards the goods bays on the other side of the Suburban Station. It is obviously not a priority for the cleaners and that makes seeing the number extremely difficult. There is a B1 in the engine yard with a Birmingham RCW diesel Type 2. Some of the Great Northern goods yard buildings are in the right background and the BR District Road Motor Repair Depot is on the left. JT Bassindale, courtesy Laurence Brownhill.

A couple of L1s are the next locos to appear and they are familiar to most spotters. Both 67787 and 67792 were transferred from Neasden on the Great Central to King's Cross in August 1958. 67787 left Top Shed for Colwick in November 1961 but 67792 stayed a bit longer, moving on to Doncaster in January 1962. JT Bassindale, courtesy Laurence Brownhill.

Every so often the shunt duties and light engine movements at King's Cross were disturbed by a main line departure, in this case 60055 WOOLWINDER. This engine was hardly an unusual sight at The Cross as it was at Top Shed from 1956 to 1961. The exhaust looks clean and there is a full head of steam for the climb through Gasworks Tunnel and past Belle Isle. JT Bassindale, courtesy Laurence Brownhill.

An Afternoon Spotting

Seen from Platform 10, the driver of A3 60065 KNIGHT OF THISTLE is vigilant as he sets off with an express on 7 August 1961. Named KNIGHT OF THE THISTLE after the winner of the 1897 Royal Hunt Cup, during an overhaul in December 1932 it acquired plates with the definite article missing. The original name was correct in terms of both the horse and the Order of the Thistle. Why it was changed is a mystery and the Order itself confirmed to the RCTS that the abbreviated form made no sense. Photograph David Knapman.

60054 PRINCE OF WALES backs out of the terminus on its way to Top Shed on 7 August 1961. This was another engine which had a change of name, uncontroversial in this case. It was new as MANNA in December 1924 but was altered exactly two years later as it happened to be the one inspected by the Prince of Wales when he visited Doncaster Works. Photograph David Knapman.

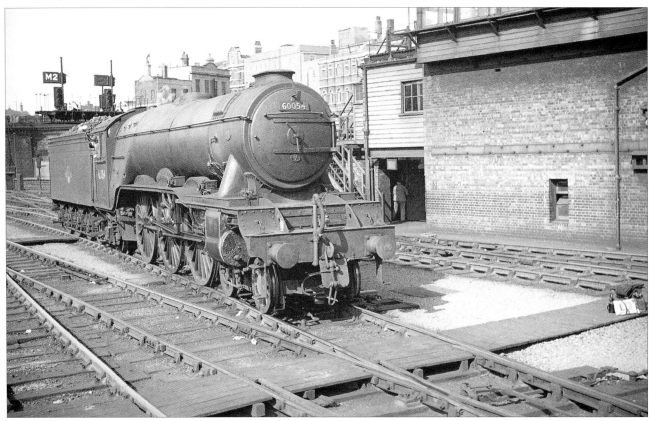

For a while, the Grimsby expresses brought Britannias to King's Cross, locos that had been a familiar sight down the road at Liverpool Street. On 7 August 1961 70041 SIR JOHN MOORE leaves Platform 6 with the 4.15pm to Cleethorpes, which will travel via Boston and Louth then reverse at Grimsby to reach the seaside. In the background a Cravens dmu pauses at York Road on its way to Moorgate. Photograph David Knapman.

A4 60024 KINGFISHER, in the usual superb Haymarket condition, arrives with the Elizabethan on 7 August 1961. From new out of Doncaster Works in December 1936 to withdrawal in September 1966, this was almost exclusively a Scottish loco, spending most of its time based at Haymarket but with spells at Dalry Road, St Margarets and Aberdeen towards the end. However, it did manage some time at King's Cross, spending six months there from July 1932 to January 1938. Photograph David Knapman.

The view back towards the terminus from the top of Gasworks Tunnel revealed another range of railway buildings and a very different skyline. It is 21 August 1956 and King's Cross A4 60015 QUICKSILVER negotiates the complex track layout as it guides an express out of Platform 7. St Pancras dominates the distant prospect on the right, as was always the intention, but the range of King's Cross platforms from 1 to 17 occupy the middle distance. To the left, an N2 on pilot duties stands alone in Platform 1 while a plume of steam rises from a barely visible J50 in Platform 4. An L1 with various vans and parcels coaches occupies Platform 11 in the Suburban Station, another N2 is alongside island Platform 15 and a second L1 is on one of the approach tracks to the goods bays. An A4 is being coaled (it still has to turn) at the far end of the engine yard and another Pacific, possibly an A2, is behind the low building on the right. New England B1 61207, which has probably arrived at King's Cross on a stopping passenger train from Peterborough, stands on the spur nearer the camera. The roller blind showing 2 in the lower left could also display 3, but this was somewhat superfluous as that platform had been abolished years before, a hint that the track and signalling arrangements at the terminus were rather backward.

2. Tracks and Tunnels

The platforms at King's Cross varied confusingly over the years; change came of course as the station grew and was re-ordered but an added perversity of logic on the part of the Great Northern made matters even more awkward, labelling the platforms as they appeared over the years in eccentric fashion. Across the wide sweep of the two train sheds, 800ft long, 105ft wide and 71ft high* ('a vista of extraordinary effect') only two platforms were laid at first, facing each other. The west side, with attendant offices and passengers' rooms, was for departures while the east (or York Road) side dealt with arrivals only. Between the two stretched no less than fourteen tracks, a standing area for spare and waiting stock, interlinked by the customary arrangement of small turntables, capstans and the like. The place was jolted out of this pleasantly relaxed working by the arrival of the Midland Railway in 1858. From 1st February Midland trains ran in from Hitchin, these and the burgeoning Great Northern traffic swiftly rendering the station arrangements inadequate.

Tunnels were delved in the 1860s to connect with the east-west running lines of the Metropolitan Railway. Down trains, leaving the Met tunnels, emerged from the Widened Lines on the west side of the station – the 'Hotel Curve' and for some years simply set back into the terminus for passengers to board or alight. Up trains curved away from the Gasworks Tunnel mouth, to call at a new platform, before diving out of sight in a second single bore, running under York Road for a distance before curving sharply eastwards and uniting

This view of the tracks and tunnels which formed the entry/exit to King's Cross was taken from the gulley between the two train sheds on the sunny afternoon of 29 April 1952. It reveals a wealth of detail and demonstrates just how much property the Great Northern owned in this area. In the foreground an A2 Pacific is backing down on to its train in Platform 6 while Gresley coaches in carmine and cream stand in Platform 5. Signal posts dominate the extremity of Platforms 7 and 8 on the left while a flock of barrows complete with the odd parcel has ventured up to the water crane at the end of Platforms 2 and 4 on the right. Prominent in the centre is the LNER signal box which was commissioned in 1932, replacing two 19th century cabins erected when operations still reflected the 'Arrival' and 'Departure' sides of the station. In the middle distance an N2 and B1 stand in the engine yard on the left as a suburban train disappears into the tunnel, while York Road station on the East Branch down to the Widened Lines is prominent on the right. The original 1852 Maiden Lane Tunnel is immediately beyond the signal box roof, while the second bore of 1878 is to the right of it and the third tunnel of 1892 is on the left. By this time the name Gasworks Tunnel had long become more or less universal. Above the portals and extending away to the left is the southern extremity of King's Cross Goods Depot, a real hotchpotch as can be seen. The first tunnel had to be carefully excavated beneath a basin of the Regents Canal, but the waterway was later modified and a new road called, with considerable ingenuity, Goods Way was created just above the tunnel mouths. This provided the main access for road vehicles and a number of mechanical horses and trailers can be seen. Also, barely credible now, two roads crossed the station throat on bridges and caused considerable operating difficulties. Battle Bridge Road ran from Pancras Road to York Road opposite Wharfdale Road and crossed the ends of the platforms. It would have dominated the foreground of this view but was removed in 1921 – inexplicably it is not shown on the 1874 Survey. Congreve Street (which *does* show on that survey) ran from York Road to the Gasworks in the middle distance and maybe the flat section of York Road station roof facilitated its passage. This obstacle was removed around 1900 with Goods Way providing access to the works. The few non-railway buildings in the right distance are between York Road and Caledonian Road.

A new signalling system was installed at King's Cross in 1931-32 but it involved overhead gantries which were intended to keep cables away from possible flood damage, though they could be vulnerable to derailments, as will be seen later. This view was taken on 24 March 1933 and shows the immense complexity of the track layout, with a single slip and three double slips prominent in the foreground. A group of gangers appear to be trying to sort something out but hopefully they are about to stand aside as N2 4761 is heading straight for them with a suburban train which includes a fairly elderly Great Northern brake at the front. This particular 0-6-2T was still at King's Cross during the 1950s as 69540, although it moved to Hitchin early in 1959 and was withdrawn from New England during 1960.

This view from above the tunnel face looking towards the station was taken on 31 March 1933 and things are relatively quiet despite it being a Friday. Prominent in the engine yard on the right is the pioneering Ivatt large-boilered Atlantic 251 of 1902, in its guise as LNER 3251. Buffered up to it is D2 4-4-0 4372 which was built at Doncaster in 1900 as 1372. Inevitably N2s feature in the scene and as was often the case they take a bit of finding. One of them is in the Centre Engine Spur behind the cables strung between the metal telegraph poles on the left. Part of York Road station and the tunnel to the Metropolitan Widened Lines is just visible beyond it. The other N2 is on the far right, beyond the low building with the slate roof. A goods train, its wagons and brake blurred by the camera time exposure, has just come up from the Widened Lines. With very little to clutter it, the very complex track layout can be examined in detail. At least four double slips are visible, together with a four-way point this side of Platform 10. There is a fair amount of fresh ballast is in evidence and the complete lack of unnecessary debris between the tracks is typical of the time.

For once, the tunnel mouth on the Hotel Curve can just about be made out, although there is still some smoke haze about. The very solid and quite ornate canopy supports on the Widened Lines platform dominate the right hand side of the view, although the gaps between them reveal a perspective of the windows which gives a clear indication of the 1 in 60 slope of the platform. Trains between Moorgate and the suburbs called here from 1 February 1878 and ceased on 8 November 1976. The island accommodating Platforms 14 and 15 is on the left in front of the wall of the original Suburban Station while peeping above them is the spire of St Pancras receiving some attention.

Another clear view of the trackwork between Gasworks Tunnel and the end of the platforms at King's Cross, again taken during the 1930s. Apart from a couple of ex-GN tender locos in the engine yard there is nothing to be seen and the ganger may be wondering what has happened to all the trains. Nevertheless it is another opportunity to study the quite remarkable layout, especially that four-way turnout a hundred yards or so away. Note the fogman's hut. JA Whaley, transporttreasury

This ancient painted wooden sign pointing the way to the Metropolitan Railway was photographed at King's Cross as late as 20 June 1984, despite that company having become part of London Transport over half a century previously! By the time the Great Northern opened most streets in the capital were so jammed with horse-drawn vehicles that some form of rail transport was being considered as a possible way of easing the problem. Charles Pearson was a solicitor in the City of London, but he also had foresight as he was the driving force behind the North Metropolitan Railway which was authorised to build a line from Paddington to King's Cross in August 1853. After joining forces with the City Terminus Company, which was planning a line from King's Cross to Farringdon Street, the project was reincorporated as the Metropolitan Railway in August 1854. There was financial support from the Great Western, which saw the line as a way of reaching the City, but public subscriptions were not forthcoming as the idea of travelling underground was wholly foreign to many people. Eventually Charles Pearson persuaded the City Corporation to subscribe a fifth of the capital so work could begin. The 3¾ mile line ran from Paddington to Farringdon Street via Baker Street, Euston Square and King's Cross. Most of it was to run beneath existing roads using the 'cut and cover' principle,

although some 12,000 people were displaced from around a thousand rather unsavoury dwellings east of King's Cross. The Great Western insisted on broad gauge track but fortunately mixed broad and standard gauge track was laid. Services over the Metropolitan Railway began on 10 January 1863 with the Great Western providing locomotives with condensing apparatus, as the Act stipulated, and hefty eight wheel coaches. There had been some bad feeling between the two companies over construction delays, but friction increased markedly concerning both financial and operating matters following the opening day so Paddington announced it would cease working the line on 10 August. The Hotel Curve and East Branch from the Great Northern at King's Cross had been put in and that company was already converting several 'Sharpie' locos for use on its 'Suburban & City' service to Farringdon Street. A number of problems had to be overcome with considerable haste but a standard gauge service commenced on 11 August 1863 using GN locos together with GN and London & North Western Railway coaches. By summer 1864 the Metropolitan had received sufficient of its own Beyer Peacock 4-4-0Ts and compartment coaches to return the borrowed motive power and rolling stock. The line was extended from Farringdon Street to Moorgate Street in December 1865 and on to Liverpool

Street and Aldgate in 1875-76. In association with the Metropolitan District Railway the Inner Circle was completed when the City Lines between Aldgate and Mansion House opened in 1884. In the west Metropolitan trains eventually reached Uxbridge, Watford, Aylesbury and deepest Buckinghamshire at Brill. It regarded itself as a main line railway to the extent that in 1904 an Aylesbury-Yarmouth excursion ran via King's Cross and a connection with the Great Eastern at Liverpool Street. Electrification had been considered during the early 1880s because of the obvious problems associated with an intensive sub-surface steam service, but its genesis was a convoluted business. Eventually full size electric multiple units began to work between Aldgate, King's Cross, Baker Street and South Kensington on 1 July 1905 and the full Circle service commenced just over three weeks later. Metropolitan stations featured impressive classical buildings at street level and magnificent interiors with glazed arched roofs. The one at King's Cross was at Grays Inn Road but closed on 16 October 1940 because of bomb damage. New platforms for London Transport services (rather than those using the Widened Lines) opened further west nearer King's Cross main line station on 14 March 1941. Photograph John Edgington.

Although the Circle was operating at full capacity it was making little difference to street congestion in the middle of London, but more 'cut and cover' lines were out of the question because of the huge cost of construction and the chronic disruption caused. The City & South London, which opened in 1890 and became the core of the Northern line through King's Cross, was the world's first electric tube railway and proved a great success. It prompted several similar schemes, rendered feasible because of the invention of the Greathead Shield which could cut circular tunnels through the soft yet watertight London Clay. Another essential factor was the growing reliability of electric traction, the only option at deep levels. The Brompton & Piccadilly Circus Railway was incorporated in 1897, followed by the Great Northern & Strand Railway in 1899. The GN itself showed a benevolent interest in the latter but did not offer financial assistance as it was more interested in the City. Both companies soon came under the influence of the American financier Charles Tyson Yerkes who formed the Underground Electric Railways in 1902 and merged the two companies as the Great Northern Piccadilly & Brompton Railway, just the Piccadilly in everyday parlance. The whole line from Finsbury Park to Hammersmith via King's Cross, Piccadilly Circus, Knightsbridge and Earls Court opened on 15 December 1906 with motor coaches and trailers used from the outset. Surface buildings were very distinctive, like King's Cross with the ghostly shadow of the main line station behind it. They were designed by architect Leslie Green and finished in glazed ruby-red tiles with the occasional 'Arts & Crafts' motif. At platform level the tunnels were lined in white tiles relieved by patterned tiles in two shades of red. This photograph clearly shows G N PICCADILLY & BROMPTON RY in the windows while posters advertise 'Later trains on the Hampstead Tube', which later became part of the Northern Line. These two merged with the Baker Street & Waterloo to form the London Electric Railway on 1 July 1910 so the view probably dates from just after then as there are signs for that company. The Piccadilly was extended from Finsbury Park to Arnos Grove in September 1932 before the London Passenger Transport Board absorbed the London Electric Railway on 13 April 1933 and out to Cockfosters in July 1933 following the merger.

35

During 1884 the London & Southwark Subway Co was authorised to construct a deep level underground line from King William Street in the City to Elephant & Castle via Borough. Powers were soon obtained for an extension southwards to Kennington, Oval and Stockwell while at the same time the name was changed to City & South London Railway. Services began in December 1890 and their success led to the opening of another extension during November 1901, this time northwards from Borough to London Bridge, Bank, Moorgate and Angel. It was now logical to press on through King's Cross to Euston where a junction could be made with the Charing Cross Euston & Hampstead Railway. This section of line opened on 12 May 1907, followed by the Hampstead tube from Golders Green and Archway to Strand six weeks later. Close co-operation at King's Cross meant that the City & South London used the existing Piccadilly entrance building. The first trains consisted of diminutive electric locomotives hauling bogie coaches with tiny windows which immediately acquired the rather unfortunate nickname 'padded cells'. Later coaches had far bigger windows and these remained in use until the line closed in 1923 for reconstruction. This view of the City & South London eastbound platform at King's Cross was taken in 1924 when work had been completed and motor cars with trailers had been introduced. Early Art Deco lamps provided illumination and large advertisements were already a feature. On 13 April 1933 the City & South London became part of the London Transport Northern Line which extended from Edgware in the north to Morden in the south and eventually took over part of the former Great Northern line from Finsbury Park to Edgware and the branch from Finchley to High Barnet, both of which were originally served by trains from the Widened Lines and King's Cross terminus.

with the line through the Hotel Curve, at Metropolitan Junction.

New main platforms opened in starts on the arrival side of the terminus, serving less than perfectly until departure of the Midland in 1868. The first 'local lines' proper at King's Cross were opened in 1875, two platforms clinging to the west side of the station and closely bounded by a new engine yard. This yard replaced the two road engine shed shown on the 1874 Survey. Trains off the Metropolitan continued to set back into these departure platforms until the line up from the depths, on the Hotel Curve, was given its own platform in 1878. In the same year a second Gasworks Tunnel was burrowed out whilst in the previous year a second Copenhagen Tunnel, for goods, had been fashioned, a skew viaduct at its northern end giving independent access from the Up lines into the goods yards.

The new Gasworks Tunnel stood to the east of the original and necessitated a rebuilt York Road station (on its latter day site). Of two tracks, like the original, it was devoted to Up trains with its predecessor now given over to Down workings. It obviously revolutionised working at the terminus (at long last) and the two tunnels, Gasworks and Copenhagen, were part of a single project, of at least two Contracts; 'No 2' for 'King's Cross Additional Tunnel', had been accepted in 1876, at £45,000.

The Gasworks portion ran of course below the Regents Canal and all the work involved the most meticulous planning and foresight. There were a number of features, two coffer dams for the canal which imply a pumping clear of its waters 'the station works at York Road' (presumably the new station) and others. These included: 'extension of Congreve Street Bridge on

a skew ... underpinning potato warehouses in York Road ... Somers Bridge and widening Regents Canal ... metalling and draining Frederick Street New Coal Yard' as well as ... 'the Viaduct in the Goods Yard, with Skew Bridge', the lot costed at £5112.18s.9d. Colonel Yolland for the Board of Trade inspected the new 'Gas Works', or 'Maiden Lane' Tunnel on 20th February and reported on 27th. He described the ballast as ...*burnt clay, gravel and coarse sand ... constructed in London clay. This railway has been made longer than intended...* [presumably referring to the new work to serve as rebuilt York Road] *...and connections are not complete. Signals are also incomplete and improvements at the York Road station are in hand. These two new lines are intended for the fast and slow Up traffic to King's Cross and the Co desire permission to make use of one of them, adjacent to York Road station, before the*

Superficially the 'native village' in front of Cubitt's screen had not changed much by August 1963, but careful scrutiny reveals that the shop on the left has a closing down sale because all the clutter at the foot of King's Cross is about to be swept away. Work on the new Victoria Line tube which was to pass through King's Cross had also started. This project began with the wide ranging improvement schemes mooted after World War Two. Five new tube railways were proposed, 'Route C' being adopted as the Victoria Line. The purpose was to establish better links from North East London and the Victoria area to the West End and provide some relief to the overcrowded Central Line. An Act of Parliament was obtained in 1955 but London Transport claimed the venture would not be financially viable; it requested government support, but this was declined. Financial support was eventually forthcoming in summer 1962 and construction work began almost immediately. Walthamstow Central to Finsbury Park and Highbury opened on 1 September 1968, the section to King's Cross and Warren Street followed on 3 November 1968 and trains continued to Oxford Circus, Green Park and Victoria from 7 March 1969. With 75% Grant Aid under the 1968 Transport Act, an extension to Brixton opened on 23 July 1971. The Victoria Line soon became the busiest on London Transport. Photograph John Edgington.

A3 60058 BLAIR ATHOLL emerges from the smoky gloom of Gasworks Tunnel into bright morning sunshine with the 7.5am from Huntingdon on 11 July 1953. When searching for suitable racehorse names for A1s and A3s the LNER did delve into history to a considerable degree, but never as far back as in this case. Blair Atholl was the winner of the 1864 Derby and St Leger, over sixty years before 2557 was completed at Doncaster Works in February 1925. The loco spent its last six years in the North East prior to withdrawal during June 1963. Photograph BKB Green.

Beyond Gasworks Tunnel the tracks out of King's Cross continue past Belle Isle where the North London viaduct passes overhead and the lines from Top Shed as well as the main goods depot trail in from the left. Immediately beyond this point Holloway bank continues through Copenhagen Tunnel which derives its name from nearby Copenhagen Fields. Emerging from Copenhagen Tunnel on 11 July 1953 and illuminated by the limited amount of morning sunshine managing to penetrate the smoke haze, N2 69523 heads north with a local working to Welwyn Garden City. It was the last N2 to leave King's Cross shed, for New England, on 26 May 1962 and the only one of the class to be preserved. Photograph Brian Morrison.

works are complete, to give facilities to alter the arrangement of lines in the station yard. The permanent way in a portion of the tunnel is laid too high, there not being sufficient clearance…

The inspector sanctioned use of the line to 'further expedite the work' but the problem of clearance had, he warned, to be attended 'at once'. Matters proceeded more or less without hitch after this and the second Gasworks bore 'was taken into use on Monday, March 4th 1878', a few days after Yolland's Board of Trade Report.

The doubling of capacity afforded by the new works meant a breathing space only; for years developments at King's Cross had only stumbled a step or two ahead of an operating quagmire. The great part of the main line departures, for instance, still used only the one original western platform, for instance, the latter day No.10, but named for many years, with some logic, 'No.1 Departure', Johns quotes Acworth in *The Railways of England*: *The King's Cross porters despatch human beings and the Finsbury Park people collect tickets, faster than on any line I know.*

Work was soon in hand to increase line capacity even further and, as before, the Copenhagen Tunnel had to be

enlarged first. A third double line bore was authorised by a Great Northern Railway Act of 1882 for 'Widening at Islington' and 'contract No 1' was accepted and signed by Mr Henry Lovatt of Wolverhampton, at £90,048.10s.4d, amended the next day to £90,298.10s.4d. This tunnel was the worst of the three in terms of construction; it had to be driven to the west of the original, was shallow in comparison to its predecessors and 'trade and industrie' had huddled about 'The Cally' (the Caledonian Road) above, variously noxious and benign but in every case a nuisance – the railway.

This third Copenhagen Tunnel consisted *of a railway commencing at four furlongs two and a half chains by a junction with the Company's Main Line at or near the south face of the bridge carrying the North London Railway over that line and terminating at one mile nine chains, 'GN mileage' by a junction with the said Main Line about three chains north of the north-east of the bridge carrying the Caledonian Road over the said Main Line.* These were the years when London, nowadays almost entirely de-industrialised, was possibly (as a city at least) the manufacturing and processing centre of *the World*. The tunnel was to run under

Blundell Street, Brewery Road, Market Road and the Caledonian Road and the factories to be underpinned read like a cavalcade of industrial ghosts: 'Messrs Gorridge & Co, Varnish Works; Messrs Crosse & Blackwell's Vinegar Brewery; Mr Kennedy's Albumen Works; Messrs Knight & Sons, Melters'. The bore was to be lined in 'good sound stock bricks', with recesses for permanent way staff ('sanctuaries') on 'each side 50ft apart'. The existing cattle pens at Holloway were to be 'removed and replaced'.

The third Copenhagen bore came into use in June 1886 and from 1890 steps were taken to replicate it with a third Gas Works Tunnel. Close to the surface and the King's Cross goods yard above, it made for some tricky subterranean work and it opened in the summer of 1892. The Great Northern had written to the Board of Trade on 6th May asking for the signalling works in connection with the new tunnel to be inspected; together with the 'first instalment of signalling of same from the West Box', it would be ready for use '10 days from 6th instant'.

Major Marindin inspected on 7th June and found the interlocking incorrect (few companies ever got it right straight off) and was obviously unhappy about the second-hand signal frame the thrifty GN had harnessed for the task. The company wrote again on 20th July, answering that 'good progress has been made with the work of altering the signalling … it will be ready for re-inspection on 7th August.' The Board of Trade was still less than keen and requested a new frame in the West Box, a demand eventually complied with the following year. 'The new frame was inspected on 20th April 1893 … there are 98 working levers and 42 spare levers'. This was just as well, for only in that year** (astonishingly, for the station had been working more than 40 years) was an additional main line departure platform provided. Late in 1893, in December, a proper double-faced platform was built, in the middle of the station, latterly numbered 5 and 6 but then termed No.5 Arrival and (on the west side) No.2 Departure.

There was now a long pause in such upheavals at King's Cross, until LNER days, though from the early 1890s a number of less obvious alterations took place. The suburban side, tucked out of the way beyond the west wall, was soon tackled and the loco yard continued its slow journey westwards. The island platform followed it to give an extra road; three tracks, each enjoying a platform face, were now available, in place of the previous two tracks/three platform faces. The curving line off the

Metropolitan was rendered somewhat less formidable and a separate platform made available on its west side. Largely cut off from view, by the waiting rooms and a wall, this became Platform A, latterly that is, No.16 and 17, and remained the most westerly at King's Cross. The building upheavals did little to dispel the pokey nature of 'the suburban side' and it remained a place of sudden turns and narrow walkways, but all was made more or less good and opened for traffic, by April 1895. Reading east to west from the platform alongside the west wall (known from 1924 as No.11) to the new line A, the platforms were titled E, D, C (loco yard in between), B and A. The whole lot was further altered in 1924, with removal of the loco yard (to its familiar site by Gasworks Tunnel) and the installation of a new double platform – but see later.

The station seems to have operated now with three Up and three Down lines; two Down in the third, westernmost Gasworks Tunnel, two Up through the second, easterly bore and a Down and Up line in the original, now the middle, tunnel. This last, original line served as 'up carriage line', for light engines, empty stock and as a shunting spur. In 1898 further alterations were made 'for the purpose of providing additional facilities for getting empty carriage trains into King's Cross'. For this 'an existing shunting neck'

(apparently 'South London siding') at Belle Isle was converted to a running line 'entered by a facing connection on the up main line opposite Belle Isle signal box. In consequence a new down box was built, 'Belle Isle Down', to give three boxes in the short stretch between Copenhagen and Gasworks Tunnels, from the south: 'Copenhagen Box', 'Belle Isle Up Box' and now 'Belle Isle Down Box'. This new line, the 'up carriage' was the only one with connection to all platforms, as Johns relates and from January 1922 it was 'renamed the up relief and resignalled to permit passenger train working, whilst retaining its usefulness for other types of movement'. With this the strict division of the station into arrival and departure sides was ended, though the effects on platform numbering and consequent passenger confusion and ire continued for many years.

*According to C A Johns, One Hundred Years at King's Cross, but 75ft according to J Medcalf – Notable Railway Stations, in The Railway Magazine.

**Johns notes the working timetable for July 1st 1893, a scheduled daily total of 539 trains, 274 down and 265 up. This included 77 down and 79 up goods working through the Metropolitan tunnels and no less than 98 passenger trains each way over the 'Met'.

An Up express enters Copenhagen Tunnel on the morning of 11 July 1953 with Doncaster V2 60867 in charge. This engine was no stranger to the GN main line and moved even closer to London when it was transferred to New England during 1955, finishing its days there in April 1962. In common with Gasworks Tunnel, three separate bores had to made here as traffic increased during the 19th century. The original 594yd tunnel opened in August 1850 when the temporary Maiden Lane terminus came into use, but congestion soon became a problem, especially following the admission of Midland trains to King's Cross in February 1858. With the situation becoming critical, the second Copenhagen Tunnel was sanctioned in 1866, but it was not ready for use until August 1877. These improvements were overwhelmed by growing demand almost immediately, an example being the 25% increase in season ticket holders between 1879 and 1881. The third Copenhagen Tunnel was authorised in 1882 and construction work proceeded with some urgency, allowing opening in June 1886. Photograph Brian Morrison.

Two great symbols of the Railway Age rise above surrounding streets, the most dramatic of such contrasts in London and one which is just as striking today. The sheer scale and Gothic exuberance of the train shed and red brick hotel at St Pancras remain awesome, although it is nearly a century and a half since they became features of the capital's skyline. It is inevitable that the Midland terminus looks down on King's Cross, that being the original intention to a certain extent, but the twin barrel roofs and simple yellow brick façade of the Great Northern station were just as much of a sensation when they were completed. Less than two decades separated the two great structures, but it is worth noting that while the building of King's Cross could only be illustrated by artists, photography had advanced sufficiently to record the construction of St Pancras. Originally King's Cross had a frontage parallel to the main road, but the Midland came along and rearranged the whole area. One outcome was a triangular parcel of land in front of the Great Northern station which became a byword for clutter and was often called the 'native village' by railwaymen. This busy scene includes early motor buses, one with an open top, and a new type in Pancras Road, together with a miscellany of delivery vehicles. Private cars are noticeably absent. Although the prominent advertisement for Jameson 'That's THE Whiskey' is relatively timeless, the posters to the right of it pin the date down fairly precisely. The Euston Cinema is showing a film about Jenny Lind with Grace Moore and Reginald Denney and the King's Cross Cinema has 'Plunder', these being released in 1930 and 1931 respectively. Meanwhile the Regent Theatre is advertising 'On Approval' from Saturday 8th August, so it is August 1931.

40

3. A Very Cheap Station

King's Cross had been built at a cost of £123,000 before 'additions in the shape of small suburban stations' took place. Fashion in taste cast it in different light over the years; at times its styling seemed at best irrelevant but now it is rightly applauded, and stoutly defended. Its future is assured and yes it's a joy to see it now so 'vibrant', which seems to be the preferred accolade *de nos jours*. Not so long ago Scots was the most exotic accent to be heard, and often, the Cross being something of a Scottish outpost. The tramp shuffling along York Way, the Porter, or the businessman stepping off the Queen of Scots Pullman could be Scottish, as likely as not. Now you are more likely to encounter a group of giggling Japanese. In the 1950s, pubs round about served stuff like Tartan bitter, the barrels coming up in the guards compartment of any convenient train; the stuff was horrible, nearly as bad as our home-grown Red Barrel, but it was different. Now, the beer – sorry, lager – will more likely have an unpronounceable name and hail from California; moreover, a pint now will cost more than a post-war porter's weekly wage.

Where once we had tea in a thick white cup, perhaps to wash down three little biscuits in a cellophane packet (you can still find these laid out for you in a certain homely type of British hotel) now there are coffees and snacks of a variety once undreamed of. It's no accident that those REFRESHMENT ROOM signs are long gone – wherever the passenger cares to look, there in front of his eyes is one food/hot drink 'outlet' or another. The problem is not finding somewhere for 'refreshment' but avoiding one!

All this was once unimaginable and we all delight in the thoroughgoing success that has been wrought from Cubitt's yellow brick masterpiece. Yet it is worth recalling that in the 1950s and 1960s almost anything 'Victorian'

A head-on view of King's Cross reveals the symmetry and basic simplicity of Cubitt's façade. In essence it is a tall brick wall across the end of the tracks with huge glazed openings reflecting the profile of the train sheds, together with projecting sections at the centre and margins. The clock tower is in the Railway Italianate style which had been favoured for some time, but at first glance this centrepiece may appear too modest for such an important terminus. Closer scrutiny reveals that its proportions are right for the overall balance of the design. Lower wings also displaying Italianate touches extend the length of the overall roof on either side, that visible here being the three-storey administrative and amenities block alongside what was the original departure platform, later No.10. On the opposite side, hidden by the tree in this view, is the covered cab road alongside the original arrival platform, later No.1. At some point it gained another storey for additional office accommodation. It is likely that this photograph was taken in 1924 during the Empire Exhibition at Wembley as a prominent hoarding reads *To Wembley, the only route into the Exhibition. Marylebone (LNER) for Exhibition Station. All trains non-stop. Buses from opposite here direct to Marylebone station.* On the right, near the open-top motor bus with the outside staircase, is the underground station, about the only touch of elegance in the 'native village'. Liptons Tea Rooms occupy the upper storey while a couple of travellers are studying a large map of the system which pre-dated the stylised version. At the street corner is another entrance signed UNDERGROUND. CITY & SOUTH LONDON RAILWAY KING'S CROSS STATION. Beyond it is a crudely half-timbered Parcels Forwarding Office with a couple of lorries outside, one lettered 'Lyons Tea'. Four horse-drawn buses appear to be stored in the yard further down the street. LNER posters are for Scarborough 'Queen of Watering Places' and 'Town to Coast Non-Stop' half-day excursions to Clacton, Lowestoft, Yarmouth, Hunstanton and Skegness varying from 6 shillings to 8 shillings. Note the tram tracks with their central conduit current supply.

Above. The oft-bemoaned clutter forming the 'native village' changed, grew and shrank over the years but it rarely became quite as shambolic as this. It is worth remembering that the miscellaneous sheds, corrugated iron lean-to, ladders propped up against a wall and sheeting draped over a weathered fence were part of the scene which greeted passengers travelling from London to Leeds, Newcastle and Edinburgh. It was not always so and many years ago a writer in the *LNER Magazine* wrote about the days when ladies in crinolines and their young men strolled unhurriedly across the open forecourt to the trains on York race days and 'a troop of Horse Guards in their gay uniforms and plumed helmets' might also be travelling. Whatever ugly manifestations might encroach upon it, the noble face of King's Cross managed to rise above the squalor, as is very apparent here. This view was probably taken in the late 1940s when work on restoring the windows was taking place.

Left. A remarkable view of the clock towers at King's Cross and St Pancras, in LNER days prior to the Second World War when the twin roofs of the former were fully glazed. The famous clock at King's Cross came from the Great Exhibition of 1851, an event which figured so large in the earliest days of the terminus. Originally it had four working faces but the one at the rear became neglected at a very early stage, which is hardly surprising as it would be virtually impossible for passengers to see it from any angle. One authority states that it was the only public striking clock installed at a railway station in Great Britain. Apparently the bells which sounded the hours and quarters were silenced in the First World War and subsequently removed for scrap metal in the Second. An intriguing feature of St Pancras was the statue of Britannia on top of the stepped gable. She was deliberately placed with her back to Euston, being part of the LNWR coat of arms, although by implication that meant acknowledging King's Cross!

This is the eastern aspect of the clock tower, probably during the early 1950s, and some repair work is about to take place by the look of the items on the parapet. The bell housing has been replaced by more lead flashing and a low wall. St Pancras station fills the background and its Gothic street level buildings are a contrast to the forest of chimneys belonging to the Great Northern Hotel on the right. King's Cross train shed in its later form with less glazing can be seen, while a corner of the 'native village' and the roof of the entrance veranda are down on the left.

It looks like the front of King's Cross is being spruced up here as the sign on the hoist cage to the left reads NEONORE STONE CLEANING and there are men at work with jets on the far side. A cab is about to enter the covered roadway to drop off passengers and the woman is striding purposefully past a building in the 'native village' occupied by the Salvation Army. British Railways are advertising March excursions on Sundays 15th and 29th from Euston to Wolverhampton (16s 6d), on Sundays 1st and 29th from King's Cross to Grimsby (19s 6d), on Sundays 8th and 22nd from Liverpool Street to Ipswich (8s 9d), every Saturday from Paddington to Oxford (13s 6d), every Sunday from St Pancras to Nottingham (15s 3d) and every Tuesday, Wednesday and Thursday from Waterloo to Bournemouth (12s 6d). The dates coincide with 1959 and 1964, and from the adjacent lettering style it will probably be the latter. That other poster observes 'I boil.. *I don't*.. I rinse.. *I won't*.. but we ALL agree on Spel. Washes everything magic. Handy 1s 0d, Giant 1s 11d'.

was routinely excoriated; 'Gothic', as typified by St Pancras was mocked and its removal presented almost as a public duty. King's Cross was a blackened hulk awaiting only a scheme for its decent but preferably speedy burial. Both stations in the end were saved by the insalubriousness of their surroundings. If there had been more money to be made, they would surely have gone...

In 1932, however, the station had been celebrated as an octogenarian marvel by the LNER – if by no-one else; Cubitt's frontage and the great train sheds were *thought a great deal of .. it wore a magnificent appearance and presented an extraordinary vista* though whoever wrote that was obviously leaving the 'native village' out of the said vista...

Some of the original shareholders however would not have been impressed by this and indeed were not enamoured of the project at the time. There were complaints of the extravagance involved: *To their criticisms Edmund Denison, famous chairman of the old Great Northern, characteristically replied, 'I am authorised to state that it is the cheapest building for what it contains and will contain, that can be pointed out in London; I am told – I am not the architect and I do not estimate it – that it will not have cost more than £123,500. If that is the case, I have no difficulty at all in saying that it is a very cheap station. Bear in mind, however, that we paid by arbitration and award, I think, about £65,000 for the two old buildings that stood there and then we*

had to excavate the ground before the station was erected; so I do not pretend to say that the whole cost is only about £123,000.'

Kings Cross, befitting a great station, was long a place of milestones in the history of British railways; in 1879 the first railway dining car left the station, provided with foodstuffs 'from the Kings Cross cellars' which is somehow not all that reassuring... In 1888 it was the starting point for the expresses of the East Coast companies in their race against those of the West Coast to Edinburgh and 1894 saw the first British track circuit...

'The longest railway race in these islands' took place in 1895: *...before a truce was patched, King's Cross witnessed the departure of an express which cut down the original timing to Aberdeen of 11 hours 35 minutes to no less than 8 hours 40 minutes – a throughout speed of over 60 mph despite the fact that engines were changed at six points en route.*

You begin to feel that the well of achievement celebrated by the LNER in 1932 was running a bit dry; 'in 1921' for instance, King's cross apparently saw 'the first restaurant car in the world to be fitted with an electric kitchen'. A worthy development, no doubt, but hardly ranking as a major milestone in transport evolution. It left King's Cross on a Leeds express, incidentally.

The year 1927 saw a new world record in non-stop train running set up by the 9.50am from King's Cross which covered the 268½ miles non-stop to

Newcastle; in May 1928, this record was broken by the Flying Scotsman which from then on (during the summer months) made a daily world record non-stop run between King's Cross and Edinburgh – a distance of 392½ miles.

While all these photographs are evocative enough, and a precious record deserving of endless study, there are of course aspects of The Cross in steam days more difficult to sufficiently bring to life. Today, at first glance, like many great stations, all appears gleaming, shiny and modern; trains *hum* in and out without even the clackety-clack of rail joints (long gone) but while this is as true of King's Cross as anywhere else, the old place still has *something* of times gone by; the brickwork while cleaned up is still a *bit* grimy, ancient archways are still there along with some puzzling passageways and the trains are still close up, within touching distance at the front, at those buffers where once sat Pacifics, V2s, B1s and tanks. Then there was *the noise*. They weren't supposed to but every now and then one blew off, rendering all conversation at the front of the station impossible till the safety valves clamped back on. Some engines at the buffers, pilot or train engine, gave the outgoing carriages a 'push' as far as the platform ends and the first slow, then quickening exhaust beats reverberated and echoed: boom, *boom, boomboomboom,* under the great train sheds, sending plumes of smoke directly up, to curl back along the curve

Left. Mist lingers around King's Cross as RT buses and black cabs travel along the streets below and men work on the station clean up. Since the earlier close-up view of the tower was taken, it looks as if the wall where the bell mechanism once stood has been built up for some reason.

Below. This 1950s aerial photograph puts the station nicely in context. Beyond York Way, which runs along the far side, a mixture of Victorian houses, factories and new blocks of flats stretch away to the Regents Canal basin and beyond Caledonian Road towards Canonbury. Nearer the terminus, Pentonville Road is lined with shops. If anything, the 'native village' looks even worse from above, but apparently there were legal considerations which made its removal problematical. The railway itself did not help matters by occupying some of the shacks itself for Departmental purposes. A London street scene for the time would not be complete without a couple of RT buses.

45

A canopy was eventually provided in front of the terminus for horse cabs to unload passengers under shelter. The structure was devoid of ornamental brick or stone work which might have made it an arcade and it certainly lacked the architectural merit to justify the term *porte cochère*. Instead, the Great Northern used a few standard components to create this covered area. For instance, the spandrels between the columns and cross girders were a characteristic feature at stations opened on the Queensbury and Leicester Belgrave Road lines in 1879/1882, so that roughly dates the King's Cross structure. Rather more exotic is the exit from the original cab road with its extravagant brick arch and very intricate cast iron fanlight, but the inside of this passage was a touch less opulent as will be seen later. The date is January 1945 and a couple of military personnel are visible. As usual, there is a range of advertisements, including familiar ones for Bovril, Picture Post, Woman's Own and Radio Times, the last one above cast iron York Road and newer York Way signs on the extreme right. Health matters are also targeted, including 'Solidox.. Protects Teeth From Tartar' on the LNER Express Parcels van and two under the shadow of the canopy for a VD Clinic.

The cab entrance at the other end of the canopy looked even less prepossessing on 19 January 1945 and rivalled the 'native village' in appearance. A ladder is propped up against the end of the roof and scaffolding against the tower suggests that the KING'S CROSS lettering is receiving some attention. Because of wartime conditions, the western arch of Cubitt's façade has lost its glass and much of it is boarded up. Beyond the policemen, the squat hut which looks desperately in need of a lick of paint is actually the Season Ticket Office. Behind the soldier striding along on the right is a scrawled and not particularly friendly notice stating 'Closed. New Cloak Room round the corner'. JA Whaley, transporttreasury

46

of the arch, continuing a slow descent well after the engine responsible had come to a stop at the platform end.

The footbridge was an abiding feature; put up in 1893 along with the new platforms (to become 5 and 6) either side of the central dividing wall, not in living memory did it serve for passengers. Like so many of the King's Cross nooks and crannies, it did seem particularly to have been put there with passengers in mind!

Finally it is fascinating (reminding ourselves of Chairman Edmund Denison boasts of cheapness) that the noble arches were originally held up by 'laminated timber girders'. They acted as 'stretched bows' and were replaced on the east arrival side, where there was no compensating office structure, in 1870 'at a cost of £13,000.' The east departure side was similarly dealt with in 1886/67 and Johns relates how a travelling wooden stage on wheels was used for the work. It was put into store, he recounts, after the first part of the work and the numbered parts reassembled for the 1880s. Cheapness again!

Right. **In silhouette the canopy ironwork looked quite refined, as illustrated by this view. It could have been taken in 1945 as the building opposite at the corner** of Pentonville Road has a large advertisement for the film 'Latin Quarter', which was a British thriller released in that year. Prominent in the foreground is the boarding point for the Inter-Station Bus Service, which went forward to Euston, Paddington, Waterloo and Victoria, as shown on the stop sign. This facility was introduced by London Transport in 1936 using eight new Leyland Cubs with a large luggage locker under the raised rear portion of the bodywork. They worked from Old Kent Road garage and were painted in a striking livery of blue and primrose with a black roof. Apart from a period during the war when the service was suspended, the Cubs continued to perform their nocturnal journeys between the termini until replaced by RT double deckers in November 1950. The development of ordinary night routes meant that the special Inter-Station service was no longer needed.

The destination King's Cross was not just carried by local trains but buses as well, although it was an irregular short working of the normal service. Trolleybus route 517 from North Finchley and Highgate to King's Cross and Holborn Circus via Archway replaced tram route 17 in March 1938. This vehicle is Class J3 1042 (EXV 42), an AEC 664T with a Birmingham RC&W body delivered to Holloway garage in July 1938. Seen here some time during the late 1950s, the trolleybus is running empty from The Cross, where it has just been turned by a road inspector, and is travelling along Grays Inn Road. It will soon turn into Swinton Street then King's Cross Road and return the way it came past the station. No less than nine trolleybus routes served King's Cross. No.1042 was withdrawn in July 1960 and buses replaced trolleybuses on this route the following February. The grand emporium in the left background is still there, as is that very fine 'Arts & Crafts' frontage, now part of a Travelodge. JA Whaley, transporttreasury

King Cross Booking Office in the glare of fluorescent lights on 5 May 1965; very traditional, with cabinets, racks of tickets, plenty of sheets of paper clipped together and clerks standing at their respective windows. One member of staff appears to be filling in a ledger at a high desk. In fact the place had been functioning in this form for less than a quarter of a century as it had to be rebuilt after bombing in May 1941. At one of the windows there is that once common notice 'You can insure your luggage here'.

Judging by the two safes, this would be the mess room for the booking office. Viewed on 5 May 1965, the room was probably arranged for the purpose of taking the photograph as it seems unlikely that the tea towel with 'BR' woven into it would be neatly folded on top of the tray of cups in normal circumstances! The stove, kettle, sink and hot water geyser all seem to be 1950s vintage. The boxes on the shelves have number sequences scrawled on them, so could they be supplies of tickets?

During the 1950s King's Cross had a variety of train indicators tucked away in various corners around the station. This one, showing main line arrivals and not long installed, was above the public telephones at the inner end of Platform 1. The hydraulic buffers and slope up to the forecourt can be seen in the foreground. The date of the photograph can be gleaned from the poster on the right announcing the appearance of Dean Martin and Jerry Lewis at the London Palladium. This was in summer 1953.

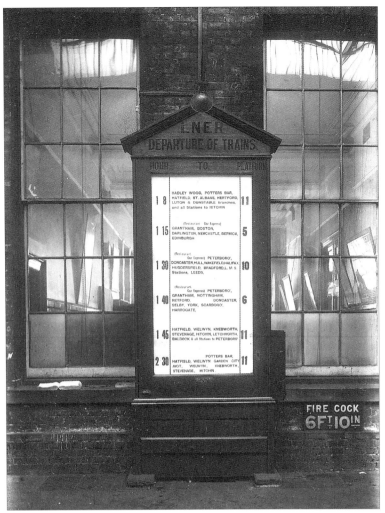

Left. This rather fine piece of LNER platform furniture was located in front of an equally grand room with, it seems, curiously hung picture or poster frames. Three long-distance services to Edinburgh, Leeds and York from the main station and three stopping trains from Platform 11 on the suburban side are due to leave over the next hour and a half. As used to be the case, places reached by connecting services are shown in the same lettering, which could be confusing.

Below. Taken from the footbridge (it provided access for the Civil Engineers offices and was not public) on 5 October 1938, this view shows Platforms 6, 7, 8 and 10 at the inner end of the western train shed, originally the departure side. The roof still consists largely of glass, which seems to have been kept reasonably clean, but much of this was replaced with boarding over the next couple of years or so. Possibly this was a safety measure in anticipation of bomb damage. All the public rooms and most of the station offices were alongside Platform 10, including the Booking Office, Ladies Waiting Room, General Enquiry Office, Telegraph Office and Tea Room. On the left is the arcade separating the two roofs, its openings leading through to Platform 5. The very restricted nature of the concourse is very apparent and the cab road is just the other side of the end wall. Below the huge end window are posters for Bovril, Guinness, Andrews Liver Salt, Player's and Laings Show House (see later) while a flower seller and the Cloak Room are housed in little kiosks on the concourse. In the foreground a rake of compartment stock has arrived behind a 4-4-0 while at Platform 10 the empty stock of The Yorkshire Pullman has been brought in by what looks like an N2.

Originally the arrival side, this is the eastern train shed from the footbridge on 5 October 1938, showing Platforms 1, 2, 4 and 5. Slightly more soot has been allowed to accumulate on the glazing it seems. The arcade leading to Platform 6 in the western half is on the right while the wall on the left also incorporates openings giving access to what was originally the cab road. This was definitely the neglected side of the station and the most prominent sign is one directing passengers to Platform 10 where they may partake of facilities offered by the Dining and Tea Rooms or Gentlemen's Hairdressing and Bath Rooms. The limited circulating area is even more obvious here, with waiting cabs visible just outside. It is interesting to note that advertising occupied virtually every space possible, which is certainly not the case today. WD&HO Wills say that the demand for their cigarettes increases daily, Craven 'A' are fine, tea revives you and Mackeson is perfection. You could use Evan Williams Shampoo, buy the new game Monopoly, see 'Break the News' or 'Midnight Intruder' at the Euston Cinema or visit Butlins Holiday Camps at Skegness or Clacton on Sea. Meanwhile, at Platform 1 a Cambridge train is leaving, or about to leave.

A very fine view of Platform 10 and the west side of the station shortly before noon one day just after Grouping. An interesting mix of main line rolling stock includes Great Northern bogies, early Gresley corridors and clerestory-roofed East Coast stock, with a Stirling saddle tank lurking in their midst. The original roof supports were of laminated timber, but their replacement with steel girders gave rise to some doubts as to whether the walls, especially the central arcade, would be able to withstand the extra strain. Such concerns were unfounded, as confirmed by a visit today. A close-up of the roof support on the left reveals the intricate and quite ornate nature of these early castings. There were few changes in the location of public facilities on Platform 10 as modern versions of the signs visible here could be seen in more or less the same places decades later. In view of the smoke haze constantly present, the advertisement for Dowbridge's Lung Tonic could be construed as appropriate!

Island Platforms 7 and 8 during the early 1950s, the modified roof allowing less light on the scene. Although there were still plenty of display boards on the walls at the time, the footbridge had long ceased to be regarded as an advertising hoarding. Pullman carriages forming The Queen of Scots have been brought into Platform 10 and await a Copley Hill Pacific. Meanwhile, the rake of Gresley coaches at Platform 7 on the right probably makes up The Northumbrian or its relief which ran a few minutes earlier. As can be seen, Platform 8 had an engine release, but pilot locos bringing empty stock into Platform 10 had to stay at the buffer stops until departure time, sometimes giving the train engine a bit of help for a short distance. Road 9, a siding, went with the widening of the island.

Despite its role as the main departure platform for long distance expresses, No.10 tended to be a haven for parcels barrows as well. In this 1950s view there is a gathering of them around an archway through to the suburban station. The sign seems to have eluded the authorities as it only refers to Platforms 11, 12 and 13 and may well be of Great Northern origin. A Gresley brake and some Thompson corridors can be seen on the centre road and no doubt the youngster is heading for his own haven, or maybe utopia, at the end of Platform 10.

Some time has elapsed and the sign has been replaced by a standard Eastern Region dark blue enamelled version, this time recognising that there are quite a lot of other platforms through the doorway. Further down Platform 10, the General Waiting Room has become plain Waiting Room. A herd of barrows is present again and there is also a lad heading for the platform end in the distance, but the most remarkable similarity between the two views is the presence of stabled Gresley and Thompson coaches in the same configuration and almost exactly the same place.

A stroll from the main platforms at King's Cross to the suburban station, often known as 'The Local', meant entering a different world. There was a provincial or even country air about it, rather than a place where long-distance expresses departed for far-off cities. Instead of a great arched train shed, the covered part had a low gabled roof which let plenty of light in and the platforms were made of timber boards which muffled the usual hubbub. This view was taken in summer 1934 and shows the entrance to Platform 11 from the homely concourse, Platforms 12 and 13 being off to the left and also under the roof. The archway leads to an open space between the suburban and main stations, which are slightly apart at this point, and a sign points potential customers to the gentlemen's emporium on Platform 10. A W H Smith bookstall can be seen on the left while there are the usual adverts for Stephens Ink and Mazawattee Tea. However, the one which deserves special applause is the whimsical effort 'Wireless Wisdom. Watt's an Ohm without Bovril'.

Platform 11 on 5 October 1938, though a casual observer might believe it to be some sort of workshop or stores area rather than part of a busy suburban passenger terminus. A selection of the ubiquitous King's Cross barrows dominates the scene, but there would not be a massive demand for them in this part of the station so they may be surplus to requirements for the time being and dumped out of the way and out of sight as far as the main station is concerned. Assorted lengths of timber and a few wicker baskets keep the trolleys company. Some work is going on, possibly to do with ducting for the rooms and offices on Platform 10, this being the original exterior wall of the west side of the terminus. A clue that this might be a passenger station is the Gresley quint-art which has been brought into Platform 12 by an N2.

Above. As suburban traffic grew, it was necessary to add further platforms to cope with peak demand and these took the form of an island outside the original Suburban Station on the site of the engine roads. Although part of one of the most famous stations in Britain, there was a curious isolated feel about the new platforms and they seemed to be shunned by the original suburban terminus, the blank bulk of the outer wall being visible on the right of this view. It is 24 September 1956 and there seems to be ample staff to deal with the volume of traffic at this particular time. The LNER vintage manually-operated passenger information contraption has been set correctly for the 11.21am departure, but could the 12.21pm be going further than Finsbury Park.

Below. If the original suburban station was a different world from the main line terminus and the island platforms were marginalised, then Platform 16 really was in the twilight zone. It stood on Hotel Curve immediately after the tunnel where trains from Moorgate left the Metropolitan Widened Lines (see also page 33). Platforms on passenger lines were normally

only allowed where the gradient was 1 in 260 or less, but the track here was at 1 in 60, having eased from 1 in 49 through the tunnel. There were catch points at the tunnel mouth, but these were only just clear of the usual eight-coach trains. Out of peak hours the island platforms tended to be quiet, but this one was usually deserted.

Returning to the east side of the main station, Platforms 2 and 4 formed an island, recorded here some time during 1957 completely devoid of trains and passengers. Platform 3 was a bay which went with the widening of No.4 beyond the footbridge. A rake of BR Standard coaches in carmine and cream, together with a couple of Gresley vehicles, stand in Platform 5. The row of shorter white posts between the tracks are taps for carriage watering purposes. A miscellaneous collection of parcels vans are waiting alongside Platform 1, a common sight with the stock often present for hours while loading took place.

Three railwaymen pass the time at the end of Platform 1 as the Daily Mirror shouts out its message. There are more modest advertisements for Pascall Sweets, Pal Hollow Ground Razors at 2d per blade and Henry Butcher & Co Auctioneers of Chancery Lane. Fortunately the approximate date can be gleaned from the poster for the London Palladium to the right of the public telephones. Gracie Fields appeared there with the Edwards Brothers, Jimmy Wheeler, the Merry Macs, Krista and Kristel and Eddie Fisher in April and May 1953. Imminent train arrivals according to the display on the left include the 10.40am Buffet Express from Cambridge, the 10.30am from Cleethorpes and Grimsby and the 'West Riding' from Leeds and Bradford at 11.49am.

This view along Platform 1 was taken just before 2pm on a winter day judging by the mix of smoke and mist just about admitting some weak sunshine. There is nothing to pin the date down this time, although there are coaches in 'blood and custard' on the left so it is probably early 1950s. The advertisement for Henry Butcher the Auctioneer is accompanied by others for Barnardo's Homes and, what a surprise, Stephens Ink. Most remarkable is that something seems to be going on high up away to the left as everybody from the footplate crew in the foreground to the old lady sitting on the barrow is looking that way!

Platform 1 could be bleak and uninviting, especially when viewed from the outer end of the train shed as in this early 1950s scene. The gloom is not helped by maintenance work on the roof which is limiting the amount of light even more. An almost continuous row of barrows is partly explained by the facility clearly signposted in the foreground, although vans and lorries swelled the influx via the cab road further down the platform. There is a flurry of activity over on Platform 4 where an express has just arrived. The brick towers this side of the footbridge are lifts.

Platform 1 in its familiar guise as a parcels depot on 20 February 1963. Anyone wishing to partake of the Gentlemen's convenience would be advised to leave plenty of time to negotiate the almost impenetrable barrier of trolleys. Despite the rather grand stairway was to provide access to the Chief Civil Engineer's offices. The once grand covered cab road ran beyond those archways in the east wall of the train shed.

Another train of mail barrows has been parked under the footbridge and a BR van has backed through one of the arches from the cab road to disgorge more sacks on to Platform 1. Considering its very substantial roof, could the Gents under the stairs have once functioned as an air raid shelter? The Chief Civil Engineers offices have been built on a solid girder frame above the roadway, as can be seen through the nearest arch.

Above. At Christmas Platform 1 tended to be overwhelmed by mail bags and this is the Festive Season chaos at 9.50am on 1 December 1960. It seems that many regular commuters from suburban stations opted for a Moorgate train, especially if it looked as if it might be the first away from Finsbury Park. After getting off at York Road, many headed towards Platform 1 and made a dash for the Underground that way. It would probably not have been particularly wise to attempt this in December! No doubt it was calmer on Platform 5 where a new Brush Type 2 has arrived with corridor stock.

Left. Beyond Platform 1 there was a particularly unkempt part of King's Cross which had once been the covered way where horse-drawn cabs collected their passengers, including nobility. By 20 February 1963 when these photographs were taken, its main function was for vans and lorries delivering parcels and post. In this view the eastern train shed forms the background and mailbags awaiting loading can be seen the other side of the footbridge. The Gents adds a touch of decorative glazed brickwork to the scene.

The view north along the cab road towards the entrance with the wall adjoining York Road, later York Way, on the right. The front of a BR Scammell mechanical horse just gets a look in on the extreme left. Almost inevitably the wall sign KEEP THE STATION TIDY is accompanied by a discarded bucket, some old paint pots, a little pile of sand, some screwed up cardboard and a mangled metal frame. Perhaps the most astonishing fact about this far from salubrious place is that it was regularly used by royalty after an overnight journey from Balmoral, departing in their limousines of course! This is now the site of 'Platform 0'.

It gets worse... The floor of the Chief Civil Engineers Office lowers the headroom of the cab road at this point, but its supports provide a little alcove which seems to have become a haven for three new baby carriages in transit. Hopefully they have not been forgotten as labelling on the covers tells everyone how good they are, 'The coach-built baby carriage, warm in winter, cool in summer, for the mother who puts her baby's comfort first'. Obviously only the best cardboard has been used as there is a warning, 'This cover if not returned will be charged 5 shillings'.

York Road station stood between Gasworks Tunnel and the point where the East Branch went underground. It was obviously associated with King's Cross and carried 'King's Cross York Road' signs in BR days, but seemed aloof from the terminus. There was also a curious track arrangement brought about by the nature of the site. The northern part of the station was actually on the Up Slow line, but mid-way along the platform this diverged from the Widened Lines track to run into Platform 1 of the main station. This view was taken during the 1950s before the canopy was cut back to the supporting columns. There was no question of spending any money renewing it in full as hardly anybody actually boarded trains there. The eastern bore of Gasworks Tunnel is on the left while buildings in York Way, formerly York Road, form the backdrop. Photograph D Clayton.

The cobbled approach to York Road station, probably in the early 1900s. Early morning sunshine brightens up the frontage and a few people trudge up the cobbled approach road. In fact the morning peak period was the only time the place came alive and as a result it had a certain hangdog air about it. This was not helped by the decidedly dull Great Northern buildings and plain canopy which spent a large proportion of their existence in need of a lick of paint. The driveway remained cobbled until the end, its fairly steep slope being treacherous in wet or icy conditions. Most people alighting here would need to continue their journey on the Underground, thus the walk alongside the bleak eastern wall of the terminus or through the obstacle course of barrows and parcels that occupied Platform 1.

Above. This fine prospect (a 'best fit' of two photographs which don't quite match) of the north London townscape around King's Cross and St Pancras was taken in 1936 and clearly shows that there was a third railway gem in the form of the Great Northern Hotel. Here it is nicely illuminated by low sunshine on a winter morning. Without the two stations the building would have dominated the area in its own right, but with their charismatic presence it was bound to be figuratively in the shade. By the mid-1930s the perimeter of the 'native village' had been tidied up a touch by a screen wall with hoardings alongside the station approach road and a row of Art Deco shops on the corner. Sally is selling lingerie and hosiery, M Janet FRS is running a chemists shop and Covent Garden Florists speaks for itself. The Great Northern Hotel was not ignored when it came to accretions. On the corner of Pancras Road is Jack's Snack Bar which proudly advertises Melbray Pies made in Hurlingham Road SW6. Newly erected behind this establishment is probably the oddest building to grace the scene, the Laings Show House urging those heading to and from local trains to consider the delights of rural living. 'Pretty villages in Hertfordshire' and 'County homes in Bedfordshire and Hertfordshire' had been advertised for some thirty years, enticing the lower middle class to flee their Islington villas and 'exchange fog for sunshine'. The Laings detached or semi-detached property, built of brick with a tiled roof and curved steel windows, was the latest manifestation of this campaign. Although London was not enveloped in winter smog on this particular occasion, the trams and taxis in Pancras Road are certainly a far cry from leafy lanes in the Home Counties.

Left. The Great Northern Hotel opened in 1854 and was crescent-shaped, its frontage facing the station and its back curving along the original line of Old Pancras Road. This view was taken on 7 August 1947 looking south west from the Booking Office roof and clearly shows all eight floors, including the basement and attic. The entrance is noble enough, but inevitably the huge hotel fronting St Pancras towers above it in the background. Inside, the Great Northern was a warren of corridors and is remembered as an almost exotic deep-piled womb of a place suffused with a peculiar redness. Having said that, it was certainly not a case of 'no expense spared' at the construction phase. In May 1852 the contractor Jay stated that he was prepared to build the hotel for £20,000 but the Board required him to confer with Lewis Cubitt. Jay attended, with plans, later in the month and it was agreed that the building would be fireproofed at an extra cost of £1,000. In August the Board heard that the work would cost £1,600 more if Ancaster stone was used for external quoins, cornices and dressings instead of brick and cement, but Cubitt 'thought he ought not to recommend it'. Sadly the bounteous times faded away and as the twentieth century drew to a close the hotel shut its doors and became derelict. Demolition looked likely, but eventually it was rescued, underwent a four year refurbishment and reopened in 2013.

65

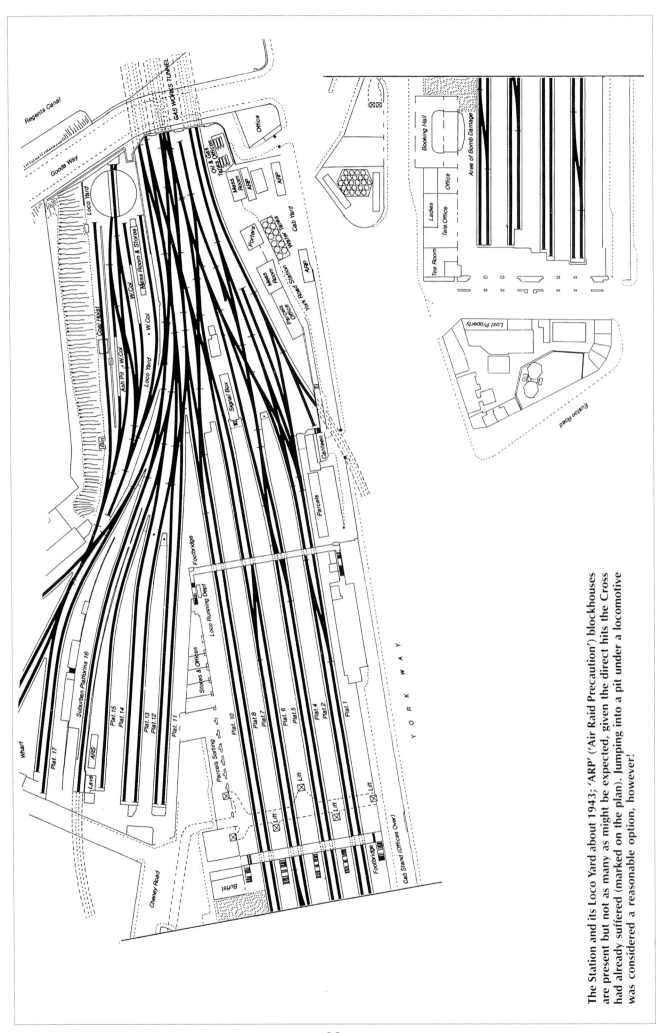

The Station and its Loco Yard about 1943; 'ARP' ('Air Raid Precaution') blockhouses are present but not as many as might be expected, given the direct hits the Cross had already suffered (marked on the plan). Jumping into a pit under a locomotive was considered a reasonable option, however!

66

4. On Shed

When a great railway entered London not only was it anxious (sometimes) to impress with the splendour of its terminus but in many instances similar, maybe greater, attention was paid to the arrangements for servicing and maintaining the locomotives. All of these were long ago overwhelmed by enlargement and rebuilding and perhaps the only reminder surviving now is the Roundhouse in Camden Town. The establishment at King's Cross was intended from the first to function as a 'engine repair station' as well as fuelling, watering and turning the locos. The result was a remarkable crescent-shaped building with no less than 25 roads set out as a fan of sidings. This was 1850-52, and by 1859 the Midland had erected a conventional roundhouse, for its own locomotives working in from Hitchin, close by. The Great Northern eight road straight shed, familiar to the end of steam, was built in front of the 'Crescent' and opened in the mid-1860s. The Midland thereupon decamped, opening its own terminus next door at St Pancras and the MR roundhouse was absorbed into 'Top Shed' as it was coming to be called. The old Crescent

was given over exclusively to repair work but with the goods depot also expanding space was limited and already the place was becoming cramped and awkward to work and throughout the rest of the century proposals were regularly examined to re-site the whole shed further out, along the line at Harringay and so on, to no effect. Improvements, alterations, re-roofings, turntables and coal stages all came and went over the years. The name 'Top Shed' presumably derived from its site 'up top' above the station. In this part of North London you went 'up' or 'down' somewhere ('Up Nag's Head' or 'Down the Cally', say). Called a Motive Power Depot under British Railways, it had attained it's greatest extent with modernisation in the 1930s, which saw six servicing pits installed, new turntable, track alterations, huge mechanical coaling plant and water softener. Bomb damage meant further repair work after the Second World War and most of the premises, straight shed and surviving parts of the Crescent building, were re-roofed. The first diesels were the 400hp shunters and the first large types, the EE 2000hp D200 Type 4s. After a short while the main line diesels were housed

at Hornsey until Finsbury Park Diesel Depot opened. Top Shed closed over the weekend of 15-16 June 1963 and was rapidly demolished and the site cleared.

Brian Bailey writes:
Recalling the period 1953-60 means quite a trip down memory lane. The rostering that had been introduced in autumn 1951 utilised frequent engine changes to reduce failures; by 1953 this was working and King's Cross had entered upon a period of stability with its main line engines that enabled regular manning of the A4s in the top link, especially on the lodging turns and the successful running of the non-stop each summer in partnership with Haymarket. A cleaning gang made up of mainly Poles, under a former driver foreman, that was not part of the progress to the footplate, enabled King's Cross to rival any other Motive Power Depot in the country in the appearance of its top link engines; anyone who can remember a King's Cross Pacific turned out for a special, from the royal train downwards, or the A4 for the first run of the season on the non-stop, will attest to that. By 1952 this was becoming apparent and by the time Peter Townend became the Shedmaster

Sometimes the smoky line-up outside King's Cross shed was made up almost entirely of Pacifics, but this one is slightly more varied. The larger engines were usually facing north ready to back down to the station or goods yard where their train would be waiting, but the J52 left of centre is no doubt on shunt duties. The photograph is undated, but at V2 60821 has a 34A shed plate and was at Top Shed from January 1953 to May 1956. Prior to that it was at St Margarets in Edinburgh and after its spell in London moved to New England then Grantham. On the far right, 60021 WILD SWAN was at King's Cross from June 1950 to when the shed closed in June 1963. In the centre is V2 60903, based at King's Cross throughout the 1950s and one of only eight to receive a double chimney, in this case during August 1961. Towards the left is V2 60912 which was a New England engine until summer 1959 and on the far left is B1 61139, allocated to King's Cross until February 1959. The roof is as rebuilt in brick and steel by BR after the War.

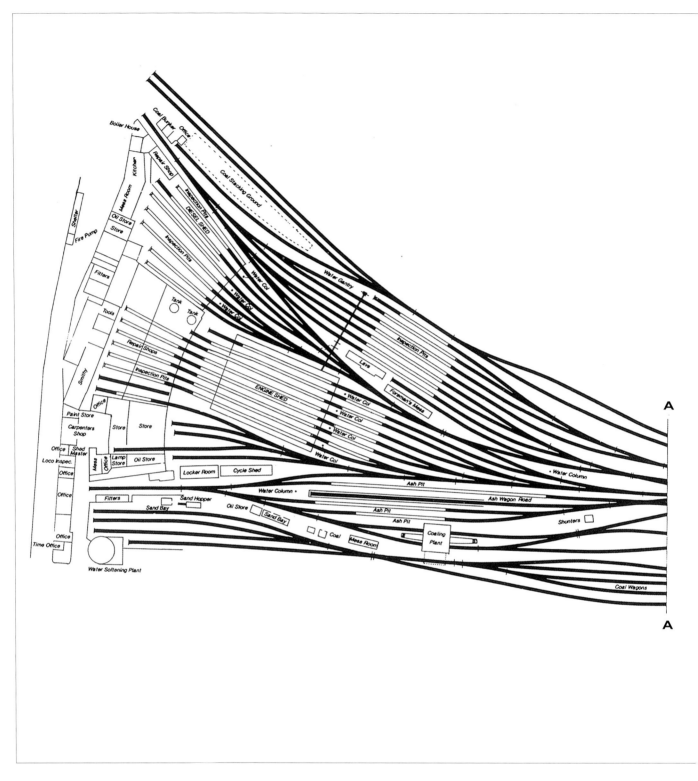

The diagram is labelled with various features including: Boiler House, Coal Bunker, Office, Shelter, Kitchen, Mess Room, Repair Shop, Coal Stacking Ground, Fire Pump, Oil Store, Store, Inspection Pit, DIESEL SHED, Inspection Pits, Fitters, Water Col, Water Gantry, Tank, Tank, Water Col, Water Col, Tools, Inspection Pits, Repair Shops, Smithy, ENGINE SHED, Inspection Pits, Loco, Foreman's Mess, Office, Paint Store, Water Col, Carpenters Shop, Store, Store, Water Col, Office, Shed Master, Loco Inspec., Mess, Office, Lamp Store, Oil Store, Locker Room, Cycle Shed, Water Col, Office, Water Column, Fitters, Sand Hopper, Water Column, Ash Pit, Ash Wagon Road, Office, Sand Bay, Oil Store, Sand Bay, Ash Pit, Time Office, Coal, Mess Room, Ash Pit, Coaling Plant, Shunters, Water Column, Water Softening Plant, Coal Wagons, A, A

in autumn 1956 the tradition was well established. At the time of his arrival there were nine A4s in the top link, with two regular crews each. In most cases the rosters were paired, so each engine did a short trip, out and home with one crew, while the other crew took the same engine on a lodging turn to Newcastle or Leeds. If there was a problem, the lodging crew took the regular engine, while the other crew were given a spare, which was either an A4 with a high mileage or possibly a good V2. The two engines set aside for the non-stop were two due for generals in March/April, so they were well run in by the end of May.

The cleaning gang were so proud of their efforts, that should it be necessary to return another depot's engine on a premier working like the Tees Tyne Pullman they polished it to Top Shed standards. Hence the rumours that a Gateshead A4 or A1 had been transferred to King's Cross if it was seen leaving at 4.45p.m. with the down train. This happened if the regular engine had failed in the NER the previous day or the scheduled engine had a maintenance problem, so the Gateshead engine for the Night Scotsman that was on lay-by was used and a King's Cross A4 was sent with the Gateshead crew at 10.15 p.m.

Because the engines shedded at King's Cross were either out on the road or under repair for regular maintenance, during most of the week the place seemed quite empty, even on a Saturday afternoon, especially in the summer. It was only on Sunday that engines were present in any numbers; not only the A4s but also the N2s and the relatively few V2s which worked in their own link on Class C goods to the North East and Scotland. The lodging turns on these were to York.

These are first memories that spring to mind, but always King's Cross had one surprise in the way of an unusual or rare engine that had worked up on a

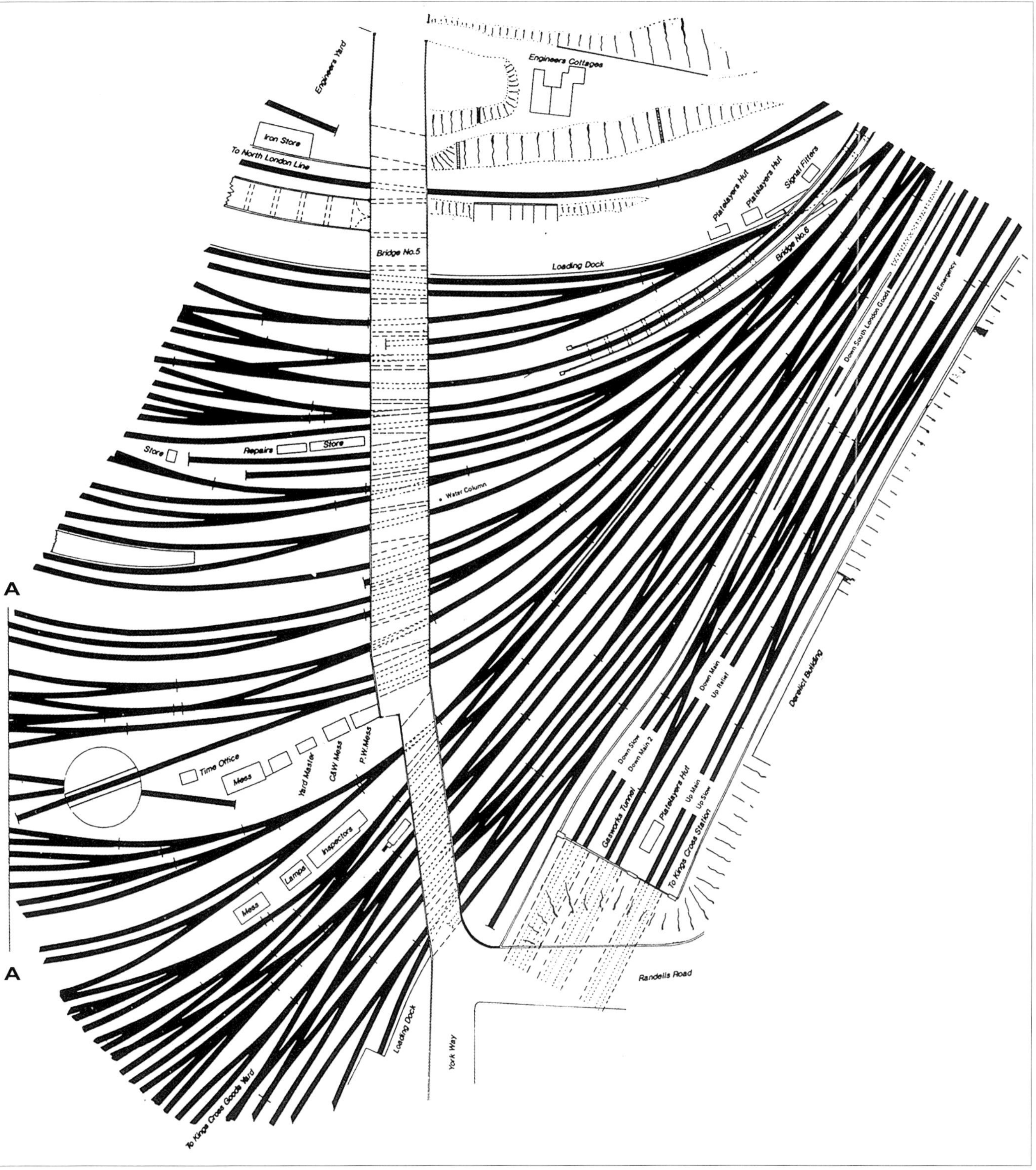
Engineers Yard
Engineers Cottages
Iron Store
To North London Line
Platelayers Hut
Platelayers Hut
Signal Fitters
Bridge No.5
Bridge No.6
Loading Dock
Down South London Goods
Up Emergency
Store
Repairs
Store
Water Column
A
A
Derelict Building
Down Main
Up Relief
Down Slow
Down Main 2
Platelayers Hut
Up Main
Up Slow
Gasworks Tunnel
To Kings Cross Station
Time Office
Mess
Yard Master
C&W Mess
P.W. Mess
Inspectors
Lamps
Mess
Randells Road
Loading Dock
York Way
To Kings Cross Goods Yard

special or while the rest of us were asleep. These ranged from NER K1s borrowed by New England to Scottish 4-6-2s running in from Doncaster, and B1s up on football specials from Lincolnshire or the West Riding. Even Dairycoates B1s appeared occasionally on fish trains from Hull.

Top Shed at its greatest extent in the 1950s, following the modernisation of the 1930s which left it with huge mechanical coaling plant, 70ft turntable and modern layout for the sequential servicing of locomotives. This is from the account in *Great Northern Railway Engine Sheds*, Volume 1, Griffiths and Hooper, Irwell Press 1989, though no one interested in the grand old place should be without Shedmaster Peter Townend's horse's mouth account *Top Shed* (various editions, Ian Allan). The LNER adopted (uniquely) the US model of open servicing roads. These are the seven parallel 'Inspection Pits' (the 'Back Pits') on the north side of the main building which were equipped with an overhead water gantry. A look at the plan will reveal how engines could move easily and judiciously through a couple of reversals between the inspection pits, the main shed or the coaling/ash pit roads. The extent of the original Crescent shed is clear to see.

Provision was made for servicing engines just outside the western train shed at King's Cross from the outset, but this had to make way for expansion of the suburban station in 1895. Fortunately there was enough land available next to the Hotel Curve to establish a new loco yard. This view, probably taken just before World War One, shows the ash pits. The stark outer wall of the Suburban Station forms the backdrop while the Widened Lines platform is off to the left at a slightly lower level. Ivatt Atlantic 1421, resplendent in Great Northern livery, is of particular interest. In an attempt to improve these large-boilered 4-4-2s, three experimental compound versions were put into service and this is the third one, following on from 292 and 1300. It was built by Doncaster Works as a 4-cylinder compound in August 1907 and despite being an improvement on its predecessors still gave plenty of trouble. The GN seems to have lost interest in the engine and Gresley had it reconstructed as a standard 2-cylinder Atlantic in 1920. As such it remained in service until withdrawn as 2851 in August 1947. Meanwhile, the loco yard was required for Platforms 14 and 15 which opened as an island in 1924. Ground had already been excavated west of the running lines near Gasworks Tunnel to create the fairly spacious area for servicing engines familiar in later years.

This view across the recently opened engine yard towards the station was probably taken early in 1932 as the new signal cabin can be seen in an advanced stage of construction towards the left. The site of the previous loco yard is marked by the island platform canopy shining through the haze below St Pancras clock tower. The Pacific is 2559 THE TETRARCH which was a Doncaster engine from April 1927 to October 1933, although it had been at King's Cross from new in April 1925 until April 1927. The N2s are 2681 (nearer) and 4734 beyond. The latter is devoid of condensing apparatus but had possessed it when delivered new to King's Cross in January 1921. The wagons of loco coal in the foreground include some from the Barber Walker colliery at Harworth on the Nottinghamshire/ Yorkshire border. The yard was not called 'Bottom Shed' but was usually termed simply the 'station loco'.

The original Great Northern Pacific 4470 GREAT NORTHERN stands in the engine yard at King's Cross on a bright day in 1931. As soon as he was appointed GN Locomotive Superintendent towards the end of 1911, Gresley expressed an interest in producing a larger passenger engine than the Ivatt Atlantics then in service. Wartime conditions and other demands delayed matters, but a firm proposal for a Pacific finally came about in April 1920. Newly built 1470 ran light engine to King's Cross where its size and fine proportions made a considerable impact during the official inspection on 7 April 1922. Three weeks later it was back in London with the 1.55pm arrival from Leeds. The second Pacific arrived in July and for the next decade both of them were regular visitors to King's Cross, although their home shed was Doncaster. For a few weeks in 1944, 4470 was actually allocated to King's Cross. With the exception of Atlantic HENRY OAKLEY, the GN had been against naming locomotives, but in 1922 the company knew that its independent existence would soon come to an end yet its first Pacific would command a huge amount of interest. As a result, the appropriate name GREAT NORTHERN was applied.

A4 4493 WOODCOCK stands over the pits in the engine yard, known to one and all as the 'Passenger Loco', during August 1938. The A4 name was originally applied to 4489 in May 1937 but that loco was renamed DOMINION OF CANADA the following month as one of those specifically allocated to the 'Coronation' streamlined trains. When 4493 was turned out by Doncaster Works in July 1937 the earlier name reappeared. This view shows the streamlined corridor tender well. Four were built for the Silver Jubilee locos and another seventeen ordered when mass production of A4s was agreed. Footplate crews had to be agile because of the nature of the job, but being supple was essential when working on these locos. The corridor was just 1ft 6in wide and 5ft 0in high. Furthermore, the floor was raised about 2ft above the base of the water tank so there was a high step at both ends. Photograph RE Vincent, transporttreasury

Blue liveried 60003 ANDREW K MCCOSH on the turntable road (presumably after halting for ONE MOMENT) in the Passenger Loco. The photograph is undated but the loco had been repainted in LNER Garter Blue from wartime black in June 1947 and acquired a coat of BR blue in April 1950, its final livery of Brunswick Green being applied in October 1951. Loco coal wagons on the left, an N2 with a Finsbury Park destination board on the bunker, an ash wagon at the far end of the pit and one or two goods yard buildings peeping over the fence. Despite the potential for ash and other debris, the yard is being kept very tidy. Photograph B K B Green.

On 23 June 1950 Cambridge B17 61636 HARLAXTON MANOR backs out of the engine yard to join its train, which is probably waiting at Platform 11 or 12. This loco had hardly ever been seen at King's Cross as it had been transferred to Cambridge less than three weeks earlier. It looks quite fresh after an overhaul at Gorton in May. Photograph Brian Bailey Collection.

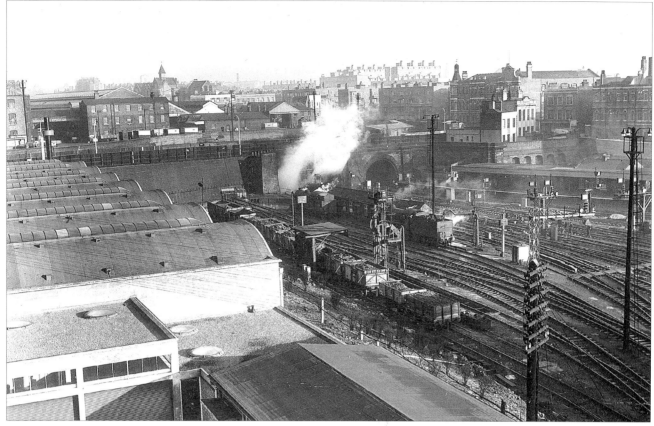

The morning of 10 January 1957 was crisp and sunny with the clear air over North London only slightly tainted by the effects of King's Cross engine yard and Gasworks Tunnel. Beyond the early 1950s BR Central Road Motors Depot (it dealt with all road vehicle repairs and maintenance in the district) the usual assortment of wagons wait, to offload their loco coal, while L1 67791 stands over the ash pit near the turntable. A B17 with LNER Standard tender rather than the Great Eastern type, is being watered. Trailers waiting for mechanical horses can be seen in the goods yard to the left, while York Road station peers through the forest of signals on the right.

A1/1 60113 GREAT NORTHERN on 29 August 1951. The rebuilding of Gresley's first Pacific by Thompson caused controversy at the time and for a long while afterwards. The controversial rebuild, as 4470, was allocated to King's Cross and employed on main line work, although there were some problems needing works visits initially. During September 1947 the Pacific underwent trials between Edinburgh and Dundee and was transferred to New England during June 1950, mainly for parcels and semi-fast passenger trains. It had no doubt made its way to London on such a working when seen here, still in BR blue but displaying a new nameplate with the GN coat-of-arms which was applied three months earlier. Photograph B K B Green.

It may look ramshackle in true railway yard tradition and a coat of paint would certainly not go amiss, but this crude hut was the 'hot seat' of motive power operations at King's Cross. The bells, engine oil cans and that most famous of headboards casually laid aside are clues that this is somewhere significant, despite its appearance. A foreman was present for 24 hours a day at the 'passenger loco', together with a variety of other staff depending on the time, day and season. A Coal Man was needed for most of the time and there were labourers who could fill a wagon with ash in a shift. There was also a procession of drivers and firemen making their way to Top Shed via the unofficial 'walk route' which involved a ladder at the Camley Street coal drops.

After a year and three months at New England, 60113 GREAT NORTHERN was sent to Grantham in September 1951 as part of the reorganisation which saw Eastern Region A4s being concentrated at King's Cross. At first it was used on top link work, but there was a tendency towards unreliability and the rebuild was eventually reduced to the role of spare engine. There was a brief stay at King's Cross again from September 1957, but during the following month it was moved on to Doncaster as Top Shed was in the process of eliminating non-standard locos. With the works where it was built then rebuilt on the doorstep, GREAT NORTHERN finished its days in quite a successful way. Doncaster used 60113 regularly on its passenger trains to London and this undated view shows it in the engine yard, probably after arriving on one of these services. The engine was condemned in November 1962. Photograph D A Potton, transporttreasury.

In December 1960 the first three Britannia Pacifics were transferred to Immingham for fast fish trains out of Grimsby Docks and the Cleethorpes-King's Cross passenger services. 70040 CLIVE OF INDIA on 3 May 1961 was one of them. The Passenger Loco existed, in essence, to save time. To run out to Top Shed might well take an hour; half an hour there and half an hour back, before even any coal was taken on board, without turning, fire cleaning and the rest. At peak times congestion made the difficulties far worse. So, 'turn round' at the terminus often meant using the station loco; on arrival at Kings Cross a relief crew always came on board to carry out disposal. The driver would start oiling round while the fireman pushed the fire over the drop grate, at the same time putting a bit of coal under the door. As soon as this burnt through some more went on, to minimise the smoke. By the time the loco got to the turntable with luck they'd be a good bank of fire to work on. Then it was over the pit to drop the clinker, the driver underneath to finish the oiling, top the tank up, pull coal forward, then back out onto the train. The engine would be back at the head of its return working in under two hours if all went to plan.

The engine yard from the embankment by Goods Way on 12 August 1959 with A1 60136 ALCAZAR on the turntable road. A Birmingham RCW diesel is on the ash pit siding and three fuel tankers stand at the end of the siding which used to be exclusively for loco coal wagons. There is also a profusion of oil drums and pieces of timber stacked around the buffer stops. New in November 1948, 60136 went to Copley Hill then King's Cross but was sent to Grantham in September 1956. It stayed until April 1957 then its time was subsequently shared between King's Cross and Doncaster until withdrawal in May 1963. Nick Nicolson, transporttreasury

Kings Cross 34A Allocations August 1950, October 1955 and April 1959

Kings Cross 34A Allocations August 1950

A4 4-6-2: 60003 ANDREW K MCCOSH, 60006 SIR RALPH WEDGWOOD, 60007 SIR NIGEL GRESLEY, 60008 DWIGHT D EISENHOWER, 60010 DOMINION OF CANADA, 60013 DOMINION OF NEW ZEALAND, 60014 SILVER LINK, 60017 SILVER FOX, 60021 WILD SWAN, 60022 MALLARD, 60025 FALCON, 60028 WALTER K WHIGHAM, 60029 WOODCOCK, 60030 GOLDEN FLEECE, 60032 GANNET, 60033 SEAGULL, 60034 LORD FARINGDON.

A3 4-6-2: 60039 SANDWICH, 60059 TRACERY, 60063 ISINGLAS, 60065 KNIGHT OF THISTLE, 60067 LADAS, 60089 FELSTEAD, 60105 VICTOR WILD, 60108 GAY CRUSADER, 60109 HERMIT, 60110 ROBERT THE DEVIL.

A1 4-6-2: 60122 CURLEW, 60128 BONGRACE, 60130 KESTREL, 60131 OSPREY, 60136 ALCAZAR, 60139 SEA EAGLE, 60144 KINGS COURIER, 60148 ABOYEUR, 60149 AMADIS, 60156 GREAT CENTRAL, 60157 GREAT EASTERN, 60158 ABERDONIAN.

W1 4-6-4: 60700.

V2 2-6-2: 60800 GREEN ARROW, 60813, 60814, 60821, 60823, 60862, 60873 COLDSTREAMER, 60892, 60900, 60903, 60909, 60914, 60915, 60922, 60983.

B1 4-6-0: 61113, 61129, 61136, 61137, 61138, 61139, 61200, 61203, 61251 OLIVER BURY, 61266.

F2 2-4-2T: 67111.

C12 4-4-2T: 67356, 67374.

L1 2-6-4T: 67792, 67793, 67796, 67797.

J52 0-6-0ST: 68764, 68770, 68771, 68772, 68780, 68797, 68799, 68802, 68803, 68805, 68809, 68818, 68822, 68828, 68830, 68831, 68832, 68838, 68854, 68855, 68861, 68862, 68864, 68873, 68874, 68878, 68881, 68884, 68888, 68889.

N2 0-6-2T: 69490, 69491, 69492, 69495, 69496, 69497, 69498, 69499, 69502, 69506, 69512, 69517, 69519, 69520, 69521, 69523, 69524, 69525, 69526, 69527, 69528, 69529, 69532, 69535, 69536, 69538, 69539, 69540, 69541, 69542, 69543, 69544, 69545, 69546, 69548, 69549, 69568, 69569, 69570, 69571, 69572, 69573, 69574, 69475, 69576, 69577, 69578, 69579, 69581, 69583, 69584, 69585, 69589, 69590, 69591, 69592, 69593.

Kings Cross 34A Allocations October 1955

A4 4-6-2: 60003 ANDREW K MCCOSH, 60006 SIR RALPH WEDGWOOD, 60007 SIR NIGEL GRESLEY, 60008 DWIGHT D EISENHOWER, 60010 DOMINION OF CANADA, 60013 DOMINION OF NEW ZEALAND, 60014 SILVER LINK, 60015 QUICKSILVER, 60017 SILVER FOX, 60021 WILD SWAN, 60022 MALLARD, 60025 FALCON, 60026 MILES BEEVOR, 60028 WALTER K WHIGHAM, 60029 WOODCOCK, 60030 GOLDEN FLEECE, 60032 GANNET, 60033 SEAGULL, 60034 LORD FARINGDON.

A3 4-6-2: 60062 MINORU, 60063 ISINGLASS.

V2 2-6-2: 60800 GREEN ARROW, 60814, 60821, 60828, 60855, 60862, 60876, 60909, 60914, 60983.

B1 4-6-0: 61075, 61139, 61200, 61203, 61331, 61364, 61393, 61394.

L1 2-6-4T: 67751, 67756, 67757, 67758, 67770, 67775, 67776, 67779, 67784, 67793, 67797, 67800.

J52 0-6-0ST: 68805, 68818, 68822, 68827, 68829, 68830, 68832, 68838, 68855, 68861, 68862, 68864, 68874, 68878, 68881, 68885, 68888.

J50 0-6-0T: 68946.

N2 0-6-2T: 69490, 69491, 69492, 69493, 69495, 69496, 69497, 69498, 69499, 69506, 69512, 69515, 69517, 69519, 69520, 69521, 69523, 69524, 69525, 69526, 69527, 69528, 69529, 69532, 69535, 69536, 69538, 69539, 69540, 69541, 69542, 69543, 69544, 69545, 69546, 69548, 69549, 69568, 69569, 69570, 69571, 69572, 69573, 69574, 69475, 69576, 69577, 69578, 69579, 69581, 69583, 69584, 69585, 69589, 69590, 69591, 69592, 69593.

Diesel Shunters: 11108, 11109, 11114, 12125, 12126, 12129, 12131, 12138.

Kings Cross 34A Allocations April 1959

A4 4-6-2: 60003 ANDREW K MCCOSH, 60006 SIR RALPH WEDGWOOD, 60007 SIR NIGEL GRESLEY, 60008 DWIGHT D EISENHOWER, 60010 DOMINION OF CANADA, 60013 DOMINION OF NEW ZEALAND, 60014 SILVER LINK, 60015 QUICKSILVER, 60017 SILVER FOX, 60021 WILD SWAN, 60022 MALLARD, 60025 FALCON, 60026 MILES BEEVOR, 60028 WALTER K WHIGHAM, 60029 WOODCOCK, 60030 GOLDEN FLEECE, 60032 GANNET, 60033 SEAGULL, 60034 LORD FARINGDON.

A3 4-6-2: 60039 SANDWICH, 60044 MELTON, 60055 WOOLWINDER, 60059 TRACERY, 60061 PRETTY POLLY, 60062 MINORU, 60066 MERRY HAMPTON, 60103 FLYING SCOTSMAN, 60109 HERMIT, 60110 ROBERT THE DEVIL.

V2 2-6-2: 60800 GREEN ARROW, 60814, 60820, 60854, 60862, 60871, 60902, 60903, 60914, 60950, 60983.

B1 4-6-0: 61075, 61174, 61179, 61200, 61272, 61331, 61364, 61393, 61394.

L1 2-6-4T: 67757, 67767, 67768, 67770, 67772, 67773, 67774, 67776, 67779, 67780, 67783, 67784, 67787, 67792, 67793, 67797, 67800.

J50 0-6-0T: 68946.

N2 0-6-2T: 69490, 69492, 69498, 69504, 69506, 69512, 69515, 69517, 69520, 69521, 69523, 69524, 69526, 69528, 69529, 69532, 69535, 69538, 69539, 69541, 69543, 69545, 69546, 69549, 69568, 69570, 69574, 69475, 69576, 69578, 69579, 69580, 69581, 69583, 69584, 69585, 69589, 69592, 69593.

Diesel Shunters: D3307, D3308, D3309, D3310, D3311, D3312, D3325, D3334, D3439, D3440, D3441, D3442, D3443, D3444, D3450, D3473, D3474, D3687, D3688, D3689.

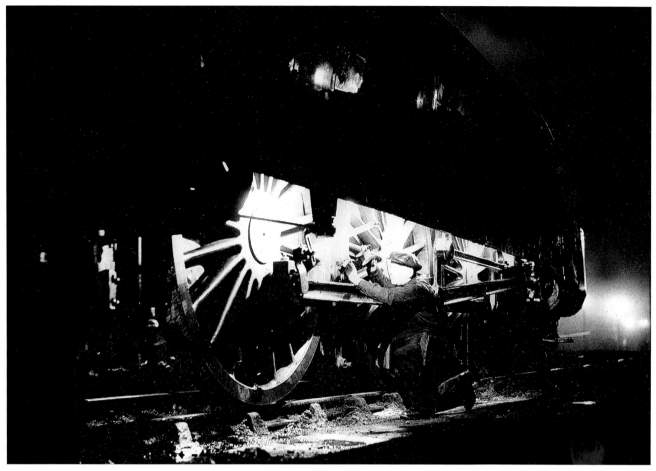

The unique W1 4-6-4 10000 receives attention at Top Shed, probably during the late 1930s and appropriately in the dead of night. It had been a revolutionary 4-cylinder compound featuring a marine-type water-tube boiler and a very high working pressure of 450lb psi, and though it did successfully work expresses, the problems were legion. It was taken into Doncaster Works in October 1936 and went through a drastic rebuild, to emerge in November 1937 with streamlined casing virtually identical to that of the A4s.

The fairly substantial repair shop which occupied the central part of the old 'Crescent' known as the 'Front Erecting Shop', 1927. This view was obviously posed as everyone, without exception, is looking at the camera. The front of what appears to be a K3 is in the right foreground while the tender of C1 3279 is prominent. The floor is seen to be laid entirely with old wooden wagon headstocks.

Amusing comparisons, especially the 'David and Goliath' type were popular with the railway companies during the inter-war years. Romney Hythe & Dymchurch No.7 TYPHOON was delivered to new Romney in May 1927 and visited King's Cross shed on the way to pose alongside 4472 FLYING SCOTSMAN. The narrow gauge railway owner and founder Captain J E P Howey already had three Pacifics based on the main line Gresley locos but wanted more power and speed from his engines so ordered a couple more with three rather than two cylinders, the other being No.8 HURRICANE. Increased running costs were not offset by the advantages so they were converted to two cylinders in 1935-36.

A4 60026 MILES BEEVOR shines at Top Shed on 29 April 1956. After leaving Doncaster Works as 4485 KESTREL in February 1937 it spent two years at Haymarket, interrupted by four months at Gateshead. Then King's Cross had the engine from March 1939 to April 1948, apart from a few weeks at Doncaster towards the end of 1947 when it was renamed after the last Chief General Manager of the LNER. Its next home was Grantham until September 1951 when it returned to King's Cross and stayed until the shed closed. Photograph M J Reade, ColourRail.

A1 60157 GREAT EASTERN in beautifully clean condition at Top Shed on 13 January 1957. When new from Doncaster in November 1949 this engine was allocated to King's Cross, but when the decision was made to concentrate Eastern Region A4s in London it moved to Grantham during September 1951. Another policy change came in September 1956 when through loco workings between King's Cross and Newcastle resumed, so 60157 went back to 34A that month along with 60149, 60156 and eventually 60158. A year or so later the influx of diesels had taken over duties previously rostered for A1s so they began to move away again.

Top right. A rather elegant Georgian porch welcomed footplate crews signing on at King's Cross Motive Power Depot, although the rest of the famous old building consisted of bricks from the less expensive end of the range. It was just a stroll from York Road round the perimeter of the yard, but was the gateway to a very different world. In this view part of the vast King's Cross goods yard can be seen on the left while the huge water softening plant is just off to the right. The alley straight ahead led to the first sidings and the sound of engines became louder. Beyond lay a part of the depot known enigmatically as 'The Continent'. An interesting curiosity is the road speed limit sign attached to the building. Rather than demanding a crawling 5mph or careful 10mph, those responsible decided on 8mph which would have been difficult to judge from the speedometers available on vehicles in the early 1950s!

Above. Rather surprisingly, 60015 QUICKSILVER looks slightly sullied at King's Cross on 13 January 1957. As 2510, this was the second A4 to be delivered from Doncaster and it was no doubt a welcome arrival at Top Shed as 2509 SILVER LINK had been working the 'Silver Jubilee' on its own for two weeks after the inaugural run in September 1935. After periods at Gateshead then King's Cross again, QUICKSILVER was at Grantham from August 1944 to the concentration of Eastern Region A4s at King's Cross in September 1951. It was withdrawn during April 1963 while still there. Nick Nicolson, transporttreasury

Right. New England V2 60908 in the yard with an A1 and A4, 13 January 1957. A wartime loco, built at Darlington in April 1940 and allocated to Peterborough until the late 1950s, it was one of the V2s sent to Nine Elms in May 1953 in the wake of the BIBBY LINE's alarming axle failure, as replacements for temporarily withdrawn Pacifics. The Merchant Navy locos were timetabled at up to 90mph on the Exeter services, a pace not expected of V2s back home. Nevertheless, once the Nine Elms crews got used to them the 2-6-2s proved they were quite capable of working on the Southern at this speed. 60908 returned to New England on 28 June 1953 and led a less exhilarating life up to withdrawal in May 1962. Nick Nicolson, transporttreasury

This re-railing demonstration took place in the shed yard on 31 May 1956 with an N2 the hapless subject of the exercise. Copley Hill A1 60133 POMMERN and Gateshead A1 60145 SAINT MUNGO are behind the van and coach on the adjacent track; maybe the best place should it all go wrong!

60017 SILVER FOX, one of the original A4s built for the Silver Jubilee, 1 November 1959; it was at Top Shed until it closed during June 1963. From the outset it was adorned with that stainless steel replica of a running fox on either side of the streamlined boiler. Many would agree that this was one of the most delightful motifs carried by a locomotive. Photograph Alec Swain, transporttreasury.

From the top of the water softening tower, King's Cross Motive Power Depot looked particularly gloomy and smoky on this occasion. On the left is the outer end of the conventional eight-road through shed which was erected in front of the original 'Crescent' in 1862. Like its predecessor, this shed became chronically overcrowded and preparation pits had to be provided on the far side in the open air. In the middle distance a long brick viaduct carries York Road across the approach tracks to the shed and goods yard, the ramp on the left being one of the points of access to the site. The main line into King's Cross passes left to right beyond York Road and the North London Railway viaduct can just be made out to the left. A prominent feature on this side is the Ebonite water tower, while away in the distance land rises beyond Highbury towards Haringey (Harringay) and Tottenham. Dominating the whole mid-1950s scene is the blackened bulk of the 'Cenotaph' mechanical coaling plant. It was completed towards the end of 1932 along with other improvements described as follows by the LNER: *The reconstruction of King's Cross Locomotive Depot has been in hand for several months and a concrete mixer, stacks of bricks and other paraphernalia of the Engineer's Department occupy a prominent place. The scheme is very comprehensive and includes the conversion of the carriage repair shop into a locomotive shed, the improvement of the layout of the yard with additional roads, the provision of wet ash pits, larger turntable, additional wheel drop and numerous other alterations such as the adoption of electrical energy, improvements to the sand and water supplies &c.*

Gateshead A3 60038 FIRDAUSSI, on 1 November 1959. It had only just been through the shops to have its double chimney fitted, so that probably explains its presentable state. The unusual name was derived from the winner of the 1932 St Leger owned by the Aga Khan. 60038 was withdrawn from Neville Hill in November 1963. Photograph Alec Swain, transporttreasury.

King's Cross panorama with the 70ft turntable apparently being cut up; the recorded date is 19 September 1961 and this would a strange course of action with the shed still open, and due to be so for a year or two. A new (second-hand) table was reportedly put in during October 1958 so this is what we could be looking at – though it has to be said RC Riley dates usually carry the authority of the Gospels. A minor mystery. Photograph R C Riley, transporttreasury

Well away from the glamorous aspects of steam-hauled expresses seen by passengers, there was of course a far less romantic side to operating locomotives characterised by grime and hard graft. Ardsley A1 60134 FOXHUNTER gets a bit of attention in North London, probably during the harsh winter of 1963. At the time Ardsley had a couple of A1s for working overnight parcels and express goods trains from Leeds to King's Cross. These two workings became notorious for derailments and collisions with other goods trains, one such incident resulting in the withdrawal of 60123 H A IVATT. The Pacific seen here was one of five which moved to Neville Hill in July 1963 where they deputised for diesels between Leeds and Newcastle and worked reliefs or specials over the Settle & Carlisle to Glasgow. During October 1963 FOXHUNTER was noted at St Enoch having arrived with the Car Sleeper on the last stage of its journey from Marylebone. Withdrawal came in October 1965 after almost exactly seventeen years service. Photograph transporttreasury.

A2 60533 HAPPY KNIGHT must have been a touch unhappy considering its condition at King's Cross shed on 5 May 1963. From November 1949 this was the only Peppercorn A2 on the Eastern Region, the other fourteen being in Scotland and the North East. When new and based at Copley Hill, 60533 worked Leeds-King's Cross expresses but its numerous trips out from New England normally involved braked goods, parcels and stopping passenger services to London. It was a Peterborough engine when this photograph was taken but withdrawal was announced the following month. Photograph Peter Groom.

60088 BOOK LAW on 1 November 1959, based mainly at Gateshead until November 1945. After then it was a Heaton loco for most of the time until withdrawal during October 1963, although the last five months were spent back at Gateshead. During the summer of 1961 it turned up on the Car Sleeper from Stirling at Sutton Coldfield and was sent to Aston shed while the authorities decided how to get it back to Newcastle. York's 60501 COCK O' THE NORTH, originally one of the five P2 2-8-2s, only survived for a few more weeks, till February 1960. Photograph Alec Swain, transporttreasury.

60029 WOODCOCK and 60026 MILES BEEVOR stand proudly at King's Cross shed on 11 March 1962, still very presentable despite the rising tide of dieselisation and the looming closure of Top Shed, a year and three months away. Both engines remained in service on that grim occasion and were moved to New England. WOODCOCK was condemned there four months later but MILES BEEVOR saw further service in Scotland. These engines had spent just over 25 years and just under 23 years respectively at King's Cross. Of the 35 streamlined Pacifics built only ten did not spend any time allocated to Top Shed, 60001, 60005, 60009, 60012, 60018, 60019, 60020, 60027 and 60031, together with 4469 which was destroyed in 1942. C Leigh Jones, ColourRail

The embankment and retaining wall above the turntable in the Passenger Loco gave a good view of the loco yard and approach tracks to King's Cross. York Road station is in the left background and empty stock for a Newcastle express is being propelled into the main station in June 1952. B17 61655 MIDDLESBROUGH saunters past, having turned after bringing in a train from Cambridge. RailOnline

Top Shed in transition on 21 January 1962. The Deltic looks new and shiny but from this angle of rather modest stature compared with its steam neighbours. On the left is A3 60065 KNIGHT OF THISTLE and an N2 while to the right is an A4 with a NOT TO BE MOVED notice. Departmental coaches complete the line up. RailOnline

Above the cavernous noise and turmoil of the approach to Gasworks Tunnel the whole character of King's Cross changed to a more private commercial world, much of it of ancient aspect. This view shows activity in Goods Way, that appropriately named thoroughfare which was driven across the roof of the tunnels at right angles to the tracks, fronting many of the goods depot buildings as well as giving access to the whole site. Many of the warehouses and sheds can be identified on the skyline of views looking north from the platforms in other chapters. Traffic remained largely agricultural in nature and a greater contrast to the nearby passenger station with its famed expresses can hardly be imagined. For example, deliveries throughout Central London were made by horse-drawn wagons in Great Northern days and an enormous volume of fodder had to be brought in to keep the animals fed. The depot was in a resolutely poor district and security was important, but it was difficult to police because there were ways in from numerous alleyways and the nearby canal. Urchins were drawn in by its mysteries, but at least they were easily spotted and ejected. Hundreds of men worked there and identifying strangers was more difficult. It was a place of smells, a vast walled-in food store where engine smoke drifted in but became overwhelmed by a distillation of farmyard Lincolnshire, vegetables and manure. Horses and carts were everywhere until the first replacements appeared in the form of steam lorries. When fires were livened up these sometimes managed to set light to street cobbles, many of which were tarred wooden blocks. Motor lorries became more common during the LNER era and after World War Two surplus army lorries flooded in to mingle with the railway vehicles. With sacks firmly roped down on the LNER trailer, a mechanical horse is ready to take to the streets.

5. The Tuber's Tale

Calculated to excite ideas on the subject of potatoes such as few people are accustomed to entertain...

For farm produce, coal and livestock, the King's Cross goods station and its yard was probably unrivalled in the capital. The humble potato lay at the heart of its greatness; it was an ancient trade which had nurtured the urban poor of England as much as any number of Irish peasants. The big London potato market had historically been at Tooley Street, Borough, and vessels laden with the tubers came to Thames wharves from all over the east coast. Once King's Cross was available this coastal trade was soon diverted, almost in its entirety, to the Great Northern.

The potato market grew up alongside York Way above the main line tunnel, on the eastern margin of the goods station. Earliest mention seems to have been in April 1853 in a Report from the General Manager, recommending a 'line of potato warehouses with two floors, estimated cost £2,000 to be erected in time for the next season in the Goods Station at King's Cross.' This was duly sanctioned by the Board which approved a further £820 a few days later for 'a third floor'.

A now long-forgotten publication, *The Leisure Hour*, observed of the place at its Victorian height: *If we go up Maiden-lane to what was formerly the passenger station of the Great Northern Railway, we shall come upon it and witness a spectacle calculated to excite ideas on the subject of potatoes such as few people are accustomed to entertain. The old station itself constitutes the market into which numerous lines of rails converge each and all of them loaded with huge trams or potato vans of a peculiar construction and built for this especial traffic. They have wide trap doors and wide folding doors at the side, for the convenience of unloading. Each one will contain some six or eight tons of tubers which are shot in bulk, without sacks and their unloading and sacking employs a considerable staff of men, who work continuously from one week's end to another. The number of vans must amount to several hundreds; they cover several acres of ground and as they stand in all directions, on the main-ways, sidings and turntables, they show like an irregular town of small houses in the labyrinths of which one might easily become bewildered and lost.*

The surrounding buildings, once the offices and waiting rooms for tickets and passengers, have been changed into depots and market houses crammed with plethoric sacks and the platform itself is heaped up with them, almost to the obstruction of the gangway. In addition to this, lofty brick edifices have arisen on the surrounding land to serve as warehouses for the salesman and potato-factors to whom the several cargoes are consigned by the growers. The quantity of potatoes sold in this market varies from 700 or 800 to as much as 1,000 tons per week and occasionally we are informed, in times of crises or anticipated dearth, almost double that amount.

Almost any of the 'dull roots' which could be produced in eastern England came to King's Cross and the Great Northern traffic grew on the essential requirements of the city – domestic heat, vegetables and meat. This had all been foreseen though its rapid growth took the company by surprise. The Islington Cattle Market Co had been in touch as early as the summer of 1849 with a prospectus and a request that the GN Board promote the undertaking. Consideration was deferred but soon, by June 1850, the GN was certainly alive to the possibilities. Cubitt was instructed to report without delay as to the availability of land for a cattle station 'at the Caledonian Road'. The London cattle traffic, the GN thought, was 'cognate to the subject of King's Cross' even though it was not 'in exact relation to it'. The two were inextricably linked, in other words.

J Medcalf, a retired Out Door Goods Manager whe began his career at the

The potato's progress, 1864. This was just a decade or so after the Market opened.

Most of the goods yard activity at King's Cross was away from the public gaze and those travelling by train saw even less of it, as this view illustrates. B3 6169 LORD FARINGDON pounds through Belle Isle with what is probably the Down Harrogate Pullman,' around 1925. The exploits of these ex-Great Central 4-6-0s out of King's Cross following Grouping are outlined in Chapter 6. The train is between Gasworks and Copenhagen Tunnels where a retaining wall separates the running lines from the fan of sidings leading to the main goods yard and engine shed. In the background a viaduct carries York Road across the tracks. Ivatt D2 4-4-0 4333 stands at the head of ten open wagons with ancient 'birdcage' carriages at each end. King's Cross had about thirteen of these locos at the time. On the extreme right is a Stirling J55 0-6-0ST engaged in shunting. Only just visible in front of York Road viaduct is another shunter, this one probably a Stirling J53 0-6-0ST which had not been rebuilt with a domed boiler. No doubt there were a dozen or more other saddle tanks in the yards beyond the bridge.

A corner of King's Cross goods yard with the usual range of wagons, including a couple of LMS vans, on 2 December 1947. The dark bulk of the water softening plant looms in the background. Daylight has gone, but fortunately the dark days of the war are over as well. The yard received several hits during the Blitz. On 8 September 1940 a high explosive bomb set fire to the Potato Market at 4.0am and caused some damage to the track. Another high explosive device knocked out part of the wall dividing the goods yard from the Down passenger lines at 11.50pm on 17 October 1940. Belle Isle box was also damaged. An unexploded bomb required closure of the Outwards Shed on 11 October 1940. Much more serious was a direct hit by a high explosive bomb at 10.30am on 9 November 1940. Extensive damage was caused to the Main Offices, Outwards Shed, Motor Garage, Invoicing and Counting Offices and Granary. Some damage was caused to the roofs and windows of other buildings. Sadly, 24 staff and a visitor were killed and 103 staff and another person injured. Finally, two high explosive bombs fell on 30 January 1941, one in the car park and another near the mess room in an existing crater. One member of staff was killed and another five injured. Information on these incidents came from *London Main Line War Damage* by B W L Brooksbank, published by Capital Transport.

Some idea of the spread of sidings in King's Cross goods yard can be gleaned from this photograph taken from the top of the water softener on 19 December 1947, less than a fortnight before the LNER became part of British Railways. A wide range of wagons are present, some lettered LMS as well as NE, and loads visible include oil drums, ridge tiles, scrap and straw. Wisps of steam from five shunters can be made out, probably saddle tanks. Hordes of men worked here, hardly surprising considering the labour intensive nature of the tasks, the incessant changeover of goods from wagon to cart and lorry, the lifting, hauling and carrying off. So it was that King's Cross goods played a great part in the economy of the grim streets round about. It had been bad in the 1930s but life was still very hard in this part of London, as in similar areas of other British cities. The winter of 1947 was particularly severe, adding to the misery of austerity and shortages following the war. In the King's Cross area child prostitution had a long pedigree, though the worst effects of poor nutrition had paradoxically been largely assuaged by the war as those who remained got a better balanced diet and those who went to war, apart from the obvious dangers, enjoyed light, air, decent food and a vermin-free bed for the first time in their lives. Back home, Copenhagen Street was typical. It was a local cobbled way leading off York Road opposite the Potato Market and had a noisome underground wrought iron public toilet, a puzzle to many residents. Who in their right mind would think to use it, particularly on hot summer days? Small boys swam 'the cut' to steal locust beans intended for cattle feed from barges, then eat them. Bed bugs made summer nights in Copenhagen Street especially unpleasant and bed legs were stood in paraffin pots to deter the vermin. In time the bugs learned to drop off the ceilings. Families lived more or less communally in the tenements, but to cram in more people the landlords had extended many of the homes forward to take up the tiny gardens. Done on the cheap, the original front steps were simply left in position in the new 'hallways' so that they ran on two levels *inside* the impossibly cramped houses.

temporary passenger station at Maiden Lane in 1850 lauded the pioneering qualities of the Great Northern with respect to the cattle trade, conducted as he saw it, 'in the lasting interests we may hope, of the people of London'. The hopes and plans of the 'Islington Cattle Co' were eventually made real through the agency of the Corporation and when the great cattle market was erected on Copenhagen Fields the GN was ideally placed for the business. It must have been the grandest cattle market on Earth; at each of its four corners stood a vast gin palace of a pub and at its centre a ridiculously ornate clock tower. Three of the pubs and the clock tower stand there still and much

of it was given over to council flats of the most unfortunate 1960s kind.

Medcalf had a keen sense of the ridiculous (probably the prime essential for the management of place like King's Cross Goods) and in his retirement he followed his first *Railway Magazine* writings by an unusual account, 'King's Cross Goods Station'. Of the cattle traffic he recalls: *direct connection was quickly made by means of the Holloway unloading pens and a private road leading straight to the market. In this way, no other railway company having similar access, we may fairly say countless droves of 'Durhams' 'Shorthorns', 'Teviots', and the rest have found their way to the stomachs of 'Her Majesty's faithful beefeaters' (meaning the*

entire population, barring vegetarians) to say nothing of untold myriads of sheep, pigs and such like 'small deer'. 'Improvements' have eaten up the old private way, but the stock still have the nearest access to the great market by crossing the Caledonian Road.

Ever after, traffic on and around the 'Cally' hereabouts was punctuated by the passing of the nervous herds, hoofs clattering and sliding on the mean cobbles. Ever and anon one bold animal would burst free to ensuing chaos, only to be run to earth in one of the numerous alley workshops round about, to the great consternation of all. It made for much laughter afterwards in one of the Market pubs. Like all the

Huge amounts of potatoes were handled at King's Cross and arrived from Bedfordshire, Hertfordshire and Cambridgeshire, but especially from Lincolnshire and Yorkshire. Considerable quantities also came from the North East and the Lothians. This scene inside the potato shed shows a glorious montage of sacks, ladders, scales and benches set in a building with ancient ironwork, hanging gas lamps and a well-glazed roof supported by slender ties. Sacks are hanging up to dry like Monday's washing and the occasional spud has escaped to languish forlornly between the rails. J Medcalf, the retired Great Northern Goods Manager quoted earlier described the business eloquently: *The Great Northern was the first Company to establish a large potato depot for London. The range of warehouses and covered siding space are the finest now extant, and in the season any number from 100 to 200 trucks a day are habitually turned into the respective "runs" for each merchant, and the contents disappear via greengrocers' vans, costers' carts and Westminster broughams into the capacious stomach of London. The trade is subject to fluctuations from two main causes, viz., weather and failure of crop, the increases and decreases being reckoned by scores of thousands of tons. In snowy or sharp frosty weather, there are sometimes a thousand trucks of this homely root standing in and about King's Cross, and the supply from sending stations has to be checked in order to prevent interference with other equally important traffic.*

King's Cross work, it was subject to great fluctuation: *when the company in turn with its competitors gets the whole of certain Scotch traffic, the work goes on, through the pens and up the lane, 'from morn till noon and noon to dewy eve', as though the universe were resolving itself into a chaos of mutton and pork, horns and hoofs, and ribs and sirloins.*

The 'chaos of mutton and pork' brought an unmistakable agricultural air to this part of London. Horses and the by-products thereof were everywhere, heaps of vegetables trundled by in carts, straw flew in the breeze, the sharp sweetness of manure hung in the air and foreign brown clay washed from the potatoes to lodge in every crevice. You even encounter flocks of geese, perhaps the most alarming animal of all of them. Coal pre-dated even the

vegetable trade into King's Cross; doubtless the two traffics waxed alongside each other but the coal did not simply fall into the waiting lap of the Great Northern. Medcalf again: *Very naturally the most ample provision has always been made and now exists at King's Cross for dealing with coal traffic. 'Coal' has been a sort of watchword of the Great Northern ever since their great fighting chairman, Mr Beckett Denison, put his back to the wall, and kept it there, session after session, with the determination to show that his railway was, amongst other things, a great coal carrying line, and that neither colliery combinations nor the schemes of rival managers, James Allport, Edward Watkins, Captain Huish, and the rest, should prevent the Company realising its destiny. King's Cross was the first great coal depot set up by a Railway Company for the supply of*

this now indispensable mineral to the inhabitants of London. Thus was the sea route in great measure 'displaced'.

It may be remembered that when merchants showed backwardness in coming forward to support the Great Northern, the latter grasped its nettle by buying coal and arranging for its disposal in the metropolis through the agency of Mr Herbert Clarke, a brother of the then General Manager, who for years was about the largest coal merchant in the world. The arrangement had to be superseded eventually, but its object was fully attained. Barriers were broken down in all directions, monopolies and privileges were broken up and free flow of the coal traffic secured for London and its immediate neighbourhood. The name of 'Herbert Clarke, Limited' still shows up amongst the coal sidings and offices at King's Cross like a battle-stained banner, the relic from some half forgotten war. When the first few trucks of coal began to trickle into King's Cross, just about 50 years ago, few could have thought the trade would ever reach the dimensions of the present day. The Midland Railway did not exist in London, the London and North Western were then too 'orty' to bother about 'coals' and the then Eastern Counties were very much of a 'negligible quantity'.

Coal drops were in operation more or less from the first and on 4 January 1852 Mr Child the 'Manager of the Coal Traffic, London District' reported to the Board upon the puzzling case of a coal labourer 'injured at the Coal Drops on 6th December 1852 when a coal waggon fell through the roof into the mess room while the men were at dinner and who subsequently died of measles. The parents are now in great distress.' They were given £5 but King's Cross was already a workplace of hazards; at the same meeting £10 was awarded to the widow of labourer John Keating, killed in the station on 14 December 1852.

By the end of the century the gross total of goods of all kinds was already close to *a million tons* a year *exclusive* of coal and of course livestock – dealt with up the road. A contract was let on 18 September 1896 for the re-roofing of the potato market, costed at £8,778. This involved 'the extension of the roof covering the present potato sidings at the back of the warehouses, the covering in of the roadway between the front of the warehouses and the York Road and other works'. Andrew Handyside of Derby, famous for many railway buildings, was the successful contractor.

There were '35 to 40' potato traders in late GN days and 28 by about 1930. By that time according to Christopher Maughan (*The Markets of London*, Pitman 1931) there were 39 warehouses, the tenants all well known as vegetable growers or merchants or in both capacities. There was in fact a long waiting list of applicants wanting a part in the trade and only lack of space prevented the construction of further warehouses for those anxious to participate. A line of track extended the whole length of the potato market termed, Maughan relates, 'the 10 o'clock Road', from its long association with a night goods. Wagons, up to 130 of them, were transferred off turntables into the warehouses, each accommodating two, three or four. The warehouses were 'the finest now extant' though Medcalf was well aware that the place was somewhat lacking in architectural beauty and classic lines. Comparison with the Regents Canal ('with its top dressing of London slime') to Venice was, he rightly felt … 'too poetic' a bias.

A long siding ran along the eastern wall of the main goods shed and this undated view, probably in the 1950s, shows rhubarb being loaded on to a lorry. The camera is pointing south westwards towards the gasometer nearest the Midland main line on the west side of Wharf Road. Girder bridges in the middle distance span the Regents Canal, later Grand Union Canal, and carry the main access road to King's Cross Goods and sidings into St Pancras Gasworks. The reinforced concrete beam and new brickwork above the lorry are probably repairs following bomb damage rather than deliberate modifications. The large main goods shed for general traffic was close to the potato market and dated from the earliest days of the depot. It featured a large number of tracks, inside and outside as well as across, all linked by a series of turntables. By the late 1890s the place was greatly overtaxed so a new but rather smaller shed for Down traffic, the 'Outward Shed', was put up to the west on the other side of the early coal yard. Tenders for the 'New Coal Yard and Goods Depot, London Goods Yard King's Cross' were signed with the aptly named Charles Wall on 9 December 1897. At a cost of £56,503 it included an inclined approach, retaining walls, coal drops and buildings on the site of the old coal yard between the old and new goods sheds. The new 'Outward Shed' was to stand on the ancient coal and stone dock by the Regents Canal and the whole of this, termed a 'barge basin', was to be pumped dry and 'efficient temporary dams' erected across its opening to the waterway.

Even the great goods shed proved inadequate to its task and in the early years of the new century was turned over to 'inwards' goods only, with 'outwards' dealt with at new premises on the site of the coal basin. The level of traffic could be quite astounding, the various peaks and fluctuations due to weather and crop failure alone being reckoned in 'scores of thousands of tons'. On occasion there might be a thousand wagons of potatoes (Medcalf calls it 'this homely root') standing in and about King's Cross. It was an incessant task to sort this lot and moving the wagons desired by each trader involved an astonishing, endless round of capstan and engine shunting work. Medcalf dryly paid tribute to the energy of the GN staff which enabled this work to be conquered season by season, 'with a moderate amount of patience and courtesy on the part of the merchants'. One of the best capstan men in the country was to be found at King's Cross, 'a mulatto and ex-sailor nearly as black as a negro' held in great regard, 'Black Jem'.

The potato market remained open 'the whole day' in earlier years and from about 5am to about 4pm by the 1930s. *The Leisure Hour* described our root with some exactness as 'not very ornamental'. The buyers attended, it was pointed out, really according to conditions elsewhere and when foreign potatoes arrived on the River the GN warehouses would be 'relatively deserted'. It was a state of affairs however 'which never lasts long, the reaction comes with the exhaustion of the sea borne cargoes and then the tide of potato dealers sets in again for the new market. The market opens at an early hour but it is not unusual to see the approaches swarming with vehicles of every kind before the gates are thrown open'.

Besides the metal-bodied open wagons, at least two venerable timber wagons have brought rhubarb from the 'Rhubarb Triangle' of West Yorkshire. Originally this referred to the area between Leeds, Bradford and Wakefield but now it is more precisely defined as lying between Wakefield, Morley and Rothwell. The Great Northern, then LNER, ran a special service from Ardsley to King's Cross every weekday night during the forced rhubarb season between Christmas and Easter. In its heyday the train carried up to 200 tons from some 200 growers, much of it destined for Covent Garden Market. Returning to the growth of the depot, before the new 'Outward Shed' was erected around 1898, the old shed dealt with both inward and outward goods in complete trains of up to 30 wagons. The practice for years was simply to draw out a Down train ready for its journey, but 'growing complexity of traffic and the pressure with regard to competitive towns' saw an alteration to the work, with individual trucks turned out over turntables from each platform to waiting trains in the parallel sidings. These were then dispatched within short intervals of each other instead of having lengthy waits between departures. The new Down goods shed clearly eliminated many of the difficulties as it was reported rather ponderously that *trucks for all parts of the Great Northern system are now loaded up simultaneously and dispatched in rapid relays to Clarence Yard, Holloway, for marshalling into the through trains for the West Riding, Manchester, Liverpool, Ireland and the Lancashire district, Scotland and the North Eastern line, Nottingham and Derbyshire, Staffordshire and the Potteries, Norwich, Yarmouth and the North Norfolk district, with of course Lincolnshire and the Home Counties, including such desirable nursery grounds for business as Cambridge and Luton.*

A trip working for the Widened Lines passes York Road station in 1934 with J52 0-6-0ST 3922 in charge. Although the first wagon belongs to the LNER the rest are private owner coal wagons as was very often the case with transfers via Snow Hill and Blackfriars to Southern Railway depots. The second wagon is the property of Barber Walker & Co which had several collieries and an extensive railway network near Eastwood on the Nottinghamshire/Derbyshire border. This wagon is lettered Bentley Colliery which was one of the company's ventures near Doncaster. Although the Great Northern main line was some way from existing collieries when it opened, a large share of the lucrative coal traffic to London was gained by spending a lot of money on new lines such as the Derbyshire Extension system which tapped the Barber Walker output in the Erewash Valley. The next three wagons are from Whitwick Colliery near Coalville in Leicestershire and after that is one from South Leicester Colliery on the ex-Midland line between Leicester and Burton on Trent. At Grouping, King's Cross had 28 of these saddle tanks and Hornsey 24. They remained an integral part of the Great Northern scene in London for another three decades, King's Cross having 30 at Nationalisation and Hornsey no less than 33. All those used on the Widened Lines were fitted with condensing apparatus, the pot on the saddle tank behind the chimney being part of it. The engine seen here was withdrawn from King's Cross as 68757 in December 1954.

It may be a dull day but there is plenty of life in J50 0-6-0T 68972 as it spins down Holloway Bank with a trip working in the mid-1950s, probably for King's Cross Yard. There are still trolleybus wires across the Caledonian Road overbridge and the fireman seems to have a teddy boy quiff! Although introduced by the Great Northern for heavy short distance coal traffic in the West Riding, this robust design was adopted by the LNER as a Group Standard and 62 were built between 1924 and 1939. One of the first batch went new to Stratford, the first to be allocated to the London area. During 1938 three existing J50s were transferred to King's Cross, another three to Hornsey and one to Hatfield, but they had all moved elsewhere by mid-

1941. Then came a major upheaval in 1952 when no less than thirty of them were transferred to Hornsey for shunting and trip workings, notably those to Southern region depots. They could handle five more wagons on the Widened Lines inclines than J52s and N1s so their introduction was understandable, but they were never fitted with condensing apparatus. 68972 moved from Colwick to Hornsey in October 1952 and stayed in London until July 1961 when it took up residence at Doncaster where it was withdrawn in September 1962.

J52 3111 shunts the eastern extremity of King's Cross Goods Yard near York Road one sunny afternoon during the 1930s. It finally finished shunting all those nooks and crannies of the King's Cross goods complex as 68803 in August 1953. A fascinating chance inclusion in this photograph is the distant building between the smokebox and the brake van. This was York Road station, opened by the Great Northern Piccadilly and Brompton Railway in December 1906 and closed on 19 September 1932 to give better line capacity when the extension from Finsbury Park to Arnos Grove opened.

The transfer of coal from railway wagons to dealers was made much easier by the 'shoots' between Regents Canal and Camley Street, just over a quarter of a mile north west of King's Cross station. These consisted of sturdy brick walls built up from ground level with rails and timber decking on top. Access was by means of a double track branch from the main goods yard which bridged the canal. This led to a traverser for conveying wagons to the appropriate siding for unloading, horse power then drawing them to the correct place. It appears that the original 'shoots' were put up by Mr Plimsoll, the former MP for Derby, but eventually they became Great Northern property when a lease expired towards the end of the nineteenth century. The waterway, by this time part of the Grand Union, can be seen on the left together with part of the bridge. Camley Street is away to the right just this side of the nearer gasometers. This view along the traverser, during the late 1950s, is looking almost directly south eastwards and the tower of St Pancras peeps above the rather rusty metal-bodied mineral wagon. If the distant gasometers were not there, the roof and clock tower of King's Cross would be visible directly down the line of the traverser.

Mr Plimsoll's depot was quite modest at first but it grew in size and complexity with the increasing quantity of coal handled. This view is looking south westwards from the canal bridge across the traverser and through some of the 'shoots' towards Camley Street which is at a lower level. The northernmost gasometer of the St Pancras works is on the left while vans in the distance are on the Midland line. The trolley which conveyed wagons on the traverser was powered by overhead electric wires, two of the supports for these being visible. Careful scrutiny reveals another trolley on a second traverser alongside Camley Street.

A standard 16 ton steel mineral wagon positioned on the trolley ready for its slow and no doubt wobbly procession above the yards and roofs of the King's Cross area. The electrical pick-up arrangement is clearly shown and rather unusually it consists of three wires. The camera is pointing roughly north west and on the right some of the sidings in a corner of the goods depot are visible above Pancras Lock on the Grand Union Canal. Top Shed is in the distance beyond the buildings on the right.

Above. Some details of the electrical equipment on the traverser trolley, viewed from the canal bridge. There are four flanged wheels taking the weight of the coal wagons, the two towards the centre being powered. An extension carries the motor and other apparatus, supported at the outer end by two very small wheels which are flangeless. The actual 'shoots' between the rails are visible below the timber-bodied wagons to the left and right.

Top right. It was quite a grim environment around the 'shoots' and this view shows the bleak access road between the waterway and the raised area supporting the rails. The bridge across the Grand Union Canal is off to the left while the traverser track continues south eastwards towards St Pancras Gasworks, one of the gasometers can just be seen through the mist. The tram-like control handle of the trolley is visible with what looks like a brake wheel to the right. Originally coal was tipped directly into canal barges, but this business declined, as related by the retired Goods Manager, 'The spacious basins provided for the now almost obsolete 'lighterage traffic' are going the way of all institutions that have served their turn'.

Right. Traders had access to the 'shoots', which became known as 'drops' in later years, via this malodorous passage next to the canal or direct from Camley Street. Coalmen arrived with their carts, then lorries, at the appropriate place and placed a sack at the end of the 'shoot'. When this was full the supply could be cut off until the next sack was ready to be filled. The traverser trolley in these views is different to the one seen earlier as it is devoid of a rudimentary roof for the operator yet has a lamp for night working.

Left. This is clearly a later view of the 'shoots' from the Regents Canal bridge as the nearer traverser is now out of use. Lengths of rail fixed by chairs and sleepers have been inserted where the trolley once ran. This means that manoeuvring wagons had to be done by the Camley Street traverser, which can just be seen beyond the wagon straight ahead. Beyond that is a diesel multiple unit on the St Pancras line. The King's Cross goods facilities were helped out by other depots, again as related by the retired Goods Manager: *The original goods station and yard have thrown out offshoots, all as busy in their degree as the parent stem, and some of almost equal importance. Royal Mint Street, Farringdon Street, Poplar and Victoria Docks are connected by North London, Metropolitan or Great Eastern Railway rails with the mother station, while extensive cartage and warehousing depots, like Bread Street, City, the 'Bee Hive', Whitecross Street and the George Inn in the Borough, besides the Company's chief City offices in Whittington Avenue, and numerous collecting and delivering centres all over London attest the constant growth of the business and the energy of the management in providing for it.*

Both below. Although this is actually Top Shed yard, it does show details of a typical four-plank timber wagon of the sort which arrived at King's Cross goods in their hundreds every day. Such rolling stock was once the lifeblood of the railway but very much unsung. This one is certainly a touch battered and by the look of the chalk notice on the side door it has been relegated to internal boiler house use. The gentlemen demonstrating the use of various pinch bars may well have been neighbours in Copenhagen Street.

The very close association between King's Cross and Pacifics started in a modest way while the LNER was being formed, commanded national attention during the late 1930s and only ebbed away with the tide of dieselisation four decades after it began. Gresley Pacifics 1470 GREAT NORTHERN and 1471 SIR FREDERICK BANBURY appeared before Grouping in April and July 1922 respectively, but before its demise the Great Northern ordered ten more 4-6-2s from Doncaster Works in July 1922, to be numbered 1472-1481. They entered service with the LNER during 1923 and, as with other GN locos, had 3000 added to their original numbers. Here is A1 4477 GAY CRUSADER leaving King's Cross with the 5.45pm express for Newcastle on a bright June day in 1933. On the left N1 4565 stands near an ex-GN six-wheel coach. These Ivatt 0-6-2Ts were built principally for suburban services out of King's Cross and cross-city goods traffic via the Widened Lines. Of the 56 engines in the class, the London area sheds at King's Cross, Hornsey and Hatfield had 51 in 1912, reduced to 45 in 1923 and 40 in 1939 as a result of N2s displacing them. Note that the throng at the end of Platform 10 was a phenomenon even in the 1930s.

6. LNER Efforts

As mentioned earlier, two new platforms were provided at the suburban station on the site of the loco yard, Nos.14 and 15 which were an island with an umbrella roof. Since 1906 the Great Northern had been promoting the delights of its rural catchment and Jackson has already noted some of the startling descriptions – 'Bracing Barnet' and among others and particularly bizarre, 'Picturesque Finchley'. These were The Northern Heights writ large; 'London's Healthiest and most Accessible Suburbs' and GN services made it possible to combine 'The Pleasures of the Country with the Privileges of Town'. The GN publicity booklet was entitled somewhat uncompromisingly *Where to Live* and though by the 1930s the LNER was glad to cast off much of the traffic to the Piccadilly and Northern lines, the new suburban platforms were much needed. 'Traffic Improvements at King's Cross', an official LNER Report on engineering progress at the terminus, appeared anonymously (though clearly provided by the LNER) in *The Railway Magazine* of 1924 and described the problems. King's Cross had begun to labour under the strict division between departures and arrivals and for many years 'quite as many' suburban trains ('on a large and growing scale') had originated or arrived at the main line station as were using the up and down Metropolitan connections. Indeed: *For a considerable time … it has been the practice during the busy periods to schedule many of the down suburban trains from Moorgate Street to pass the platform provided for them on the steep incline from the Metropolitan Railway (the Hotel Curve), suburban traffic from the main line station itself being largely provided for by separate trains.* These latter trains of course had to shunt across the station after their arrival to gain the departure platform. Some sophistry was needed to overcome the obvious drawbacks of all this and the key was the conversion of the 'Up carriage' into a standard running line, the 'Up relief'. Up trains could thereby run directly into all the platforms on the departure side. 'No point alterations' were involved but there was extensive re-signalling 'and in connection therewith the principles of three-position and upper-quadrant signalling have been adapted to the circumstances of the situation in a manner which introduces several interesting and novel features'.

The LNER, principally through Mr Brown CBE, the Chief Engineer, provided an exhaustive description of the new signalling. The crucial feature was that Up trains could now directly enter the suburban side and although the station approach remained 'very complicated' (an understatement) and certain movements had a profound blocking effect (principally those outwards from 1 to 5 which halted all inward movements) things were nevertheless much improved. There were now eleven roads in the main station and the old separate designation 1-5 for arrivals (all of which served platforms) and 1-2 for departures (these served platforms with 4 sidings in between) was abandoned. All lines (not

A decade after the LNER was formed there were 47 A1 Pacifics in service and 23 A3s with higher pressure boilers, five of which had been converted from A1s. As a result these locos were a very common sight at King's Cross, as is apparent in this photograph, which was probably taken in mid-1933. Four A1s are visible, including 2547 DONCASTER which is departing from Platform 8 with what is likely to be the 'Junior' Scotsman. This was a relief to the 10.0am Flying Scotsman waiting at Platform 10 with 4475 FLYING FOX in charge. Other A1s stand in Platforms 7 and 11 at the head of secondary expresses. The signal box, only a couple of years old but already carrying a veneer of soot, is on the left while the Suburban Station, including the island and Widened Lines platforms, is on the right. Three N2s are in view and there could be a fourth one at Platform 6 behind the steam.

platforms, note) were now renumbered from the original No 1. Thus 1-5 remained the same, No.2 departure became No.6 and the ancient No.1 departure, No 10. This slightly perverse sequence (maintaining a long history of the same) gave 1-6, 10 in the main station, allowing for one of the four sidings on the old departure side to be taken out and a long narrow platform inserted, numbered 7 and 8 in September 1926. No.9 siding was absorbed when Platform 7/8 was doubled in width in 1938. In the meantime in 1934 the LNER had abolished the stepped platform 3, for the series to run, by the end of the 1930s: 1 and 2, 4-8, 10. The local platforms beyond the west wall were numbered 11-17 in the scheme, incorporating the new umbrella roofed 14 and 15. It still made little obvious sense, and total confusion time – say five minutes for every new or occasional passenger – could possibly add up to centuries.

A1 2546 DONOVAN leaves Platform 6 in early 1932. Although the photograph is undated, it can be pinned down fairly well as the old Departure Side signal box has yet to be demolished but the new box is complete, apart from the extension which could only be erected when the redundant cabin was cleared away.

C2 3990 HENRY OAKLEY leaves Platform 11 with the 1.45pm to Cambridge one day in February 1925. Fifteen years previously, the 22 early Ivatt Atlantics had already been displaced from top main line duties by the far more numerous large-boilered variety, but that did not detract from the fact that they were very much pioneers. Photograph F R Hebron, Rail Archive Stephenson.

The last of the original Ivatt Atlantics at King's Cross on a stopping service, probably during 1925, in LNER livery but bearing its GN number 258 together with an N suffix prior to 3258 being applied. Doncaster completed the loco in June 1903 and it worked from Grantham for seventeen years.

The east side of King's Cross with the clock showing 12.40pm in 1924 – there is a large banner over the concourse advertising non-stop trains from Marylebone to the station for the Empire Exhibition. An N2 has brought in the empty stock at Platform 5 while the loco which arrived with the carriages at Platform 1 in the foreground has no doubt used the release road near the buffer stops. Great Northern bogie coaches are in evidence, including what appears to be 10036 in the foreground and 10042 in the right background. There are advertisements for Concord Port, Foster Clark's Cream Custard, National Gas and Oil Engines, Pears Soap (Matchless for Complexion), Maple & Co Furniture (London, Paris, Buenos Aires, Montevideo) and Wincarnis Tonic Wine which is said to cure, among other things, depression and sleeplessness.

From 1 May 1928 the 'Harrogate Pullman' was extended to Edinburgh Waverley and Glasgow Queen Street, becoming The Queen of Scots. This view from the footbridge showing the train standing at Platform 10 before commencing its long journey north was probably taken soon afterwards. The new all-steel Pullman cars are a marked contrast to the assortment of rolling stock, including an early GN bogie carriage, which has just been brought into Platform 6 beyond by an N7. Attendants sporting carnations are there to welcome and assist passengers while a constable keeps an eye on proceedings. J A Whaley, transporttreasury

Looking in the opposite direction along Platform 10, a large Ivatt Atlantic is at the head of The Queen of Scots. Less prestigious coaches occupy No.9 road while the rest of the train at Platform 6 is visible. There is a delightful cameo of Pullman car attendants performing their duties to the lower right. The dowager lady still looks a touch bewildered and anxious despite the reassurance being offered, while the gent in the hat could have a minor gripe about something as the official offers his full attention by dutifully bowing his head. All the signs in these two views are vintage Great Northern. J A Whaley, transporttreasury

The first large Ivatt Atlantic emerged from Doncaster Works towards the end of 1902, therefore prior to the last ten of the earlier variety entering service in 1903. Eventually 94 of the new type were built up to November 1910 and despite a disappointing start, together with four experimental locos, the class eventually put in some very fine performances. Photograph F R Hebron, Rail Archive Stephenson.

Grantham had large Atlantics from the outset for express duties as far as King's Cross and York, mainly on Edinburgh and Newcastle services. Even when Pacifics were available in abundance the shed retained plenty of C1s and still had fourteen of them in 1933. As far as is known, the engine seen here leaving King's Cross with the 1.40pm express to Leeds and Harrogate in February 1925 was at Grantham throughout its existence. It was completed at Doncaster Works as GN 1405 in June 1905, became LNER 4405 in January 1925 and was condemned in August 1947, just four months before it could have become BR 62835. Photograph F R Hebron, Rail Archive Stephenson.

In some ways this double-headed stopping train at King's Cross presents a rather melancholy picture, with the small Atlantic in its twilight years and the large Atlantic on a duty far removed from express work. This undated photograph was probably taken between May 1932 when the signalling became fully operational and April 1937 when 3258 was withdrawn. Although the glory days of Pullmans and prestigious race specials had faded away, the C1s did gain a new lease of life during World War Two when motive power was at a premium. The train is standing at Platform 13 in the covered part of the Suburban Station; the canopy of island platforms 14 and 15 can just be seen above the tender of the C2.

A prospect of the approach tracks from the station roof on 31 March 1933. The Gasworks Tunnel portals have disappeared from view, a reminder that the combination of dull mist and drifting smoke from the engine yard were not uncommon here. Engines making a contribution to the murk include two N1s, three Atlantics and a Pacific. King's Cross goods depot forms the skyline to the left while York Road station and York Road itself are on the right. Platforms 11, 10, 8 and 7 are on the left, the N2 and its train are at Platform 6 and Platforms 5, 3 and 2 are on the right. No.3 was abolished the following year and incorporated in a widened No.4.

Left. There were one or two unsung innovations during the LNER era, this being one of them. A portable drill for making holes in sleepers ready to take the chairs is being demonstrated on sidings at Belle Isle between Gasworks Tunnel and Copenhagen Tunnel during December 1933. The nifty machine was manufactured by B E N Patents of London and appears to consist of a petrol-driven generator driving an electric motor on the drill itself. The 150ft edifice in the background was built by John Tylor & Sons in 1870 and contained three water tanks. The firm made water-measuring instruments and the tower enabled them to be tested under a constant pressure. By 1960 the factory had been taken over by the Ebonite Container Co which made plastic accumulator boxes and the tower continued in use as a chimney, prominently displaying the firm's name. Unfortunately the landmark Ebonite Tower was demolished in June 1983. If the demonstration was staged officially by the LNER, surely someone should have thought more carefully about the ownership of the wagon standing prominently in the background!

Below. A shimmering B3, 6167, leaves King's Cross Platform 10 with the 11.15am Harrogate Pullman, this time in 1925. The engine went new to Gorton for hauling Marylebone trains, although Director 4-4-0s were still favoured for the best work. It was one of the three B3s transferred to King's Cross in 1923, the remaining three moving there or to Copley Hill in 1924. 6167 was in the Top Shed Leeds Pullman Link at this time with a dedicated driver. Photograph F R Hebron, Rail Archive Stephenson.

Similarly sparkling B3 6168 LORD STUART OF WORTLEY makes a stirring sight as it leaves King's Cross with the 11.15am Harrogate Pullman one day in 1924. Having been completed at Gorton Works in October 1920, the engine was only just over two years old when the LNER was formed, but it was transferred away from its native metals because the Locomotive Running Superintendent of the new company had held a similar post with the Great Central and wished to see how Robinson's largest passenger locomotives would perform on the GN main line. Although these 4-6-0s proved to be fast and strong, they burned a great deal of fuel and required different techniques from drivers and firemen accustomed to Ivatt Atlantics. Photograph F R Hebron, Rail Archive Stephenson.

D16 8783 is turned at King's Cross as an A1 Pacific exits Gasworks Tunnel with parcels vehicles. 8783 was new in July 1923 while 8787 went into service the following month. They were rebuilt with extended smokeboxes in 1928-29 and that is the form in which both locos are seen in these views.

During the 1930s, ex-Great Eastern D16 'Claud Hamilton' 4-4-0s 8783 and 8787 were a familiar sight at King's Cross and they invariably looked immaculate as these two engines had been moved to Cambridge in 1930 specifically for working the Royal train when the monarch or members of the family visited Sandringham. A special link of three crews was created for the purpose although this also involved ordinary timetabled trips from Cambridge to King's Lynn, Peterborough and, notably, King's Cross. Those to and from the capital were the 1.55pm slow from Cambridge and 6.55pm back, also a stopper. The latter is waiting to return to Cambridge behind 8787 one evening in the mid-1930s. During 1932 the LNER introduced five new weekday services between Cambridge and King's Cross which were lightweight, had fast timings and included a buffet car. At first D16s hauled them, but they became increasingly popular and acquired the sobriquet 'Beer Trains'. More coaches were provided so GN Atlantics were drafted in to Cambridge to cope with the heavier loads and B17s took over in 1937. Wartime conditions meant that 8787 lost its once immaculate green livery in 1941 and was painted all over black. Although going back to green in 1949 it never returned to Royal train duties but remained at Cambridge as a common user engine until February 1958.

Seen from York Road station, the Royal train leaves King's Cross for King's Lynn and Wolferton on an unknown date in 1931. 'Claud Hamilton' 8783 carries the appropriate headcode comprising a disc on all four lamp brackets and the cab roof has been painted white, a custom usually observed. Another D16 stands in the loco yard. The first occasion on which one of these GE 4-4-0s ran over the GN from Cambridge to King's Cross via Hitchin is thought to have been on a special working in February 1924, while the first Royal train to come this way was on 17 October 1924. This view also features an N2 on the left, a fogman's hut on the right and that curious workbench complete with drill and vice.

Another Great Eastern design to appear at King's Cross, this time actually allocated to Top Shed, was the N7. 2643, at King's Cross shed on 5 May 1935, had appeared from the Dalmuir Works of Beardmore during July 1927. All twenty engines produced in Glasgow went to the King's Cross District, most of them to Top Shed, and they immediately went into service on suburban passenger workings.

The LNER also added 47 more N2s to its stock and 2662, the first of twenty built by Hawthorn Leslie, at King's Cross in 1931. Modified condensing apparatus with the pipe entering the tank mid-way was fitted, but it proved as troublesome as the earlier type. Although 2662 was renumbered 9568 in 1946 a fierce chemical cleaning plant at Top Shed had scoured two numerals off one side, causing confusion. In desperation, someone had boldly chalked on the tank 'this engine is 9568 NOT 2668!' As 69568, this was the last of the class to leave Top Shed for storage on 26 May 1962.

There were changes to the 'native village' during the 1930s, as illustrated by these two photographs which were taken five years apart. This one is not dated, but with a bit of detective work the year and month can be pinned down fairly accurately. It is 12.10 pm on a dull summer day with the huts, sheds and larger accretions exposed to the public gaze, although a feeble attempt to hide them from the main road has been made in the form of a high wall which is a bit of an eyesore itself. Large sections of glazing have been removed from the end screens as there are clearly smoke dispersal problems with the original roofs. Some of the painted letters GREAT NORTHERN RAILWAY are showing beneath the raised characters forming LONDON & NORTH EASTERN RAILWAY while the Underground Group logo is prominently displayed beyond the ruby red tiled façade of King's Cross tube station. The poster at the *Evening News* stand in the foreground announcing 'Mystery of a Great Earthquake' is the clue to the period. At 1.30am on 7 June 1931 the Dogger Bank earthquake proved to be the strongest in the United Kingdom since records began. Despite its epicentre below the North Sea, it twisted the church spire at Filey, caused chimneys to collapse in Bridlington and, worst of all, knocked the head off the Dr Crippen waxwork at Madame Tussauds in London!

The King's Cross area at 10.50am in pleasant winter sunshine in 1936 – a view contemporaneous with the 'composite' one on page 65. Although the angle and altitude are different, a number of changes to the 'native village' are quite obvious. Firstly, some of the huts alongside the station approach road have gone and a wall plastered with posters has been erected. Secondly, one of the big sheds this side of the Underground station have been demolished, although the other has been retained for the LNER Parcels Forwarding Office necessitating a gap in the wall. Thirdly, the largest change has been the cutting back of both

the pavement and building line facing the main road and the construction of a row of small lock-up shops with an Art Deco façade aligned with the exterior of the tube station. Similar retail premises have been provided towards York Road and Pancras Road. A new type of ST bus, now London Transport, picks up passengers outside the Underground. There is a poster this side of the Parcels Office entrance for travel via Harwich to the Olympic Winter Games, at the Bavarian town of Garmisch-Partenkirchen 6-16 February 1936. They were organised on behalf of the 'German League of the Reich for Physical Exercise' and were the last before World War Two.

113

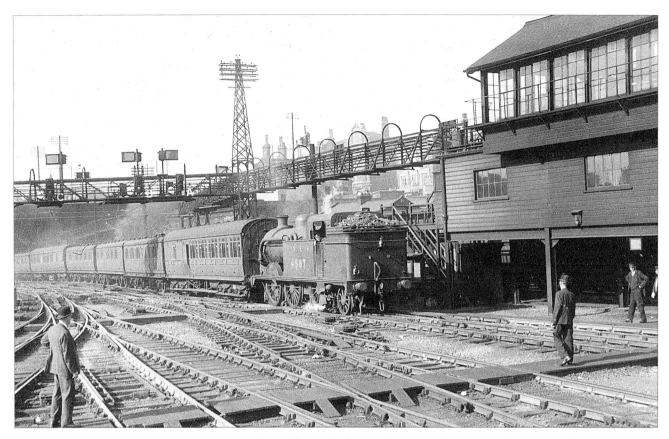

Gresley N2s displaced Ivatt N1s on the more demanding suburban work out of King's Cross, but many of the latter were retained for lighter work, such as in this view from the end of Platform 10. New out of Doncaster Works as 1587 in March 1912, 4587 is drawing empty coaching stock, including some early Great Northern bogie carriages, towards Platform 7 on 27 July 1935. A couple of railway officials in suits and hats seem to be particularly interested in what is going on.

K2 2-6-0 4668 leaves Platform 6 with what is probably an outer suburban service on 27 July 1935. King's Cross had some of these 'Ragtimers' from the outset and fourteen by Grouping. As long distance freight traffic from London mainly ran at night, the K2s filled in with daytime passenger workings to places such as Hitchin and Baldock. With the advent of more powerful K3 2-6-0s in 1924-25, the K2s were largely confined to slower partially-braked goods trains which they might take as far as Peterborough. Passenger workings continued, as seen here but by 1936 there were just four K2s left at King's Cross, including 4668, and they were all transferred to New England that year.

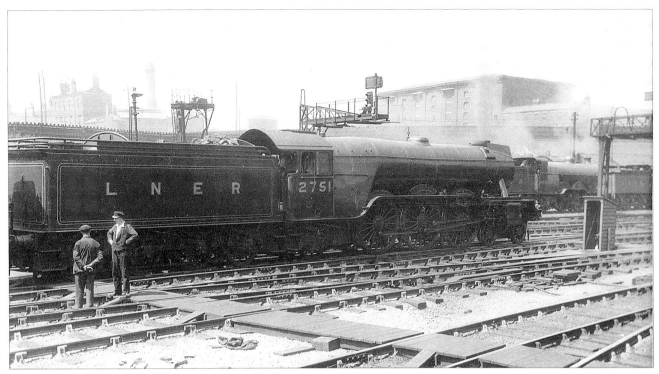

2751 HUMORIST in 1933 with one of the various arrangements fitted (in vain) to lift smoke upwards when running. Here the top of the smokebox is cut away and wind vanes fitted. In 1937 this engine was fitted with a Kylchap blastpipe and double chimney, anticipating the conversion of the rest of the class in 1957-58 by two decades. HUMORIST was at Doncaster shed until August 1942, then Grantham until October 1946 when it moved to King's Cross. Shortly after Nationalisation there was a strong Union representation in Scotland about the use of right-hand drive Pacifics, so four of theirs were exchanged for an equal number of left-hand drive locos from the south. 60097 HUMORIST was one of them and moved from King's Cross to Haymarket in July 1954. It continued to be based north of the border until withdrawn from St Margarets in August 1963.

It is a rather cool and overcast April day in London but King's Cross is festooned in flags, banners and bunting for the Coronation of King George VI on 12 May 1937. Every lamp post has some sort of decoration and pennants are strung between them. This was clearly a time of joy and celebration, although in retrospect it was a brief interlude of optimism between the despair of the depression and the horrors of the Blitz. The 'native village' is undergoing some changes again. The LNER Parcels Forwarding Office has been forced further down the station approach road as its former site is now partially occupied by an excavator. The timber structure stretching out into the street with, it appears, a heap of spoil on the roof, has a sign stating 'Work in connection with the installation of escalators and ticket hall King's Cross St Pancras Underground station'. The Euston Cinema is showing 'General Sparky' and 'Southern Roses' and while Sally is still selling lingerie and hosiery, damp and smog have taken their toll on the once sparkling Art Deco stonework of the shops.

The Coronation of King George VI gave rise to the 'Coronation' express which began running between King's Cross and Edinburgh Waverley on 4 July 1937. This was the second of the three high-speed streamlined trains that brought so much prestige to the LNER in the mid to late 1930s, the first being the Silver Jubilee to and from Newcastle which commenced on 30 September 1935 and commemorated the 25 year reign of King George V. This was the train which introduced Gresley A4 Pacifics to the world. On 27 September 1937 the West Riding Limited began to run between Bradford Exchange, Leeds Central and King's Cross and is seen here on arrival in London one day in June 1938 with 4496 GOLDEN SHUTTLE in charge. Photograph R E Vincent, transporttreasury

A4 4490 EMPIRE OF INDIA backs down on to its train, possibly the Coronation, during the late 1930s. It was a firm favourite for the train and had made 125 appearances on it before it was withdrawn prior to World War Two. Photograph R E Vincent, transporttreasury

Looking magnificent in immaculate Garter Blue, 4492 DOMINION OF NEW ZEALAND leaves Platform 5 with the Coronation on 19 April 1938. The A4 had only just come back to Top Shed from Haymarket the previous month, having been there since July 1937. As noted elsewhere, this engine put in almost continuous work on the Coronation and non-stop Flying Scotsman in summer 1937. The Pacific remained at King's Cross until withdrawn in April 1963, apart from a couple of years at Grantham in 1948-50. Photograph L Hanson.

For over a quarter of a century A4s worked alongside the earlier Gresley Pacifics, literally in this view. Blasting up Holloway Bank at Belle Isle one afternoon in the late 1930s are A4 4467 WILD SWAN on the 4.0pm Coronation and A3 4480 ENTERPRISE with the 4.0pm to Leeds.

On 11 September 1938 the Railway Correspondence & Travel Society organised 'The Old Flying Scotsman' special from King's Cross to Peterborough East and back using Stirling Single No.1 and seven six-wheel coaches. Here, the return train arrives back in London and this could well be a genuine late Victorian express were it not for the signal box completed just six years previously. This most famous of Stirling single-wheelers was built in 1870 and withdrawn during 1907 when Ivatt Atlantics were firmly established on the principal main line workings. The railway recognised the historic importance of this engine and it was stored in the Repair Shop at Top Shed for many years before its final preservation. It was a monumental failure when the same principle was not applied to SILVER LINK in the 1960s.

4903 PEREGRINE in June 1938; clearly, even with regular cleaning the garter blue livery could be sullied when it came to those awkward places. The RCTS guide notes that this A4 was notable as the only one not to haul any of the three streamlined trains, but after all it was the last to be completed, in July 1938. The engine made up for this omission in June 1948 when, having acquired a corridor tender for the first time and the new identity 60034 LORD FARINGDON, it hauled the first Down non-stop Flying Scotsman after the war. Photograph R E Vincent, transporttreasury

Away from the glamour of the high speed trains there were normal day to day services and occasionally a visitor to generate interest. Many years after the B3s had ceased to haul expresses out of King's Cross, engines from another class of former Great Central 4-6-0s were fairly regular visitors to the terminus on specials from Yorkshire. The date is 14 May 1938 and B4 6101 has reached London with an excursion from the West Riding consisting of modern Gresley corridor stock. A H Lucas, transporttreasury

The streets outside, probably in early spring 1937 just as the streamlined era was getting underway but when ominous noises were emanating from Europe. There is a poster (top right) for Frank Capra's 'Lost Horizon' starring Ronald Colman and Jane Wyatt, released in March 1937. A tram on Route 7 from Parliament Hill to Holborn is followed by London Transport STL double decker. At the time there were eight tram routes past King's Cross, Nos.3, 5, 7, 9, 15, 17, 21 and 59 from Hampstead Heath, Parliament Hill, Highgate and Waltham Cross in the north to Holborn Circus, Moorgate and Farringdon in Central London. Three services were replaced by trolleybuses on 6 March 1938, followed by another four on 10 July of the same year. This left just Route 59 from Waltham Cross and Caledonian Road past King's Cross to Grays Inn Road and Holborn Circus which went over to trolleybuses on 16 October 1938. Tram routes in Central London did not use a conventional overhead wire system but collected current by means of a conduit mid-way between the rails, an arrangement clearly visible in this illustration. When trolleybuses were introduced it was necessary to erect numerous poles and quite elaborate overhead line at complex junctions like that between Pancras Road, Euston Road, Grays Inn Road, King's Cross Road, Pancras Road and Caledonian Road. JA Whaley, transporttreasury

King's Cross during the Second World War is the subject of a later chapter, but this 15 July 1942 photograph of the inner corner of Platform 10 is a reminder that the LNER had to maintain passenger and postal services as far as possible despite the huge amount of goods traffic associated with the conflict. A woman in services uniform examines the timetable while to her right is that classic wartime poster 'Is your journey really necessary?' Most of the windows are covered by anti-blast material while out of view to the right is the gaping hole in the roof and offices caused by a direct hit in May 1941. Behind the mail barrows is a reminder that it had all happened before, the Great Northern War Memorial containing a huge list of employees who had fallen during the Great War.

The period between the end of the Second World War and Nationalisation was one of continuing austerity for the LNER and pretty bleak for King's Cross as well. It also saw the whole convoluted motive power numbering system sorted out into a logical pattern which made it the easiest of the former 'Big Four' loco stocks to understand during British Railways days. With the familiar backdrop of St Pancras Gasworks, this view of the engine yard was taken in the summer of 1946. A3 2561 MINORU was converted from an A1 just two years earlier but is still in wartime black livery. It will be given the number 62 in October 1946 and eventually become BR 60062 and carry the Brunswick Green livery which suited the big Eastern Region Pacifics so well. In the right background is N2 9545 which officially changed from 4766 in June 1946. Application of the new number must have only just happened as that clean patch on the tank would not remain like that for very long. It will eventually become 69545 and look splendid in BR lined black. Photograph transporttreasury

The 1930s resignalling – taken from *The Railway Gazette*, 1931.

UP SIGNALLING ARRANGEMENTS

DOWN SIGNALLING ARRANGEMENTS

7. A Signal Event

Prior to 1932, much of the appearance and mode of operation of King's Cross was derived from the early LNER work of the 1920s. The station had always been an inordinately complicated place and the new upper quadrants for instance represented a way of overcoming the permissive nature of much of the movement. With empty carriages and light engines, nevertheless, 'you went everywhere at caution'. All movements thus provided for, including those of trains or engines on the up carriage line as far as the disc signal within the tunnel were, therefore, of a shunting character. Owing to the complications, and the large number of points and connections crowded into small space, it was virtually impossible to give complete indications of all movements, and discs controlling movement from stage to stage had to suffice. This arrangement had worked well for many years, but obviously trains conveying passengers could not be worked into the station by this route, hence the need for alterations and the new equipment. The new

signals satisfied the rules as they applied to passenger running and were also equipped with miniature arms which controlled the movements of empty trains and engines, as previously provided for, with the further improvement that, by using route indicating appliances, drivers were then given full information as to where they were proceeding, whether with passenger trains or under shunting conditions.

The LNER Board heard of the antiquated signalling at the terminus on 2 January 1930: 'The signalling at the King's Cross Passenger Station which is manually operated – is controlled from two signal boxes known as 'King's Cross East' and 'King's Cross West'. The number of working levers in the East box is 76 and the West box 137, a total of 213. The existing plant is worn out; it requires constant attention and repair and is becoming difficult to maintain in a safe and satisfactory condition.

'The signal boxes also require renewal. With the present system of

manual working, it is not considered practicable to combine the two boxes in one, partly because it would be difficult to find a site large enough to accommodate a box of the requisite dimensions and partly on account of the dislocation and risk which would result consequent on new runs of rodding and wires having to be put in places where there is inadequate room for the purpose, seeing that they would have to be installed, as far as possible, before the existing runs are interfered with.

'It is therefore proposed to install power working on an all-electric system, with colour lighting. This would enable the working to be concentrated in one box, for which there would be no difficulty in finding a site on account of the requisite dimensions being much smaller: Estimated cost ... £46,200. The power system would enable the present operating staff of 13 men and 4 boys spread over 3 shifts, to be replaced by 8 men and 3 boys, while the existing maintenance staff of 12 could be reduced to 10. This amounts to a decrease in annual costs of £1114...'

This magnificent study dates from February 1925, a little less than eight years before the new signalling scheme was commissioned; latticework and somersault signals abound. East Box is on the extreme left, West Box is behind C1 4401 and some of the Great Northern signals they controlled are prominent features. Photograph F R Hebron, Rail Archive Stephenson.

East Box at the outer end of Platform 1, 27 May 1931 just before it became redundant in connection with the new signalling scheme. The two cabins dated from an earlier signalling reorganisation during the 1870s and 1880s when the original rudimentary arrangements on the southern part of the GN main line had to be substantially improved as a result of increased traffic. They were commissioned around 1881 and were, frankly, quite ugly compared with the attractive GN cabins being erected elsewhere on the system. In this view there is a glimpse of York Road station in the left background while part of a building which at one time incorporated the staff canteen is on the right.

The interior of East Box on 27 May 1931 showing a fair proportion of the 100-lever frame, which had 76 levers in operation at the time. The cabin was responsible for the Arrival side of King's Cross station and a hint of the complexity of the track

layout can be gleaned from instructions on levers in the foreground, for example *77 Signal Home Indication Green Up Main to Platform Line No.1 76* (just beyond the out of use white levers), *88 Points Crossover Up Slow to Platform Line No.1 89* (in the right foreground) and *93 Signal Disc Southern Spur to Up Slow 97, 94, 89* (at the extreme right). Although the windows let a reasonable amount of light into the box, working conditions are not helped by the dark boarded ceiling of the flat-roofed cabin.

The approach tracks from a vantage point above the southern portal of Gasworks Tunnel on 5 June 1931, before the new signalling system came into operation, showing the complexity of the track layout. East Box can just be made out on the far left, in front of the two-storey gabled building and behind the van on the Centre Spur. West Box is hidden behind the new cabin which is under construction beyond the nearest signal. The prominent signal posts in the foreground are for inbound trains and incorporate main arms 98 and 93 together with miniature arms 97 and 99, all of which are controlled by East Box. Illuminated roller blinds manufactured by Siemens indicate the route for arrivals, in this case Platform 5. York Road platform and the track down to the Metropolitan Widened Lines can be seen on the extreme left while the suburban platforms and the southern extremity of the loco yard are to the right. Present at the latter are N2 4730 and Atlantic 4458.

Even bright sunshine on 27 May 1931 fails to cheer up the dismal appearance of West Box, the eastern elevation of which is portrayed here. Virtually everything about the cabin is grim, from the cowls and tilting stove chimneys on the roof to the cables dangling below the windows and the tired ground floor woodwork. There appears to be some sort of temporary signalling arrangement in force, judging by the makeshift bracket attached to the window frame, and the new box is under construction on the left. An Atlantic is just visible at the far end of the loco yard in the right background.

The western elevation of West box was in shadow 27 May 1931 but despite this the structure looks marginally tidier on this side. It must also be admitted that the huge gas lamps on swan-neck brackets are rather fine. There are men working on the new cabin and it is likely that the chap on the extreme right is a lookout man, complete with flag. Since the earlier view of the gantry was taken in 1925, the second signal in has changed from a short lattice post to a taller solid version with twice the number of arms. There is another glimpse of York Road station can be seen on the left beyond the gantry and box.

The interior of West Box on 27 May 1931 when 137 of the 140 levers were working. Back in 1881 the cabin had 90 levers. The length of some of the lever labels shows the complexity of the locking system, a good example being one of those nearest the camera displaying *120 Signal Platform Lines Nos.6 or 7 to Down Main No.2. 88, 89, 128, 129. Back 128, 140, 124, 111. Back 124 or 88, 89, 128, 129. Back 128, 140, 124, 111, 112. Back 124.* Complying with those instructions and many more like them had to be done in very noisy conditions with levers rattling and crashing in their elderly frame and locos blasting away a few feet from the windows. An impression of phantom levers has resulted from a long time exposure in a busy box.

There was a convenient space between the existing West Box and the end of Platforms 5 and 6 for the new cabin, as is clear in this view of 27 May 1931. Steelwork supplied by Sanders & Forster of Barking is in place and carpenters are busy putting together the infill and superstructure. The lookout is still there beyond the water crane bag, another railwayman peers at the photographer from behind the planks stored beneath the steel frame and a signalman looks out of the old cabin to see what is going on. A D2 4-4-0 stands in the engine yard on the left, loco coal wagons and narrow gauge tubs can be seen to the right of it and a smoke haze hangs around Gasworks Tunnel on the right of the picture.

These proposals were recommended by the Chief General Manager, Ralph Wedgwood; work went ahead and all seemed well. The General Manager returned to the issue, in mournful mood, on 25 October 1932: 'The Directors will have seen reference in the press to the dislocation at King's Cross at the commencement of this month, consequent upon alterations in signalling at that place and it is thought they would like to have before them a report of the matter. The scheme is that sanctioned by Traffic Committee Minute 4512 of 30 January 1930 at an estimated cost of £46,200 which, briefly, provides for the replacement of the two mechanical signalboxes known as the East and West boxes respectively by one central 'all-electric' box. The Directors authorised the placing of the contract with Messrs Siemens & General Electric Railway Signal Co at a cost of £34,901.0s.10d on 24 July 1930.

'A programme was drawn up for the changeover to be effected in three stages, as under:
First Stage: Signals at Belle Isle – North end of Gas Works Tunnels, 19 June 1932.
Second Stage: All West Box working. 2 October 1932.

Third Stage (final): East Box working. 30 October 1932.'

'The First Stage was carried out to programme and no hitch occurred. The Second Stage was commenced at 1 o'clock on the morning of Sunday October 2nd and the schedule of operations provided that all points and signals should be capable of being worked from the new box by 6pm, the period from 6pm on Sunday to 6am on Monday 3rd – during which it was arranged we should have possession of the west side of the yard – being utilised in testing all signal circuits and controls.

'Trouble began however with the first pairs of double ended points which were coupled up as it was found that when being operated one of the motors, after the movements appeared to have been completed, was rotating for a short period in the reverse direction, sufficient to cause a movement of the point detectors and break down the detection contacts. The breaking down of these contacts prevented the running signals from being operated, thus causing delay to traffic operations, hand signalling being resorted to.

'Investigations showed that this was

brought about by the fact that the two motors had been connected up in parallel with only two wires from the cabin to the first pair of points and as their movements did not exactly terminate at the same moment, current from the motor which had not quite completed its stroke passed through the field coils of the other one causing the short reverse movement mentioned above. Each motor should have been operated by an independent pair of wires and double contacts, involving running four wires from the box, but for reasons of their own the contractors had altered this and utilised one pair of wires only, as previously stated.

'As a temporary measure, the motors have been 'cascaded', by which, one motor has to complete its movement before the other beings to operate, thereby preventing the reverse action which gave rise to the trouble. This has the effect of slowing up the combined movement where double ended points are concerned and the question of installing separate pairs of wires from the cabin to each motor of double ended pairs of points is in hand with the contractors.

Here is the new box, which was built by E R Hipperson & Sons at a cost of £1,811 0s 0d and became fully operational on 24 May 1932. Although the position at the end of Platforms 5 and 6 was ideal, it was not quite large enough so the outer bay of the first storey and the far end of the top floor could not be completed until resignalling had been completed and the old West Box demolished. The lighter paintwork on the timber planking is obvious but on the original photograph a slight difference in the colour of the new roof tiles can be discerned as well. There is a hint of the extensive gantry system for the cables and signals while York Road station and N2 4745 are in the background.

Without doubt the new 'Electric Signal Box' was considerably more comfortable to work in than the elderly East and West cabins and it even boasted 'hot water heating' supplied by Dilworth & Carr for £133. Its operation was much quieter and it was well above the constant rumbling of trains on adjacent tracks. There was also a floor covering as opposed to bare boards, although there is a distinct possibility that some of that furniture would have been familiar in the old box! Seen here just before mid-day on 11 November 1932, it was a very familiar feature of King's Cross to enthusiasts who visited in steam days, although its internal workings always remained a mystery.

The new diagram on 11 November 1932. Compared with the old diagram in West Box, which is visible in an earlier view, this one is large, very clear and shows the whole station layout. Bay Platform 3 and No.9 Road were still in operation at the time. Although long gone, it would be nice to think that some relics, mementos, of this very familiar box still survive, maybe unsuspected, in some cherished collection.

It was a dismal episode: 'Owing to the time occupied in altering temporarily the wiring to the more important of these points it was not until 4.30am on Monday that the last of them which it was necessary to couple up to the box were completed, and even then, those leading into the loco yard had to be left uncoupled, and operated by hand signalling and clamps. By the morning of Tuesday 4th the last of this 'cascading' was done, thereby removing this trouble. 'The fault here rests with the contractors, who should not have adopted the system of wiring they did.

'Another difficulty which was experienced in the initial stages were those from the rather fine setting in the first instance of the detectors. This was done in the interests of safety and is not a matter in which we can find fault with the contractors but is incidental to the bringing into operation of such works as these. By slightly coarsening the detection, the vibratory action of the trains on the detection contacts was counteracted, though, of course, the points which fitted up quite closely to their stock rails were not affected. The necessary adjustments in this case were completed by the evening of Tuesday 4th.

'The most serious trouble however was the false indication given by the point detector relays in the signalbox, which began to show itself on Tuesday.

This was found to be due to the fact that in some cases when the point lever was operated by the relay contacts swung right over to the reverse instead of into the neutral position and at times held in that position even though the points themselves were normal. The effect of this when it occurred was not only to give wrong indication to the signalman but would have enabled him to obtain conflicting movements. The danger of allowing such a condition to continue is self evident and the steps to remedy it were taken without delay. The whole of these point detector relays so far as the new signalling has been brought into use have been replaced by those of the Westinghouse type, the work being done on the weekends of the 8th/9th and 15th/16th instant, these being the only periods on which possession of the track could be obtained for times necessary for the changeover to be made.

'It will be appreciated that the defects which made themselves felt on the morning of 3rd October caused a dislocation of traffic. Great difficulty was experienced in dealing with the 'rush hour' suburban trains and this reacted on the main line trains, which suffered heavy delay both outward and inward. Every effort was made by the traffic department to mitigate inconvenience. Serious delay to main line trains was practically confined to the Monday,

October 3rd, normal working being virtually restored on Tuesday October 4th.

In an attempt to relieve the situation with regard to suburban working, the fullest possible use was made of the Moorgate lines, whilst a number of trains due to run to and from the terminal station were terminated at Finsbury Park and the public advised to use the Underground to and from Finsbury Park and King's Cross. In spite of this, however, very numerous delays took place and it was not found possible to run the full suburban service until Monday 24th October.

'It has been deemed advisable to defer the carrying out of the Third Stage of the changeover until all the difficulties which arose on the Second Stage have been satisfactorily dealt with. The question of the liability of the contractors has been fully considered by Mr Brown, whose report thereon will be submitted with this memo to the Works Committee.'

Despite the initial setbacks, King's Cross had been entirely transformed by 1933. The Siemens scheme was operating, much of 'the gubbins' carried in the distinctive 'access gallery'. The two bridges straddling the yard had long gone, to be replaced by 'Goods Way' and even the upper quadrants so acclaimed in 1924 had gone.

Left. This view from the top floor of the Parcels Office building on 31 March 1933 reveals the full expanse of the lines south of Gasworks Tunnel. The new 'Electric Signal Box' is shown in its context at the end of Platforms 5 and 6 while some of the quite intrusive cable and signal gantries are visible. On the Arrival Side, Platform 1 is in the bottom right corner and N1 4599 stands at Platform 3 while Platforms 7, 8 and 10 on the Departure Side are on the left. There are a couple of engines in the loco yard and a wagon stands in the Centre Spur near York Road station on the far right.

Bottom left. The gantries were particularly prevalent on the Departure Side and dominate this view north from the end of Platform 10 on 24 March 1933. A couple of tapering lattice towers carrying telegraph wires were also prominent features here.

Below. Resignalling King's Cross had been a prestige project from the outset and one which attracted fierce competition. Two tenders were received for electric pneumatic systems and four involving the 'all electric' principle. Charles Brown, the LNER engineer responsible, was inclined to favour the latter and Siemens submitted the best quote. Brown wrote to the Works Committee '...as to which system should be adopted, the all electric type is the more modern one and I should prefer to see it installed.' Siemens was given the go-ahead in October 1930. Here are the new signalling arrangements for the suburban station 31 May 1933, with a C2 Ivatt Atlantic at Platform 11. Two blokes wait for the photographer to finish his work, one taking the opportunity to enjoy a smoke.

A combination of smoke and late autumn mist make for a rather grim prospect from the train shed roof on 11 November 1932. An N2 and 4-4-0 in the engine yard and an N7 shunting stock near York Road station add to the murk. This was only nineteen days after the new signalling system was fully commissioned, but the old West Box has already been demolished and the new cabin extended, as shown by the lighter portion of the roof. In less than fourteen years the vista changed again, spectacularly and unintentionally. On 4 February 1945 2512 SILVER FOX, resplendent in wartime black, left Platform 5 with the 6.0pm to Leeds Central consisting of 17 coaches and weighing 590 tons. As the stock had been propelled in there was no engine at the rear to give a helping shove and there are suggestions that there had been problems with the sanding gear of the Pacific earlier. Furthermore, new rails had recently been laid in the tunnel and these provided less adhesion than ones that had been in place for some time. Eventually the train slipped to a stand in the tunnel and because of the amount of smoke the driver was unaware that it had started to slide back. The signalman became aware of what was happening but had already set the road for Platform 10 where coaching stock was awaiting its loco. He altered the points to divert the runaway into an empty platform, but was just too late and the bogies of the Gresley Brake Composite at the rear went their different ways resulting in the coach derailing, turning on its side and rearing up. It demolished a length of the signal gantry which crushed a first class compartment and killed two passengers, one of them the head of the MG car company. Hand signalling was necessary for Platforms 6 to 17 and it was nearly three weeks before everything was back to normal. Many of the signal cables were laid underground, a much less obtrusive arrangement. This view clearly shows the narrow island comprising Platforms 7 and 8 in the centre, Platform 10 on the left and, on the right, Platforms 5 and 6 with timber boarding, clutter from the resignalling and a couple of forlorn looking barrows.

King's Cross signal box in the mid-1950s; several changes have occurred, notably the protective brickwork added during the Second World War. Cowls have appeared on the roof, presumably after complaints about inadequate ventilation, and a large sign has been added to the wall leaving passengers in no doubt where they are about to arrive, or even leave! The site of the old West Box has been occupied by a squat brick building with a flat concrete roof, the sort of structure erected by the railway authorities in places where even a hint of aesthetically pleasing design was deemed unnecessary.

Left. By British Railways days changes had also been made inside the cabin and it is interesting to compare this 1950s view with that taken during the 1930s. The new panel is still in three sections but it is shallower and installed almost vertically, with brackets securing the top to the ceiling. Bay Platform 3 and No.9 Road are no longer shown, these having been abolished before the war. The levers are of a more substantial design and the clock has been transferred from the end of the cabin to a prominent position above the panel.

Below. A cheerful scene inside King's Cross box during the 1950s, complete with bowl of flowers. In an earlier photograph the LNER signalmen are wearing a kind of suit with trousers and a light jacket top, but the attire is rather more casual here. Black trousers and a regulation white shirt with rolled-up sleeves are common factors, although an official waistcoat, a cardigan or just braces seemed to be optional accompaniments!

A1 60134 backs out and the railwayman on the lights up on 23 April 1949. The tunnels and complex layout made this a hazardous place, for men had to cross it on the level constantly. Both sides of the indicators adjacent to the colour lights showed which road the points were set for. One of the new signal installations is visible on the left. The Pacific is less than six months old, having emerged from Doncaster Works in November 1948. It was new to Copley Hill and that shed has kept its apple green paintwork in fine condition. The name FOXHUNTER was not applied until October 1950. Photograph R H Fullagar, transporttreasury

The much neater replacement signal supports had been around for almost as long as their predecessors when this photograph was taken on 7 March 1958. One aspect of the scene which had not changed was the King's Cross winter mist fortified by outpourings from the engine yard. Yet however smoky the place might look to us now there were rigid instructions – adhered to as much as possible – forbidding 'black smoke'. The indicator shows M1 as A3 60066 MERRY HAMPTON backs out of Platform 6 and a couple of men cross the track in safety. At King's Cross and a daily sight by this time, it had nonetheless moved no less than 22 times during its 39 year career. In England by 1950, it went back and forth between King's Cross and Doncaster several times prior to withdrawal from Grantham in September 1963. Although the engine celebrated the winner of the 1887 Derby, its name caused a few ribald comments in later years and it was also prone to misfortune, suffering a couple of notable derailments. Photograph D Clayton.

King's Cross box is prominent in this view of the main station from York Road platform on 10 October 1964. The cabin has recently had a coat of Eastern Region paint, possibly as part of a clean up prompted by the end of steam, but this attempt to smarten up the scene is countered by the appalling brick buildings this side of the box. A Brush Type 4 looks as if it might be starting from Platform 1, possibly with a parcels train. The Centre Spur is prominent in the left foreground while the hazy outline of St Pancras can just be made out in front of the Suburban Station roof on the right. The lattice post signals to the left of the cabin are a reminder of the 1930-32 changes, while the girder support on the extreme right post-dated the 1945 accident.

Looking out from Platform 10 towards Gasworks Tunnel, around 1965. A Brush Type 4 and a Deltic are in the yard while a Brush Type 2 acting as station pilot stands in the North Spur near the tunnel portals. Proceedings are being observed from the end of Platform 10 by gentlemen who were probably more in their element when the scene was dominated by A4s and N2s by the look of them, while the younger enthusiasts seem to have colonised the end of Platforms 7 and 8. They have the company of barrow loads of corridor end doors, somewhat in excess of requirements it would seem. Careful scrutiny reveals the rails climbing through the tunnel bore on the left and it will be noted that York Road station has had its canopy cut back. Apart from losing one of the cowls off its roof, the signal box appears to be in reasonable condition. Unfortunately its days are numbered as it became redundant when a new power box was commissioned in association with track rationalisation and electrification during the early 1970s. Photograph ColourRail

The appearance of Platform 10 was altered abruptly at 3.15am on Sunday 11 May 1941 and with part of the roof blasted away by the bomb, sunlight streams in to illuminate the scene of devastation the next morning. N2 4761 and a Gresley full brake peer out from beneath the roof debris as firemen damp down still smouldering rubble some hours after the explosion. The view was taken from the top of the footbridge stairs looking towards the concourse, but hardly a square inch of the actual surface of Platform 10 can be seen. On 11 May there were nine known fatalities, four railway staff serving as firewatchers and five soldiers.

8. A Direct Hit

The Second World War brought appalling conditions of toil, hardship and fear, not least to King's Cross, punctuated and relieved by valour and a grim good humour. As the dread of the first days faded there came months of almost comic disruption and overcrowding. Inconvenience and delay were the worst experiences and even the grim harvest of Dunkirk made for traffic difficulties more than anything else. When the bombs came a new War began.

As the campaign hardened, bomb damage across the great empire that was then the LNER grew and by 7 September 1940 had been costed at £29,650 in the Southern Area, £9,150 in the North Eastern Area, £2,100 in Scotland and £2,100 at the various docks. After then, attacks were increasingly concentrated on the Southern Area. King's Cross engine shed and the potato market were hit,

four engines were damaged in Peterborough engine yard, killing an engineman and injuring ten others, and in January Colchester and Liverpool Street were attacked. Ipswich station was machine-gunned, killing a guard, and at Lowestoft eight LNER men and a customs officer were killed and 34 railwaymen injured. On the night of Saturday 10th and Sunday 11th May 1941 King's Cross, Liverpool Street and Marylebone were all hit, with the Cross the worst. A high explosive bomb struck part of the main station building, the western block facing No.10 platform, and considerable damage occurred. There were unfortunately nine fatalities, four of the company's men and five soldiers. A length of approximately 75 feet situated between the booking hall and the footbridge was destroyed including the buffet, grill room and kiosk, dining car stores, hotels department central stores, 'RTO's office' (formerly the ladies third class waiting

room) and a number of the headquarters offices. In addition five bays of the station roof including three trusses were wrecked. The adjoining portion of the station buildings to the north for a length of about 60ft with the gentlemen's lavatories below the platform and a length of 190ft to the south were seriously damaged. This latter portion included the enquiry office and the ladies first class waiting room and the headquarters offices above. The roof girders fell across the platforms blocking Nos.6, 7, 8, and 10 platforms. Measures were taken to strut the centre wall against any unbalanced steel ties across the undamaged span, to tie the centre wall to the main office block on the York Way side of the station.

The explosion took place only yards from the booking office and by a miracle two members of staff escaped serious injury, but the office itself was wrecked and millions of tickets, together with books, records, dating presses and all

Although this scene was more than nine years before King's Cross itself became a victim of international conflict, the little W H Smith bookstall at the entrance to Platform 6 displays newspaper posters announcing hostilities elsewhere which had echoes in World War Two. One reads 'Japanese Bombard Nanking' and another 'Four Big Powers Say Ceasefire'. On 3 February 1932 Japanese cruisers and destroyers launched an intense attack on the Chinese city of Nanking in the Yangtze Estuary inland from Shanghai. American warships were ready to sail in order to rescue US citizens and counter Japanese aggression. Other posters refer to the economy, announcing 'Cabinet and Debt Cancellation' and '£111,000,000 Income Tax Collected'. Modern Transport has a feature about 'Railway Shareholders and Competitors'. The ubiquitous enamelled advertisements for Bovril, Virol, Mazawattee Tea and Stephen's Ink festoon the walls and there is a joint LNER/LMS poster for trains to the Winter Sports in Scotland, subject to weather conditions. It all seemed quite normal.

King's Cross looks sombre in this grey scene, probably in 1936 or 1937. It is raining and the war clouds are gathering on the Continent. Attached to the very ornate lamp in the centre is a notice pointing to 'Metropolitan Railway King's Cross & St Pancras Station. Electric Trains Every Few Minutes', so the publicity had not yet caught up with the formation of the London Passenger Transport Board in 1933. The picture also shows two forms of road transport providing a remarkable contrast. On the right is a horse-drawn LNER parcels delivery cart with a canvas cover. On the side there is an advert for long-forgotten N&C Butter, while above the driver is a sign stating 'Marylebone for the Midlands'. This still applies, although not in the way intended back then. To the left is a coach belonging to Birch Brothers of Rushden on Route 203 from King's Cross to Rushden via Hitchin and Bedford. On the way it served the RAF Camps at Henlow and Cardington. The vehicle is one of ten with Leyland Lion chassis and exotic centre-entrance American-style bodies built by Birch Brothers themselves in 1935. The company had started a horse bus service between Pimlico and Mansion House as early as 1847 and was finally wound up as a coach hire business in 1971. JA Whaley, transporttreasury

Although shadows and shafts of sunlight through the smoke create a rather ethereal picture, the troops are a reminder that there are more weighty matters to contemplate. The Second World War brought the tramp of service feet, unfamiliar uniforms and weapons to all the great stations of Britain. There were also previously unheard accents. Yorkshire, Geordie and Scots were familiar enough at King's Cross, but with the enormous increase in service journeys French, Poles, Norwegians, Canadians and others (including Germans and Italians!) made the station one of the most cosmopolitan in the country. In these conditions the awkward layout, narrow inadequate concourse and concentration of facilities on one side tested the place severely.

the paraphernalia of a large booking office were buried under debris. In pitch darkness, these two men made their escape from the wreckage, and then, badly shaken and with clothes torn, sat down for a while to consider how they should carry on the work which had been so suddenly interrupted. Apparently they decided that the passengers for the next train must be booked somehow, although they could not shut their eyes to the fact that the virtual disappearance of their office and all that was in it presented some difficulty. However there was another office near by, very much smaller and not equipped with the requisite tickets, and with no staff on duty. They decided to install themselves there. They scoured surrounding offices for excess ticket books and blank cards, and, with the aid of the staff who came on duty later, the first morning train was successfully booked. The Georgian Tea Room was chosen for the new booking office and

passengers were being served within 36 hours.

A report a fortnight or so later, on 27th May detailed progress: 'Nos.7 and 8 platforms are fully in use again but No.6 is available only northwards from the footbridge as the strutting overlaps the platform track opposite the damaged area. No.10 platform road is clear but is being utilised to accommodate the vehicles clearing the debris from No.10 platform. In the destruction of the booking office the whole of the ticket stock was either lost or had to be scrapped and an entirely new stock of tickets is now in use. All the cash in the safe in the main line booking office, about £3-4000, was recovered and there was very little loss of loose cash. The tea room on No.10 platform is being used as a temporary booking office and is proving fairly satisfactory although there has been a certain amount of congestion. The enquiry work is at present being conducted in the seat

reservation section of the enquiry office but it is hoped the remainder of the office will be available for use in a few days time. A buffet car has been placed at the south end of No.10 platform for the sale of light refreshments to passengers and is being well patronised. Temporary arrangements have been made for the restaurant car stores and for the preparation of meals. Approximate estimate of the cost of restoration of the above work is £121,000; one locomotive, eleven coaches and four other vehicles were damaged – estimated cost of repairs is between £1500 and £2000'.

Temporary arrangements made for the comfort of passengers comprised simple shelters, put up with old rail and spare girders. The roof was properly rebuilt, more or less in the original style of the station during 1947, though not before several alarming schemes for complete rebuilding had emerged from various dark corners. The tender for

It looks as if the Home Guard has everything under control in Belle Isle as the railway strives to keep wartime traffic moving. This is the southern portal of Copenhagen Tunnel, looking down the gradient towards King's Cross from the most westerly of the three bores. The other lines through the tunnel are at a lower level, thus the parapet on the left, but the land rises to the right so there is a retaining wall and steep bank up to the branch serving Caledonian Road Yard. This line actually passed over the tunnel mouth above the photographer. What looks like an ex-Midland 2F through the mist is drawing a goods train tender first across the North London Railway viaduct. The profile of the N2 is unmistakable. As will be seen in a later chapter, this is the precise spot where the would-be 'Ladykillers' were to meet their fate one by one!

This very busy Platform 10 during the early days of the war prior to the bombing, possibly in the spring of 1940. Servicemen greatly outnumber civilians. Of the ordinary passengers, there is quite a contrast between the girl in the light skirt behind the porter and those formidable ladies on the right. The W H Smith bookstall is doing brisk business and is carrying advertisements for the *Illustrated London News*, *Autocar* and *The Motor*, which announces 'Wartime Motorists Assistance'. Soon, the area this side of the footbridge, including the cigar kiosk and the underground gentlemen's lavatory, would be transformed in a very nasty way.

Sunday 11 May turned out to be a bright sunny day, but the bomb had struck. Seen from a precarious position in the centre gutter of the train shed, a kiosk survives near the footbridge but the stairs down to the gents are completely drowned in debris and the underground lavatories themselves were severely damaged. On the left, destruction of part of the main station block led to the loss of the Buffet Grill Room, Hotels Department stores, RTO's office and several headquarters offices. Serious damage was done to the adjoining Booking and Enquiry Offices as well as the Ladies 1st Class Waiting Room. Platforms 7 and 8 in the foreground were back in use on 12 May but Platform 10 was not fully operational until 27 May. The poster for National Savings demanding 'Hit Back' could not have been better sited!

repair work, the culmination of extensive discussions stretching back over much of the previous year, was finally accepted in May 1946 from Samuel Butler & Co of the Albion Works, Stanningley, Leeds, at a cost of £11,738.1s.0d. The LNER was unable to enforce a penalty clause 'due to the uncertain position of steel supplies'.

These were uncertain times; there was a tremendous call on the services of construction firms but they in turn were hamstrung by shortages of labour and materials. A year earlier, on 4th July 1945 LNER Secretary, W H Johnson, had in fact accepted Messrs Johnson Bros tender, 'for sheeting, glazing, slating and boarding to the four bays of the western span of the King's Cross Main Roof' at £4,762. This work is presumed to have been additional to Butler's steelwork contract but if so it is odd that it was tendered a year earlier. It could not be carried out of course until the girders were erected. Other plans were surfacing…

On 26th October 1945, with Sir Ronald Matthews is the chair (an A4 had carried his name since before the outbreak of War) discussions took place regarding the 'Committee appointed in August to consider the question of the reconstruction of the roof at King's Cross'. The Board decided that the portion of the roof destroyed by enemy action should be replaced at 'an estimated cost of £21,000'. On 28th

August 1945 consideration was deferred and by September no less than six schemes were submitted, mostly involving umbrella awnings and ranging from £180,000 to £235,000!

FitzHerbert Wright (a B1 was later to carry his name) wrote to Johnson the LNER Secretary, from his Invicta Works at Grantham on 6th September 1945, recalling his comments at the meeting … 'my view with regard to the station is that we should spend as little as possible now in view of the plans there are in the future such as electrification etc. This means in other words that I am in favour of repairing the hole in the station which I believe with the Government contribution will cost the company £10,000.' This was sensible.

In August 1945 there had been considerable discussion about 'removal of smoke' and 'the new station' (note the term) it was determined, 'should be like the LMS portion of Leeds City'. With proceedings headed 'private and confidential', on 22nd August 1945 it was decided that 'the present roof of the King's Cross station … be replaced by a roof of more modern design, this includes an umbrella roof in reinforced concrete'. Lord Balfour of Burleigh (later to furnish yet another name for a B1) had written to Johnson on 31st July 1945; the good lord was interested to know 'the possibility that some day the roofs may have to accommodate overhead electrified stock.' Incredibly (Johnson

underlined this – can we guess his feelings?) Balfour then mused: 'I wonder whether all the possibilities of future air traffic have also been taken into account?' Balfour continued: 'It may be that such has been ruled out ex-hypothesis', opining that 'in such case (it) will be considered at Lloyds Bank.' (Balfour was writing from the Head office of that very bank, where he was also a Director).

So we see that, years before the various redevelopment proposals swirled so threateningly around King's Cross and St Pancras, even more radical – nightmarish even – plans were afoot. All through one cursed German bomb!

Hopes had already been expressed, earlier in 1945, concerning the doing away of the 'expensive arch span upon which maintenance costs are so high'. Alarm bells will be ringing for conspiracy theorists. These discussions, unusually, were announced beforehand as taking place in 'Private Rooms' and again unusually (and pointedly) declared private, confidential etc. There are a lot of absentees (almost unprecedentedly) who are otherwise engaged, on holiday and so on. Everyone came to their senses, we must assume; the financial position of the time and the dire shortages of labour and materials rendered a wholesale rebuilding wholly out of the question. After this there is nothing, until the simple repair tender of the Albion Works noted above.

The battered brake coach, which was part of a newspaper train, had its far end crushed by fallen roof girders and overlooks a carpet of splintered wood on Platform 10 a few hours after the explosion. Five hundred German aircraft dropped over 700 tons of bombs on London during the night of 10-11 May 1941 and 1,436 people were killed. Although one of the worst attacks, this turned out to be the last raid of the horrific 1940-41 Night Blitz. There were nearly sixty blazes considered serious or worse, more than thirty important factories and works were badly damaged or destroyed and at least six hospitals were hit. The Houses of Parliament, Westminster Abbey, the British Museum, St James's Palace, the Tower of London and even the War Office were also victims of the onslaught. Dozens of bombs fell on the railway network, with Paddington, St Pancras, Fenchurch Street, Marylebone, Liverpool Street and Waterloo all sustaining damage in addition to King's Cross.

Early morning sunlight is just beginning to shine through the hole in the roof, illuminating 4761 still in steam alongside Platform 10. With a sprinkling of debris the N2 looks as dazed as any inanimate object could do, but the only substantial damage is the staved-in cab roof. The engine was twenty years old at the time, having been built by North British for the Great Northern in April 1921. It was dragged out of the ruins and back to King's Cross shed then soon repaired and put back into traffic. As BR 69540 the engine continued to work from 34A until February 1959 when it moved to Hitchin for four months and New England for just over two years prior to withdrawal in August 1960.

The last of the flames resulting from the bomb are damped down on 11 May 1941 and by now some wagons have been brought in to help with the clear up. Those men with brushes have made a neat job of the little piles of debris on the platform, but no doubt something more hefty was required to shift the roof girders! Although this part of the office block was simply demolished by the high explosive, fire did spread to the rooms off to the left. Just visible on the extreme left is the W H Smith bookstall, still displaying advertisements for journals which, for the time being, are not on sale. In the distance, the skeletal roof of St Pancras has reverted to the mid-1860s when it was under construction.

Several temporary measures were put in to stabilise the buildings and train shed as well as provide a degree of comfort and convenience for passengers. A substantial horizontal bar attached to the roof girders by ties helped to counter new forces on the screen wall now that part of the western arch was missing. The sections of Platforms 6, 7, 8 and 10 beneath the gap were provided with very rudimentary shelters, but no doubt they were appreciated in a downpour. Remarkably the W H Smith bookstall on the left more or less survived the blast and was soon back in business.

Practical considerations rather than elegance and craftsmanship were the order of the day when the temporary platform canopies were installed. In any case, both money and materials were in short supply. Spare girders and old rails bent to shape formed the framework while lightweight sheeting kept the rain off. This is the shelter over Platforms 7 and 8, probably about six months after the attack and it looks like the Christmas mail is piling up.

The entrance to the Booking Hall on the west side of the terminus on 15 July 1942. A couple of officers are having a chat with a railwayman at the nearest entrance, although the individual lurking in the doorway is doing a good impression of a spy. The group of porters look as if they have been assembled for the photograph. There are four ladies among them, as well as a short chap with an unfortunate *Nationalsozialistische* visage and a tall chap who seems to be more intent on observing the military in a rather stern manner. Some of the posters convey wartime messages such as 'Save fuel', 'Is your journey really necessary' and 'If you have to take a long journey take your food with you'. On the extreme left some construction work is taking place in the bomb hole.

A further study of austerity on 15 July 1942. The group has rearranged itself in a more casual manner but some of the staff look even less cheerful. Inevitably, you have to think, the porter with the toothbrush moustache would have been nicknamed Adolf by now, if not perhaps to his face.

The hole in King's Cross from the outside some time after patching up had been completed in 1942. Inevitably the tidied up bits were a stark contrast to the original Fletton bricks which had accumulated nearly a century of soot. A corrugated metal shed occupies the gap in the main three-storey block and though the new work was clearly a temporary measure, there is evidence that it was going to be there for some time. The wall on the right has a properly installed drainpipe while the letters A and B above the barrow openings suggest that some sort of procedure has been established, probably in connection with parcels traffic.

This murky view of the temporary canopy over Platform 6 was probably taken in November or December 1941 as there is a notice on the right headed 'Christmas Parcels'. Above it is a sign pointing the way to the Forces Canteen. The loco of the stopping train which has just arrived cannot be identified, although it is clearly of Great Northern origin.

The temporary canopy over Platform 6 on 15 April 1942 in brighter conditions. It seems that the advertisements on the screen wall are a permanent feature, the same ones for Stephens Ink, Dr Barnardo's Homes and Beecham's Pills being visible. As usual, Bovril introduced a touch of railway humour by announcing 'The Fit Express their Thanks to Bovril'. Oddly, there appears to be a picture of some sort propped up behind the cables in the lower right corner.

Looking along Platform 10 towards the concourse on 15 July 1942. It is all very grim, with the upstairs windows either partially boarded up or missing because of the bomb and fire damage. The bookstall is advertising Robert Donat in 'The Young Mr Pitt' and announcing 'Problem of Sleeplessness Overcome by Aspro', but an almost flippant poster states 'The London Illustrated London News, the Greatest Record of the World at War'.

Platform 10 showing the hole, the temporary canopy and probably the most uninviting entrance to a booking office anywhere. A couple of civilians and a soldier lounge beneath a boarded up window and casually observe the photographer. 'Boy's Own', 'Girl's Own' and 'Woman's Magazine' are on sale at W H Smith, along with an unidentified periodical featuring 'War at Sea'.

Although the Booking Hall on the west side was not actually demolished by the bomb, a corner of it collapsed, the ceiling fell in and a great deal of damage was done inside. The balcony giving access to first floor offices was supported by very robust brackets which survived the explosion, but the ticket office had to be rebuilt and the result was rather bleak. Seen on 15 July 1942, the eight windows all convey the message 'Is your journey really necessary'. Half the positions dispense Third Class tickets for stations beyond Peterborough and others are for Advance Tickets and First Class tickets for all stations.

L.N.E.R.
DEPARTURE OF TRAINS

2.20	(SATURDAYS EXCEPTED) POTTERS BAR. HATFIELD INTERMEDIATE STATIONS TO CAMBRIDGE Ely	7
2.25	(SATURDAYS ONLY) HATFIELD AND INTERMEDIATE STATIONS TO CAMBRIDGE St. Albans Branch Ely	7
.5	THIRD CLASS ONLY (SATURDAYS ONLY) HATFIELD AND INTERMEDIATE STATIONS TO BALDOCK	7
.5	THIRD CLASS ONLY (SATURDAYS EXCEPTED) INTERMEDIATE STATIONS TO HITCHIN Luton and Dunstable Branch Letchworth Baldock	13
10	THIRD CLASS ONLY (SATURDAYS ONLY) NEW BARNET AND INTERMEDIATE STATIONS TO HITCHIN Luton and Dunstable Branch	13
.15	PETERBOROUGH Spalding Boston Firsby Skegness Louth Grimsby Town Cleethorpes GRANTHAM Nottingham NEWARK RETFORD DONCASTER WAKEFIELD HOLBECK LEEDS Harrogate	8

PETERBOROUGH M&GN Stations

Please put Your Waste Paper in this Box

Train indicators were easily overlooked at King's Cross as they were often camouflaged by the dense thicket of posters, signs and other clutter on the platforms. Once discovered they were straightforward enough to interpret, as in the case of this one lurking somewhere in the corner of a building where presumably the public had access. It is probably 1942 again, judging by the blackout curtain. The incidentals are intriguing, such as the little drawers, the wooden crate with the notice 'Please put your waste paper in this box' and the pot and brush on the floor to the left.

Something was happening to the clock from Platform 10 on 28 August 1944 and judging by its condition this is either a new face or the old one which has had a very good clean. The most remarkable aspect of the operation to modern eyes is the complete lack of safety barriers. In fact it is quite probable that the whole platform would be out of use nowadays! Men and women from the armed forces make up the vast majority of people leaving a newly arrived train. This fascinating scene is courtesy of the Luftwaffe which enabled sunlight to stream through the hole in the roof.

Army vehicles dominate the approach road to the Booking Office and Suburban Station on 19 January 1945, although there is a lorry with a container in the Parcel Yard. A cheery note is provided by the Salvation Army which advertises its Caledonian Canteen and Rest Room on the awning of the canopy. The apex of the canopy itself is missing some cladding, possibly as a result of bomb blast damage which is yet to be put right. Just about readable on the original print is a distant sign announcing 'LNER King's Cross Local Station'.

Pentonville Road on 19 January 1945, and the girl on the left has a war-weary look despite the winter sunshine. The end of hostilities is still months away and the roof of St Pancras, battered yet unbowed, is a constant reminder of the blitz. By this time German cities know very well what it is like to be on the receiving end of bombs. Cubitt's clock tower, proud as ever, overlooks the clutter around the Underground station while The Victoria pub advertises Nicholson's Gin and Bass on draught. Vehicles range from a London Transport trolleybus and a greengrocer's motor lorry to two horse-drawn LMS delivery carts. Most people in this scene are civilians, although three army personnel in greatcoats stroll along the pavement to the right, another reminder of the times.

Those greatcoats suggest there was a chill wind on 19 January 1945 despite the sunshine and no doubt this followed a lean Yule. This is the driveway separating the Great Northern Hotel from the west side of the station and at least three army vehicles are parked near the welcoming signs 'Tea Room' and 'Canteen'. There is still a demand for cabs and three of them wait for customers on the left. Their drivers are faced with an instruction on the gate in front of the RTO stating 'LNER. Taxis discharge fares under arcade except for cloak room. By Order'.

Above. On 19 January 1945, only the canopy in front of King's Cross gets a look in beyond Bravingtons and the Bass sign attached to The Victoria. Dominating the scene as always is Gilbert Scott's mighty Gothic tower at the corner of St Pancras. With the shattered train shed behind it, the grand edifice looks even more defiant than usual. Although the blitz was long over, flying bombs and rockets were a terrible fear. A doodlebug had blocked the main line at Wood Green less than a week earlier and in June 1944 one of these 'pilotless aircraft' had landed in Tiber Street off York Road, shattering windows in King's Cross and bringing down ceilings in the general offices. Nevertheless, there was hope in the air and a firmness of step. The scene is completed by a couple of trolleybuses, a taxi with white-wall tyres and a dray without a horse.

Left. This is the east side of King's Cross on 9 April 1946 with re-roofing taking place. The direct hit in May 1941 would have removed practically every pane of glass from the station roof, or at least any that had not been thrown down and smashed by earlier bombs falling around the terminus. Putting all the glazing back would have been a hazardous task in any case, but this skimpy system of planking suspended from the station roof would be totally unacceptable today. The gaps between the boards look wide enough for feet to come through as well as bits of putty and other debris. There are a few people waiting at Platform 5 on the far side, but otherwise this part of King's Cross seemed to be fairly quiet at the time, apart from the activities of workmen.

It is 17 November 1946 and with much of the new roof in place the awkward task of repairing the hole begins. A sign announcing 'Steelwork by Samuel Butler, Stanningley, Leeds' is displayed on the scaffolding beyond the temporary shelter on Platforms 7 and 8. The local steam crane and associated staff coaches, presumably made available to the contractor, is in attendance with N2 9498 in charge. On Platform 10 part of the shelter has been removed so that construction work could proceed and by now two of the supporting girders were in place. They are very similar but not exactly the same as the originals. There are a fair number of people waiting on Platform 10 but this is obviously a quiet time as one of the bookstall shutters is down.

Although undated, this view was probably taken towards the end of 1946 as all three replacement girders are now in place. The trappings of construction work such as ladders are evident, but the scene is dominated by barrows of postal sacks which may well be associated with the Christmas peak. What looks like an N2 has brought a rake of Gresley main line stock with carriage boards into Platform 10. Most people on the platform are civilians or railway staff, although a couple of people in military uniforms are present.

Left. This prospect of Platform 10 from the footbridge looking towards the buffer stops was taken around 1954 and the bomb damage might never have occurred. It is worth comparing this scene with the earlier view of the crushed coach and dented N2 taken from almost the same place. The subterranean gentlemen's emporium incorporating baths, a hairdresser and wash and brush up facilities besides the lavatories was badly damaged but it is well and truly back in business. Careful scrutiny of the top right of the photograph reveals the three replacement girders. An N2 has brought in empty Mk.1 stock to form The Heart of Midlothian which is loading prior to its 2.0pm departure from Platform 10. On the left an Immingham B1 has arrived with the through train from Cleethorpes and Grimsby Town via the East Lincolnshire line and Peterborough. Most appropriately, there is a soldier striding along the platform with his leave suitcase.

Although this is Platform 10 some time during the 1960s and memories of the war are fading, or non-existent for some of those waiting for their train, there is still a strong reminder of that bomb. Above the 'Gentlemen' sign between the bookstall and the footbridge those three roof supports which replaced the ones knocked out by the explosion can be seen. They have solid metal rather than diminishing hoops in the acute angles between the base and the apex, the circular bracing in the middle is thicker and there is no decorative work at the springing points above the corbels. Presumably these girders were rolled rather than cast. Furthermore, the new section of building, which can be distinguished by its lighter colouring, is set further back so the girder uprights protrude from the wall rather than being set in it. Continuity was provided by installing corbels of an identical design to the originals.

The lure of King's Cross during the 1950s is encapsulated here on the afternoon of 9 July 1955, as 60014 SILVER LINK departs from Platform 7 with the Yorkshire Pullman. An A1 stands at the head of another express in Platform 10 accompanied by the usual gaggle of youngsters, while a rake of BR Standard coaches in 'blood and custard' stands at Platform 8. In the right foreground is A3 60053 SANSOVINO. It occupies the road usually assumed to be reserved for the main line 'standby' pilot but matters weren't really that straightforward. It wasn't quite that a prepared pilot stood there ready all the time; in LNER and early BR days there had always been a pilot, often an Atlantic, for assisting heavy trains to Potters Bar, though it would also be hurled into the fray in the event of a failure or extra train being required. In BR days there was always a 'pilot' prepared at Top Shed, though this was a Pacific that would be required later for a booked turn; another 'pilot' would have been prepared by then. SANSOVINO, if indeed it is a 'pilot (the tender is pretty empty) would head north soon and another 'pilot' take its place, either here or 'up the Top'. There were also pilot locomotives prepared and ready at Peterborough Station, Doncaster Station and Darlington MPD. These were turned during the day to face the most likely direction that they might be needed. It was routine of course for a spare to be ready and fully prepared for the Non Stop and any Royal. In the Centre Spur on the left is spick and span N2 69525 patiently waiting for its next task. Just visible to the left of the signal box another clean N2 stands at Platform 2 with empty coaching stock and is making a good deal more smoke. Photograph D M C Hepburne-Scott, Rail Archive Stephenson.

9. 1950s Remembered

Following Nationalisation the lettering above the soaring semi-circular end screens at King's Cross had to be changed again, but there are still hints of its previous ownership behind BRITISH RAILWAYS. It seems the opportunity was also taken to re-point some of the mortar. The 'native village' is still going strong, although the 'Underground' sign has gone from the end of the surface building and Fay Harris rather than Sally now runs the lingerie business in the Art Deco shop on the other side of the station approach. The incongruous Laing show house now looks very sorry for itself, with curtains drawn and no sign of a welcoming estate agent. Two generations of London black cabs are in Pancras Road and the trolleybus wires are still in place. It is 2.55pm on a dull afternoon and austerity measures still abound, but the slow recovery from the War has at least begun.

Very clear signing was provided on the approach road to the west of the main part of King's Cross. Those heading for the Suburban Station are advised to turn left and the entrance to the local platforms can be seen beyond the canopy. Entrances to the main Booking Office are in the covered area and a cab has just dropped off a passenger near them. A number of shiny black motors, together with one audacious light coloured car, complete this sunny scene. Photograph ColourRail

Thompson A2/1 60507 HIGHLAND CHIEFTAIN stands at Platform 8 on 18 April 1949. Before long, Top Shed would have a reputation for keeping its Pacifics in beautiful condition, but obviously that was not the case here. The depot did have an excuse as the engine was still in unlined wartime black which it had carried since new out of Darlington Works in May 1944 as 3696. It even retained this austere livery when it went through the shops for a heavy in October 1948, but eventually acquired a coat of Brunswick green in October 1949. Furthermore, it ran un-named until May 1947. Edward Thompson had succeeded Sir Nigel Gresley, who died in office during April 1941, and these engines were his Pacific version of the V2 2-6-2s, although only four were built. Photograph M J Reade, ColourRail

60022 MALLARD backs out of King's Cross during the summer of 1950. The A4 is in British Railways blue livery though it had been the only one to pass to British Railways in black. It went into the shops during January 1948 and emerged a couple of months later in Garter blue livery, numbered E22 and allocated to King's Cross. BR blue was applied in September 1949, together with the commemorative plaques, then during summer 1951 this was one of the engines assigned to regular top link crews. 60022 finally became Brunswick Green in July 1952 and '22' remained at King's Cross until withdrawn for preservation during April 1963. Photograph Brian Bailey.

On 23 June 1950 two Pacifics have made their way to the engine yard at King's Cross having brought in expresses from the North East. On the left is Heaton A2/3 60512 STEADY AIM which has arrived with a through working from Sunderland. To the right of it is A1 60158 off the Tees-Tyne Pullman and in the BR blue livery applied when it was new from Doncaster Works in November 1949. King's Cross originally had eight new A1s and three more were soon drafted in from Grantham and Doncaster, but the summer 1951 decision to concentrate A4s at Top Shed meant that the new Peppercorn Pacifics all moved away, although this one was back again for a while in 1957-58. Photograph Brian Bailey.

Later in the 1950s, 60128 BONGRACE leaves King's Cross with The Flying Scotsman, the engine now with nameplates and rather more stylish lipped chimney. It has a 35B Grantham shedplate and was there from September 1951 to September 1957 having been transferred from King's Cross when A4s were concentrated there. The houses of Suffolk Street next to the gasworks are on the right.

Watched by the usual flock of devotees at the end of Platform 10, A1 60148 ABOYEUR makes a volcanic start from King's Cross with the Aberdonian in mid-1952 as an N2 on its usual perch, the Centre Spur, awaits its next duty. Beyond this loco is York Road station and the inconspicuous tunnel entrance leading to the Widened Lines and Moorgate. It looks as if BR has found enough funds to paint the signal box, all the signal posts and York Road canopy. The A1 and its crew would have worked a Leeds express from Grantham to London and are returning with the 7.0pm Aberdonian, a sleeping car train. A second set of men took over at Grantham and the loco continued to York, returning on a parcels train. ABOYEUR was withdrawn from Ardsley in June 1965. Photograph B K B Green.

Low sunshine nicely picks out the front of Grantham A3 60112 ST SIMON at Platform 8 with the 7.15pm from King's Cross to Aberdeen on 5 July 1952. This could have been a relief for the 7.0pm Aberdonian. Thompson and BR Standard coaches in 'blood and custard' are standing in Platform 5 on the left while an N1, presumably on empty stock, is at Platform 10 to the right. Photograph Brian Morrison.

On 28 September 1952 a special train ran from King's Cross to York to celebrate the completion of the 'Towns Line' from Peterborough to Grantham, Newark and Retford on 1 August 1852, thus completing the Great Northern portion of the East Coast main line, and the opening of King's Cross station on 14 October 1852. The 'Centenaries Express' was hauled by Top Shed A4 60007 SIR NIGEL GRESLEY in spotless condition. Here the train awaits its 9.0am departure from Platform 6 amid plenty of attention, as was to be expected. Photograph Philip J Kelley.

The driver and fireman lean towards the immaculate paintwork of SIR NIGEL GRESLEY on 28 September 1952 before they take the 'Centenaries Express' forward to York. Photograph ColourRail

A view on the last day of the Centenary Exhibition at the station, held 13-18 October 1952. It included a small exhibits gallery and various items of rolling stock. The only indication on the exterior to indicate that anything special is going on are the two flags. The trolleybuses are still flourishing, for the time being, and a London Transport RT is about to pass the 'native village'. Bedford Fish & Co Ltd continue to function as printers and stationers from their Art Deco premises, King's is still selling jewellery, cutlery and watches, while Brandons remain 'Progressive Tailors'. F.W. Goudie, transporttreasury

60800 was the first V2, new as 4771 in June 1930 and named GREEN ARROW in recognition of the fast goods service of that name which had just been introduced and was to be worked by these locos. It was allocated to King's Cross from the outset. Apart from six weeks at Woodford on the Great Central in May-June 1953, GREEN ARROW remained at King's Cross until withdrawn in August 1962. It also worked passenger trains and in its BR guise as 60800 the V2 is seen on such a duty during the early 1950s. Its importance meant that preservation deservedly followed withdrawal. JA Whaley, transporttreasury

With a broad backdrop including one of the train sheds, the Suburban Station, the German Gymnasium and St Pancras, 60008 DWIGHT D EISENHOWER in BR blue is in charge of the Scarborough Flyer (it was 'Flier' before the War) on a Friday in June/July 1950. Bizarrely, it looks as if the first coach has been derailed, yet the loco crew, passengers and bystanders all appear unconcerned, so it must be an optical illusion. After spending nearly all of the 1950s and early 1960s at King's Cross, the engine was withdrawn in July 1963, received an immaculate paint job at Doncaster and was presented to the National Railroad Museum at Green Bay Wisconsin in spring 1964.

King's Cross A4 60006 SIR RALPH WEDGWOOD stands at Platform 4 having arrived with the Flying Scotsman on 24 May 1953. Besides the customary headboard it bears a plaque for a very special event which is just a few days away. This loco was new as 4466 HERRING GULL in January 1938 and was allocated to King's Cross, but after only three months moved north to Grantham. It moved back to London in August 1944 by which time it had been renamed. The original SIR RALPH WEDGWOOD plates had been on 4469, but this was damaged beyond repair during an air raid on York shed in April 1942. 60006 was at Top Shed until it closed in June 1963 but there was a further lease of life in Scotland prior to withdrawal from Aberdeen during September 1965. Photograph T B Owen, ColourRail

Although there is less in the way of bunting for the Coronation of Queen Elizabeth II on 2 June 1953 than there was for that of George VI in 1937, King's Cross still has a few flags on display and there are flourishes in the centre of each semi-circular window. Furthermore, the frontage is beautifully picked out by floodlights. An E II R banner is attached to the lamp post on the traffic island and the snack bar has put up a couple of flagpoles but there is still a hint of austerity about. Since the pre-war views, the lingerie and hosiery business has shrunk and the chemist's sales increased by the look of it, as one of the shop units has changed hands from the former to the latter. Fay Harris now advertises blouses and knitwear as well and there is a Photographic Chemists in addition to the Dispensing Chemist. Melbray pies and cakes still seem to be going well at the café, although it has changed hands. Some new lamp standards have been erected and the stairs down to the underground station have been moved. The attempt to conceal the 'native village' by a wall was clearly thwarted by the escalator and booking hall works in the late 1930s and a new hut has been put up where the LNER Parcels Office once stood. It is about 10.7pm and the

area round King's Cross is relatively quiet in contrast to the scene today. A bus has picked up passengers outside the underground station and moved on, although it is blurred because of the lengthy time exposure for the photograph. Nevertheless it can be identified as a London Transport RT, a type extremely common by this time.

A very worthy effort was made to decorate the Booking Hall for the Coronation in 1953, embellishments including garlands, shields and flags on the balcony and plaques displaying crowns, E II R and the Queen's profile between the ticket windows. Of the hatches, the three nearest the camera are for 'Third Class Stations beyond Peterborough' and the furthest two are for 'Third Class Stations to Peterborough & Cambridge Branch'. Second Class had recently been abolished. One of the remaining pair of windows is for 'First Class All Stations' while the other is for 'Tickets in Advance, Dogs, Cycles, Prams, Horses, Motors etc'.

On 11 July 1953 60017 SILVER FOX bursts out of Copenhagen Tunnel with The Elizabethan a fortnight after the service was introduced. Following World War Two, main line schedules were a shadow of the heady days of the late 1930s and eventually an attempt was made to increase the speed of expresses. In May 1949 SILVER FOX was chosen for a test run from King's Cross to Edinburgh and back and achieved 102mph on the descent from Stoke summit during the return journey. Unfortunately, it was concluded that the A4s were up to the task but the track was not, so it was another two years before 90mph was permitted on certain sections. Photograph Brian Morrison.

To celebrate the completion of Doncaster Works in August 1853, special trains were organised for successive weekends in the early autumn of 1953. On 20 September 1953 'The Plant Centenarian' ran from King's Cross to Doncaster and back, this being the scene of anticipation at Platform 6 before the stock and locos had arrived. Away from the excitement, an N2 makes its presence felt at Platform 8 as it moves out of the station, no doubt having brought in the stock of a now departed express. Photograph Philip J Kelley.

A lovely atmospheric study of a V2 and B1 at the inner ends of Platforms 7 and 6 respectively, with mid-day sunshine through the big semi-circular window highlighting steam and smoke, parts of the engines and the porter strolling down the platform. Unfortunately it is undated, although some time during 1954 seems to be a reasonable guess. The V2 is 60962 and appears to have worked up to London on a parcels train while the B1 is 61394. Photograph ColourRail

Thompson A2/3 60514 CHAMOSSAIRE climbs Holloway Bank on the morning of 5 October 1955 with what could be the 10.10am relief Scotsman from King's Cross. If so, this engine would take the train as far as Peterborough. It was frowned upon – forbidden really – at King's Cross for a loco to take any coal if working a Cambridge, Peterborough or Grantham turn. It was regarded as 'taking coals to Newcastle' and any coal needed would be taken at one of these 'country' sheds. Every ton thus taken on board was a ton that did not have to be transported south to London – hundreds of thousands of 'ton-miles' a year if you think about it! When the A2/3s were completed at Doncaster Works, three of them took up residence at King's Cross, including 514 in September 1946. They immediately went into top link work as most of the older Pacifics were very run down because of lack of maintenance following the war. The influx of A1s displaced them and all those on the GN section migrated to New England, this one in December 1948. Their main line work at that shed included the overnight Aberdonian from Peterborough to London followed by the relief 'Scotsman' back. CHAMOSSAIRE did not move from New England and was withdrawn from there in December 1962. Photograph transporttreasury

Although 12 April 1955 was a dull day, A4 60015 QUICKSILVER added a gleam to the scene as it departed at 2.10pm with The Heart of Midlothian for Edinburgh Waverley. The particularly concentrated gathering at the end of Platform 10 would no doubt have agreed. The Heart of Midlothian made its first run on 3 May 1951 and was discontinued as a titled train on 4 May 1968.

A fascinating insight into parcels handling techniques at King's Cross during the mid-1950s. Passengers seemed totally oblivious to the wayward mail bags and were perfectly used to negotiating their way round them. An N2 has brought some Gresley stock into Platform 10 and Bravington's display cabinet brightens up the scene. This jewellery firm had premises at 189 Brampton Road SW2 and 22 Orchard Street W1 as well as its main shop at King's Cross N1 'just outside the station' in case anyone suddenly felt the need to buy a ring. By some miracle, the very flimsy glass cabinet managed to survive the May 1941 bomb intact. Holiday traffic was buoyant by this time and there are posters proclaiming the delights of beaches at Mablethorpe and Great Yarmouth.

On 29 April 1956 the Stephenson Locomotive Society ran a special train from King's Cross to the Stratford on Avon & Midland Junction Railway. The loco selected for the initial leg was Cambridge D16/3 62605, seen here in the engine yard prior to backing on to its train. The headboard was made by the photographer and the cab roof of the loco has been painted white for the occasion. After a punctual departure at 9.14am, the train travelled via Hertford North to Hitchin where ex-Midland 43222 took over for the journey through Bedford, Olney, Towcester and Kineton to Stratford on Avon SMJ station. The 0-6-0 then continued to Alcester, Redditch and Selly Oak to Birmingham New Street. Standard 5MT 73099 was provided for the return via Coventry, Leamington Spa and Rugby to Euston. Photograph Philip J Kelley.

The most unlikely loco to carry a 34A plate was Black Five 44911 which was allocated to Top Shed from February 1956 to May 1957, an odd blip in an otherwise conventional career. Along with 73071 it was there for testing over the Barnet-Huntingdon Automatic Train Control trial section. Carrying a stopping train headcode and piloting L1 67785, it is at Platform 15 with the 4.21pm to Royston on 31 August 1956. The scene is completed by N2 69497 at Platform 13 with an inner suburban service. Photograph T J Edgington

Copley Hill A1 60141 ABBOTSFORD in charge of an express for Leeds Central on 27 June 1956. In May 1950 it had begun a stay of over thirteen years at Copley Hill which had three loco and crew workings to King's Cross, two of which were lodging turns. The latter were the Up Queen of Scots, and an evening express which acquired the nickname 'Bradford Flyer'. The crews returned on an early morning business train and the Down Queen of Scots respectively. Another loco worked an early morning train to London and returned on the afternoon 'West Riding'.

The lure of Platform 10, at least its extremity, is quite obvious on 15 October 1956 as A4 60032 GANNET guides a morning train from the West Riding out of Gasworks Tunnel and into Platform 8. This was one of the last LNER streamlined Pacifics to be completed at Doncaster Works and went into service at Doncaster shed during May 1938. It did not stay in Yorkshire for long as a transfer to King's Cross came in September 1938, but it was back to Doncaster during May 1939 then on to Grantham in October 1943. Although the motive power crisis of summer 1951 saw a concentration of A4s at King's Cross, GANNET anticipated this development and moved back to the capital in June 1950. It was there until Top Shed closed in June 1963 but the move to New England was its last, withdrawal coming during the following October. Photograph Brian Bailey.

On a grey and murky 13 January 1957, A4 60033 SEAGULL leaves Platform 5 with an express, the first coach of which appears to be an LMS Stanier vehicle. This was the last but one of the class to be built and began its career at King's Cross in June 1938. It was one of the four with a double chimney from new, the others being MALLARD, CAPERCAILLIE and PEREGRINE.

On 6 April 1957 A1 60149 AMADIS is ready to leave Platform 10 with what is possibly a Newcastle express. Fresh from Darlington Works in May 1949, this was one of four A1s allocated to new to Grantham, but a decision was soon made to increase the number at King's Cross from eight to twelve so 60149 moved south the following September. The motive power reorganisation of September 1951 meant that all the A1s left King's Cross, this one going back to Grantham that month. During September 1956 another policy change resulted in locos working through from London to Newcastle again so King's Cross acquired three A1s from Grantham once more, including this one. Photograph Brian Bailey.

On a particularly sunny day in June 1957, 60028 WALTER K WHIGHAM is about to depart with The Talisman for Edinburgh Waverley. This was a relatively new service, the inaugural titled run having been on 17 September 1956. This engine, as 4487 SEA EAGLE in Garter blue, worked the last Down 'Coronation' at the end of August 1939 and the first Down 'Elizabethan' on 29 June 1953 in the guise seen here. In between these momentous occasions the loco was painted wartime black in 1941, LNER blue again in 1947, BR purple in 1948, BR blue in 1950 and finally Brunswick green in 1952. The engine was renamed after the last Deputy Chairman of the LNER in October 1947. Photograph B K B Green.

On 10 August 1957 New England A2/3 60513 DANTE eases past the loco yard. Along with 514 and 523, this was one of the three locos of this class allocated brand new to Top Shed. 513 was there from August 1946 to December 1948 when it moved to New England having just been renumbered 60513. A typical job for a Peterborough A2/3 at the time would have been the 11.42am to King's Cross, which had left Newcastle at 8.0am, then the 4.10pm from the capital, due in Peterborough North at 6.29pm. In 1957-59 Grantham acquired three New England Pacifics for varying periods and this one was there from June 1958 to June 1959. They were employed on certain parcels duties during their stay. 60513 was withdrawn from New England in April 1963. Photograph J Robertson, transporttreasury

Beyond Platforms 1 to 10 and the two great train sheds, the hotchpotch of suburban facilities and goods docks carried on much the same during the 1950s. This photograph shows a good slice of that different world and although no date is recorded, it is probably the 1956-58 period. N2 69575 on the left has a passenger train at Platform 13 (part of the original Suburban Station with its overall roof) and another local working with an unidentified N2 is at Platform 14. This is the eastern side of the island, built on the site of the earlier engine yard. More coaching stock is at Platform 15, the other side of the island. Then comes Platform 16 serving trains from Moorgate and still on a rising gradient at the top of the notorious Hotel Curve. The slightly higher canopy to the right of it is Platform 17, the outermost bay. Behind the nearest signal post a third N2 is standing in what were originally called the Milk Bays. The soaring roof of St Pancras overlooks this intriguing corner of King's Cross. Photograph P Moffat, ColourRail

The inclined nature of Platform 16 is very noticeable here (the period would be 1956-58) emphasised by the gradient levelling off at the far end. The tunnel is behind the camera and it can be observed that timber was used for virtually everything, including the platform, canopy supports, the canopy itself and waiting rooms. The newer structure sheltering Platforms 14 and 15 up on the right has plain lightweight ironwork supporting the roof. Photograph P Moffat, ColourRail

As the 1950s drew on, the era of steam-hauled suburban trains out of King's Cross was coming to an end, but N2 69534 at Platform 12 in the original suburban station maintained the tradition when this photograph was taken in spring 1958. The engine was a touch unkempt and its stock consisted of modern BR non-corridor coaches rather than Gresley articulated sets, but the essentials are still there. Some older carriages occupy Platform 13. New from North British as GN 1755 in March 1921, this was one of the engines delivered to King's Cross but soon moved away to Hornsey where they were kept in immaculate condition. During the heyday of suburban traffic from the late 1920s to the early 1930s, King's Cross had 45 weekday diagrams for N2s and Hornsey six. After periods at Hatfield and King's Cross during the 1950s, 69534 was withdrawn from Hornsey in February 1959. The cheeky lads and the old brazier keeping the water crane company are incidentals setting off this scene to perfection. Photograph Brian Bailey.

Although the A4s usually looked smart and the principal expresses still had a sparkle, King's Cross was looking very drab by the late 1950s. Here, a filthy J50 deals with parcels stock at Platform 1 beyond a row of forlorn barrows. Stonework, brickwork, roofs, end screens, huts, platforms and lamp posts all have a generous coating of soot. In fact the only bright spot in this view is the rolling stock of The Northumbrian at Platform 5.

A4 60025 FALCON waits to leave Platform 8 on 9 May 1958. Photograph J Robertson, transporttreasury

There was a fairly strong westerly breeze blowing on this bright July day in 1958 as V2 60829 waited at Platform 8 as N2 69568 went about its duties at Platform 7. Photograph T J Edgington.

The N2s were certainly one of the most endearing features of the King's Cross scene and although some of them eventually worked in other parts of the country they looked most at home on the southern reaches of the Great Northern main line. With steam to spare on 28 March 1958, 69528 is on empty stock duties just outside the Suburban Station. Photograph ColourRail

On a wet day, possibly in 1958, 69535 is well prepared to move a rake of main line stock out of Platform 4 to Hornsey Carriage Sidings. It was quite usual for an N2 to haul trains weighing 400 tons or more out of the terminus, although it was always the practice to provide a clear road so that momentum could be built up for the climb through Gasworks and Copenhagen Tunnels. Inevitably progress was fairly slow up the bank, but after Holloway summit a fair turn of speed was achieved. 69535 is in lovely condition here, a sign of care and attention by regular crews. Note the upturned Hatfield destination board on the smokebox. Photograph P Moffat, ColourRail

N2 69493 beyond Platform 17 at the dock once known as the Milk Bay, 15 November 1958. This appears to have been one of the N2s overhauled at Stratford Works where the cream and red lining was omitted, although it has been kept clean and the number together with the early version of the BR emblem are clearly visible. 69493 was withdrawn from service at the end of 1958. Photograph L Rowe, ColourRail

Peppercorn A2 60538 VELOCITY moves past the engine yard on 31 July 1959. It went new to Gateshead in 1948 with its BR number but painted in LNER green, although it acquired a double chimney and Brunswick green livery as early as October 1949. VELOCITY worked regularly from Newcastle to Edinburgh and London until the rapid spread of diesels. A move to Heaton in May 1960 was followed by a more ominous one to Tweedmouth during October 1961. When the extra summer season traffic was over in September 1962 the loco went into storage at Blaydon and was condemned there the following November. Nevertheless it had nearly 900,000 miles of useful work behind it Photograph ColourRail

L1 67787, an occasional resident at King's Cross, gathered at Platform 4 with another L1 and an N2 on 16 August 1959. It too is probably bound for Top shed, coupled to the 0-6-2T in front. Photograph Nick Nicolson, transporttreasury

It was the practice at King's Cross to couple two or even three locos together to get them from the station to Top Shed, thus saving paths at busy times. On 26 June 1959 an A3 and A4 are ready to make the move up the bank through Gasworks Tunnel on 26 June 1959, 60060 THE TETRARCH and 60006 SIR RALPH WEDGWOOD Photographs D Clayton.

New housing developments in outlying districts and the resultant increase in demand for suburban services was one of the reasons the LNER decided it needed more N2s. On the Centre Engine Spur on 12 August 1959 with a J50 0-6-0T, 69589 was one of those built by Yorkshire Engine Co of Sheffield and in this case delivered as 2683 during October 1928. By 1929 King's Cross had nearly sixty N2s. These later engines could be distinguished by the 'improved' condensing gear. The external pipe was pitched higher, supported by a bracket and originally entered the top of the tank about half way along, but this was later modified so that it went into the tank at the front. None of the systems worked particularly well and the crew would isolate the apparatus whenever possible. In this view, on 12 August 1959, King's Cross is embracing a fairly dense smoke haze. 69589 is making its contribution to the murk, although its days are numbered. Photograph Nick Nicolson, transporttreasury

On a very bright summer day in the late 1950s, Immingham B1 61406 arrives with the early morning Cleethorpes through train via Louth, Boston, Spalding and Peterborough. This was one of the longest regular passenger workings for a B1 and its crew and after spending the afternoon in London the loco returned on an early evening service. There was a similar working just before 9.0am from Cleethorpes, but this time Boston men took over the train at their home town. 61379 MAYFLOWER was a regular performer. Immingham B1s also worked fish trains from Grimsby Docks to King's Cross, but Britannia Pacifics took over both passenger and freight workings in 1961. Photograph Nick Nicolson, transporttreasury

Top Shed's 60032 GANNET with an express at Platform 7 on a sunny afternoon. Because King's Cross kept its big engines in such fine condition, it is impossible to say whether this loco is ex-works or not. In November 1958 GANNET and UNION OF SOUTH AFRICA were the last two A4s to go through the shops to receive double chimneys, so this could be spring 1959.

60007 SIR NIGEL GRESLEY waiting to leave London with 'The Stephenson Jubilee' special to Doncaster on 23 May 1959 makes a fitting finale to the 1950s at King's Cross. It proved to be a day when records were broken and for many enthusiasts set the seal on the A4 story. The headboard seen here was made by the photographer. Although diesels had been introduced on main line services out of King's Cross in winter 1958 they had to be rescued by A4s on numerous occasions, but nevertheless it was realised that the end of express steam workings was in sight. As a result the Stephenson Locomotive Society organised this train and with 60007 in the hands of Driver Hoole of King's Cross there was an air of anticipation, especially as it was known that the operating authorities had agreed to relax the 90mph maximum for this one occasion. On

the northbound journey speed rose to 101mph beyond Hitchin and Stoke summit itself was breasted at 82 mph, an all-time record for steam. Speed during the descent of Stoke bank on the way back reached 112mph and another maximum of 100mph was reached near Sandy. As the RCTS guide comments, this was another epic performance by an A4 a quarter of a century after the amazing debut by SILVER LINK and although the streamliners were not finished it was realised that there would never be another run like it. Photograph Philip J Kelley.

King's Cross V2 60814 does its bit during filming of *The Ladykillers* at the south portal of Copenhagen Tunnel, probably during the winter of 1954-55. The original Copenhagen Tunnel is on the left while the later portals accommodating the Down Main and Up Main respectively are to the right of it. Copenhagen Junction box is also prominent on the right and the North London line viaduct is immediately behind the camera. Factories of York Road and Pleasant Grove in Belle Isle are above the tunnel to the left while terraces at the end of Frederick Street form the skyline to the right. The mock rear wall of the ramshackle house can be seen below them. Photograph Philip J. Kelley.

There is just a glimpse of the tracks between the wall and the windbreak as preparations are made for another scene, probably involving a body and coal wagons. *The Ladykillers* was a huge success in the USA as well as Britain and these extracts from an American review sum up their enthusiasm for the film, albeit without much reference to the Great Northern main line! 'Meet Mrs Wilberforce. She's a kindly old lady who lives alone in a house at the end of a line by some train tracks. Nicest woman you'd ever want to meet – but she does get some rather crazy ideas though … you know, about extraterrestrials and whatnot. What seems to be a simple comedic caper becomes more and more complicated and everytime you turn around there's another giant *Klong!* In one of the coal cars out back. It's just too brilliant to be believed. Fact of the matter is, this is as good as its going to get and its damn funny to boot. I'd say plonk down the coin, because this is a classic. *Klong!* Photograph Philip J Kelley.

10. 'The Ladykillers'

Paddington may have had its bear and Waterloo its sunset, but King's Cross and its approaches became stars of the silver screen. *The Ladykillers*, actually filmed in colour, was the last of the classic Ealing Comedies and its premiere in 1955 coincided with the sale of Ealing Studios to the BBC. The cast included several famous names but during its 1 hour 37 minutes of dark humour which occasionally verged on broad farce, the film featured scenes shot at Belle Isle and The Cross to the extent that this stretch of railway should have been nominated for an Oscar. Its central character is dear sweet little old Mrs Wilberforce who lives alone in a wonky bomb-damaged house at the end of a street with a view of St Pancras. Inside, there is an aura of faded Victorian gentility helped by a portrait of her long departed husband and a parrot which answers to the name of General Gordon. Louisa Wilberforce, played by Katie Johnson, often visits King's Cross police station chatting about crimes she has witnessed, supposedly, and reporting sightings of flying saucers. The benevolent policeman on duty, almost inevitably portrayed by Jack Warner, has heard it all many times before but always lends a friendly ear. Our heroine wants a lodger, more for company than the rent money, and one day there is a knock at the door followed by the seemingly innocent question 'Mrs Wilberforce? I understand you have rooms to let.' The gentleman making the request is Professor Marcus, featuring Alec Guinness in one of his most remarkable guises with floppy grey hair, shifty eyes and extraordinary protruding teeth which make every utterance sound sinister. One critic said his creation was creepy enough to make you shudder and eccentric enough to make you chuckle, but nervously. Before long Mrs Wilberforce is pleased to find out that the professor regularly has four friends round so they can practise playing their musical instruments in the string quintet they have formed. Of course she is totally oblivious to the reality that the professor is actually a demonic criminal mastermind and his amateur players are a gang of thieves. Together they are plotting the perfect heist using their 'Mrs Lopsided' as an unwitting accomplice and her rickety house as the operations

Phil Kelley was the official railway photographer while sequences for *The Ladykillers* were being shot near the south portal of Copenhagen Tunnel and mixed freely with the actors and production crew. Towards the end of the filming he took this memorable photograph which is signed *Good wishes Alec Guinness, Herbert Lom*. During this break the former has set aside the wild grey wig and hideous dentures of unhinged Professor Marcus while the latter is grinning, not a familiar characteristic of Soho gangster Louis Harvey. These two world-class actors had very different beginnings. Alec Guinness de Cuffe was born in London and joined the Old Vic during the 1930s. After War service in the Royal Navy he eventually became a household name because of films such as *Kind Hearts and Coronets*, *The Man in the White Suit* and *The Bridge on the River Kwai*. In later years he was George Smiley in the BBC serialisation of John le Carre's *Tinker, Tailor, Soldier, Spy*. Herbert Lom was born in Prague as Herbert Charles Angelo Kuchacevich ze Schluderpachern, so it is perhaps as well he changed his name. Having acted in Czech plays and films he escaped from the Germans and worked in the German section of the BBC in World War Two. Of his hundred or so film appearances, one of the best known is as dithering Inspector Dreyfus in the *Pink Panther* series. Herbert Lom, with trusty camera, was a railway enthusiast and would often completely miss instructions from the Director as a passing Pacific claimed his attention. Photograph Philip J Kelley.

base. The gang is a wonderful mixture of characters. Major Courtney, a rather doddery ex-officer and upper class charmer is played by Cecil Parker while the lumbering heavyweight '(don' call me stoopid') One-Round Lawson is portrayed by Danny Green. The twitchy Jack-the-Lad teddy boy Harry Robinson is played by Peter Sellers and the suave cold-hearted assassin Louis Harvey is Herbert Lom. With Boccherini and Haydn playing on the gramophone, the door is locked and the payroll robbery at King's Cross station planned. Unfortunately the rogues have reckoned without the constant interruptions by Mrs Wilberforce who brings tea, coffee and cakes then asks for help giving General Gordon his medicine. The parrot decides to bite Harry and promptly escapes causing chaos as frantic attempts are made to retrieve him. In due course the payroll van is successfully held up and the money transferred to a trunk. Willingly and totally innocently, Mrs Wilberforce collects the luggage under the noses of unsuspecting detectives, but the gang are alarmed when the old dear suddenly goes back to collect a mislaid umbrella. There is more chaos when she has an altercation with a barrow boy, a cameo role by Frankie Howerd, who is outraged by a horse eating his fruit. She eventually manages to get the trunk home with the assistance of a policeman and the gang drag it upstairs. After gloating over their haul they transfer the used

banknotes to their instrument cases. Nothing can go wrong now... or can it?

As they bid farewell to Mrs Wilberforce, One-Round gets his cello case stuck in the door and as the clod attempts to free it, the lid opens and the 'lolly' spills out. A rapid exit is the first thought, but it dawns on the villains that their landlady might tell the 'bogeys', so they try to come up with a plausible explanation. Their utterances are interrupted by the arrival of four more old ladies who are guests for afternoon tea and one has brought the latest edition of a newspaper which contains the story of the robbery. Suddenly the penny drops and Mrs Wilberforce is appalled, dressing down the gang as if they are little boys who have misbehaved in the nursery. She demands they stay for tea but afterwards the rogues try to convince her to stay silent and when this fails warns her that she will be implicated and faces jail. A policeman calls and she tells him to 'naff off' on the instructions of the gang, but still insists the money must be returned. There is no option now other than dispose of her and that will be the end of the matter. Not for the first time, intentions do not quite work out as planned, but this time it falls apart in a terminal way for the ruffians.

None of them really want to be the 'ladykiller' so they draw lots and the Major loses. The others go downstairs

and send Mrs Wilberforce up to him, but he loses his nerve, tells her he is going to the police and climbs through the window with the money. By now the rest of the gang realise what is happening so Louis gives chase and recovers the money, but Major Courtney falls to his death. One down, four to go. Lots are drawn again but One-Round, who had always been well disposed towards the old lady, rebels and insists she should live. To distract

V2 60814 obliges the film crew with plenty of smoke and steam as preparations for further shots proceed. The mock-up of Mrs Wilberforce's house is just visible behind the smoke at the end of Frederick Street. The critics also had plenty of praise for Katie Johnson who achieved fame and won a British Oscar for her part in _The Ladykillers_ when she was 77. One wrote 'The cast of criminals are uniformly excellent, but it is Katie Johnson as the oblivious old lady who carries the film with a sweet determination'. Another commented: 'The characters are some of the smartest dumb people ever put on screen. Katie Johnson as Mrs Wilberforce is simply wonderful, acting with such little effort, she is extraordinary'. A third declared 'But the film really belonged to 77-year-old Katie Johnson as the apparently dotty but utterly indefatigable Mrs Wilberforce.' Photograph Philip J Kelley.

Other reviews remarked: 'Herbert Lom's thuggishness, Peter Sellers' nervy twitching and Danny Green's lumbering cloddishness are a treat, but are wickedly done away with one by one under cover of locomotive smoke plumes' and 'Accompanied by a noirish cacophony of screeching trains, parrots and little old ladies at afternoon tea, a series of unlikely events builds to the hilarious surprising finale'. King's Cross V2 60821 on film duty as well seen from above the south portal of Copenhagen Tunnel. Photograph Philip J Kelley.

him, Marcus asks for help getting rid of the major's body into a passing goods train. Back in the house, Harry draws the short straw this time but instead of killing her he decides to do a runner with the cash as well. One-Round returns while Mrs Wilberforce is having a doze and comes to the conclusion that she is dead, so he runs after spiv Harry and finishes him off. Two down, three to go. Marcus and Louis dispose of Harry's body in the established manner amid smoke and steam but One-Round later overhears them plotting to kill him. He pulls Harry's gun on them but the safety catch is on and Louis dispatches him with a knife. Three down, two to go. With the prospect of securing all the loot rather than sharing it, the professor and Louis fight it out and the latter eventually falls to his death. Four down, leaving just manic Professor Marcus who wanted all the money for himself in the first place, but as he smugly celebrates a signal arm strikes him and he falls as well. With the gang obliterated, Mrs Wilberforce now has £60,000 in her possession and dutifully makes her way to King's Cross police station. Once more, the amiable policeman listens politely to what he deems to be yet another fantasy then sends her home. Bemused, she walks back to the rickety house wondering what to do with all the money. After all, the gang told her the insurance company would never want it returned!

More volcanic exhaust, this time from A4 60030 GOLDEN FLEECE climbing towards Copenhagen Tunnel with a Down express. Another great actor who witnessed such scenes was Peter Sellers, born into a touring family at Southsea in 1925. After becoming a 'drummer, pianist and general funnyman' for RAF gang shows during the war, he rose to fame on radio as the source of several idiotic voices in *The Goon Show*, a national cult in the mid-1950s. Following *The Ladykillers*, Sellers starred in many films including *I'm All Right Jack* and *Dr Strangelove*, but his lasting achievement may be the character Inspector Clouseau in the *Pink Panther* series, a legendary comic creation whose disastrously misplaced 'French' vowels have entered the vocabulary. Jack Warner was born in London in 1896. His role as PC George Dixon in *The Blue Lamp* established him as the image of benevolent community policing. Translated to television in 1955 as *Dixon of Dock Green*, his Saturday night homilies on the British way of life ran until 1976 by which time, according to one critic, both Jack Warner and the image of the police he represented were ready for retirement. Photograph Philip J Kelley.

Preparations are made for filming the heist in the shadow of St Pancras Gasworks behind King's Cross. Considering the police presence, it seems that someone thinks that a real robbery is about to take place.

1. Ealing Studios organised a Tea Party for the children of Frederick Street and the weather was kind.

2. Herbert Lom and Alec Guiness have a game of cards between filming.

3. Herbert Lom does not look much like cold-hearted assassin Louis Harvey as he enjoys the company of five local nurses.

4. One-Round Lawson, alias Danny Green, hands out goodies to the youngsters.

5. Professor Marcus, otherwise known as Alec Guinness, looks shifty outside the shop where he saw the advertisement for a 'room to let'.

6. Frankie Howerd puts the final touches to his barrow of fruit before the horse begins to claim its share.

There were several landmarks in the development of motive power working out of King's Cross and the introduction of the Deltics was certainly one of them. 'The peculiar 'Golden fing' on the front was a startling sight to those of us used to the more restrained headboards of the steam era but the Deltics, even allowing for our early prejudice, made for a fine sight in their dashing livery. The subsequent popularity – idolatry – of these big diesels was a contrast to our typical urchin's reaction in 1961 – then they were shunned. There was some disappointment, nay, mystification I seem to recall, that they were not painted 'like the blue one'. Allan Baker, who operated the locos out of the gleaming new depot at Finsbury Park (see the excellent *Deltics at Work*, Baker & Morrison, Ian Allan, 1985) has pointed 'to the astonishing mileages the introduction of the big 'Type 5s', brought, working 'the first true cyclic diagrams'. They roared and whined and blasted their way in and out of King's Cross for nearly two decades, and were particularly impressive screeching and throbbing around the groaning curves of 'the passenger loco', given over to diesels with the construction of a proper servicing shed. This dealt with the lesser periodic exams and so avoided the need to travel light out to Finsbury Park, which was a maintenance depot only – apart from one of two sets for movements it had no crews like Top Shed had, for instance. The awesome twin blasts of a Deltic exhaust as it 'lit up' were almost thrilling, in a less environmentally-conscious age, rocketing up and outwards to signal the issuing forth of yet another monster from the yard. The Deltic seen here is D9000 ROYAL SCOTS GREY, new from English Electric Vulcan Foundry in February 1961 and one of those allocated to Haymarket as reflected by the name. In May 1979 the diesel moved to York and was withdrawn as 55 022 in January 1982 with preservation following. Photograph Brian Morrison.

186

11. Latter Days

Within weeks of the 1955 BR Modernisation Scheme being announced long cherished ideas had surfaced in many areas of the network, some going back decades, and detailed plans were being produced in almost indecent haste, without revisiting the premise on which they had been devised in the first case. The result was many expensive projects like flyovers and marshalling yards in a few years became expensive and redundant white elephants. Change in traffic flows, the speeding up of transportation, and habits of travel brought this about, along with failures in financial rigour.

Keen as any other Region, the East Coast authorities first decided on long term infrastructure projects that were fundamental to any long term improvement, but which by their very nature would take years if not decades

to complete. This had the advantage of allowing for public funding drying up because of changes in government policy or public finances. At the time the line out of Kings Cross was already undergoing change as the enlargement to four tracks to north of Welwyn Garden City had been started in 1953 with the provision of three new tunnels alongside the existing ones between Hadley Wood and Potters Bar and all the rebuilding of stations. This project was completed in May 1959 and was accompanied by the complete recasting of the local services with diesel power and diesel railcars.

By the time this work was nearing completion from 1957 onwards, new schedules were introduced which would pave the way for new motive power ordered under the 1955 Scheme to be introduced in numbers. By 1963 diesel

power had swept away steam from the southern end of the East Coast main line. The first main line diesels had appeared in April 1958 with English Electric D201 hauling the down Flying Scotsman on 21 June. But the early diesels in 1958-59 only prepared the way for the second generation of locos, especially the Deltics, BR and Brush Type 4s, and the Brush Type 2s that monopolised the scene from the formal abolition of steam on 15/16 June 1963.

This book in concerned with the past, present and future of Kings Cross station which held its centenary in 1952 and is now 174 years old. During the past 40 years it has received as much attention, both in maintenance and upgrading as it has ever received during the rest of its existence. Consequently it is more fit for purpose than ever and at the same time the architects and

The prototype Deltic waits to leave King's Cross Platform 10 with The White Rose on 7 July 1959. Having been on loan to BR from English Electric since October 1955, it had arrived on the GN earlier in 1959 with some degree of success. There had been periods out of use with radiator trouble, though being a single example, spares for minor problems would always have a disproportionate effect. It had returned to 'its usual King's Cross-Doncaster diagram' on May 28th and in the first weekend of June it had gone to Scotland via the LMR for a weeks trial. *Trains Illustrated* at the time lauded its feats, including 'the working of a 550-ton train over the 29.1 miles from Peterborough to Grantham in 25 minutes'. DELTIC's stay at Hornsey 'had not been the most fruitful of its career so far'; tight clearances apparently had restricted it to a daily mileage well below potential, for it could not 'freely work beyond Doncaster'. Shadowed in Platform 11 of the Suburban Station is 'Baby Deltic' D5906.

Until subjected to close scrutiny, this view from the engine yard in August 1959 gives the impression that King's Cross has gone over entirely to diesels. On the left is North British Type 2 D6104, which was new to Hornsey depot in February 1959. After an indifferent start the loco went into store during February 1960 then moved to Eastfield in April 1960 for use on the West Highland line. Withdrawal came in December 1967 after less than nine years, much of it in store. Its companion is a 'Baby Deltic' while in the Suburban Station a Cravens DMU stands in Platform 12, a Birmingham RCW Type 2 waits to leave Platform 13 and another diesel of the same class is to the right of it, possibly emerging from 'The Drain'. However, there are loco coal wagons on the right and some reassuring smoke rising above Platform 10, so all is not yet lost.

engineers have established in London one of the finest early Victorian buildings for us to appreciate as a public space. Its stark, striking outline is in sharp contrast with the later Victorian period manifested alongside it by the Gothic exuberance of St Pancras.

D206 arrived at Hornsey at the end of July 1958, slotting unobtrusively into the crew training jobs of D201. From the winter timetable of September 15th five intensive weekly rosters began with only five of the Type 4s, booked for 4,500 miles a week each ... 'the first real British test of all the advertised benefits of intensive use over long distances of a stud of standard units.' Full implementation was delayed until 29th September ... 'pending delivery of the fifth unit.' Type 2 diesels for freight and passenger work were also soon being delivered to Hornsey and Birmingham RC&W Co D5300 made its debut on Hertford passenger turns in September 1958. North British Type 2s began their particularly inauspicious and brief GN careers in 1959. Diesel performance generally was 'less than impeccable' but the Sheffield Pullman trains were something of a flagship and every effort was made to preserve Type 4 haulage of the Master Cutler. In the autumn and winter of 1958 many trials and much

exasperation was endured and despite the worryingly frequent ignomy of multiple failures, the D200 programme of 1958 was a bold one, with perilously meagre resources.

DELTIC arrived in January 1959 and though out of action at Hornsey in May it was soon back on regular King's Cross-Doncaster jobs. Most of the EE 'Baby Deltics' reached Hornsey by the end of May but nerves were frayed and hopes faltering badly by the summer of 1959. The BRCW locos had piston troubles and spare DMU sets from country districts were being requisitioned, some of their home jobs reverting to steam. *Trains Illustrated* in October reported that a King's Cross steam locomotive was prepared as stand by for every one of the Type 4 duties. Though there could have been few things worse for a BR engineer to hear, in the trough of teething troubles this long lamented journal followed with the devastating and fascinating point that *in such a situation there will be many who will wonder whether the construction of new boilers to save the double chimney A3s from extinction might not be a worthwhile investment – particularly as there is evidence that the much more youthful – and nominally Class 8 A1s are beginning to promise more trouble than the Gresley*

Pacifics ever did at the same age, whereas the Class 7 double chimney A3s have become the apple of every East Coast Route shedmaster's eye and are used on the most exacting workings the line has to offer.

In the event, twenty new diagram 107 boilers were put onto A4s and A3s from July 1959 to July 1961. Brush Type 2s (class 31), D5563 and D5564 turned up at Hornsey on November 20th 1959 for trials, considered more suitable, through reasons of power, on such workings as King's Cross-Peterborough. They were to prove a success and the BRCW/Sulzer and NB Type 2s went to Scotland.

The first A3 Pacific was condemned at the end of 1959, SOLARIO with a cracked frame. Traction changes at King's Cross from hereon would be extraordinary. Brush Type 2s in multiple worked the 'Heart of Midlothian' and 'Northumbrian' in February/March 1960. The first through diesel working King's Cross-Edinburgh came in 1960, a Type 4 on the 'Car Sleeper'. Britannias displaced from the GE were an unexpected development, working from Immingham on Cleethorpes trains.

Finsbury Park (Clarence Yard) diesel depot opened in April 1960. Diesels were bearing its shed code 34G and the lifeblood of Top Shed was inexorably

North British Type 2 Bo-Bo D6107 stands in the yard on 3 October 1959 with the BR Road Motor Depot in the left background and Gasworks Tunnel to the right. These diesels had 1,000/1,100hp NBL/MAN engines; this one was new to Hornsey in March 1959 but was stored unserviceable by February 1960. It moved to Eastfield a couple of months later but was out of use again by March 1964. After a few more years of work in Scotland it was withdrawn in October 1971.

'Baby Deltic' D5908 waiting to move out of Platform 11 on 16 August 1959 presents the modern image in contrast to the Gresley coach in maroon and BR Mk.1 still in carmine and cream occupying Platform 10. These machines were noisy, smoky and had character like their big brothers, but unfortunately their longevity was just as poor as that of the North British Type 2s. This one was new to Hornsey in May 1959 and was withdrawn from Finsbury Park in March 1969. Nick Nicolson, transporttreasury

Around 1959, D5903 leaves a pall of diesel exhaust hanging under the roof as it departs with a local service made up of BR Standard non-corridor stock. These Type 2s were built by English Electric at Vulcan Foundry and had 1,100hp Napier Deltic engines. This one arrived new at Hornsey in February 1959 and moved to Finsbury Park during April 1960. Withdrawal came at the end of 1968 after just under ten years allocated to suburban work out of King's Cross, a fair proportion of it laid up. Nick Nicolson, transporttreasury

flowing away to 'The Park'. The first production series Deltic, D9001, arrived in London in January 1961 for an exhibition at Stratford and Type 2s of a different make (but destined to be relatively short-lived on workings out of the terminus) also date from about this period: Sulzers in the D5000 series from GE line depots. The Deltics now began their prodigious mileage feats, Haymarket examples bringing up the morning Talisman to work back with the Aberdonian and so on.

The great event was to be the new winter timetable of 1961, 'to restore the highest pre-war standards of express passenger train speed between London and the West Riding, Newcastle and Edinburgh...' Delays, and problems meant only a proportion of the order for 22 Deltics was available and only a tenth of the accelerations were possible. Moreover crucial reconstruction work, especially the easing of the Peterborough curves, was in abeyance on the instruction of the Ministry of Transport. It was a bit of a mess and derived principally from the halt to electrification plans. As *Trains Illustrated* put it in rather frustrated but anonymous tone in 1961: *what we now have is a comparatively hurried*

extemporisation forced on the East Coast Route by the abandonment of electrification, even though at the time the decision was taken there was not available a high powered British diesel engine or locomotive complete, which was sufficiently proved for mass production, so that the East Coast Route could still provide something like the service envisaged with electric traction.

In June 1962, with a complete fleet of Deltics, six hour schedules could be introduced on King's Cross-Scottish services. By 1963 with EE Type 3 and 4 (class 37 and 40), Peaks (class 45 etc) and Deltics, there seemed to be diesels galore: D1500 in a debut heavily rodent of symbolism, displaced MALLARD on October 8th 1962, on the 5.23pm Doncaster train. The end of steam at King's Cross was not greatly heralded, probably because it was still commonplace across much of the country; the *Railway Magazine* reported June 15th 1963 as the last day and the *Railway Observer* the next day, the 16th. This was 60158 ABERDONIAN, on the 10.45pm Leeds train. 'Top Shed' closed that day but the engines proved persistent. Pacifics were still turning up as substitutes and on freight through

the summer. A1 and A3 Pacifics, V2s, 9Fs and B1s all turned up for failed diesels, into November 1963. SILVER FOX worked a Leeds train on October 29th, despite 'its official withdrawal nine days earlier'.

What followed was demonstrably the Deltic era, in which King's Cross took on an almost unique air amongst the great railway stations of Britain, or at least the capital. The Cross was amongst the most 'active' to be found. There remained a marvellous variety for a start – the colossal Deltics, the boxlike and rumbling Brush Type 2s, whistling class 40s, Peaks from the North East, handsome 47s and others, as well as clattering, fussy DMU sets, lurching and careering between the platforms and the tunnels. A ghastly 'sixties redevelopment proposal floundered but a new concourse in the early 1970s was hardly more uplifting; fighting your way through threading, ill-tempered queues, it was nevertheless still possible to soak up the choking spaces of the train shed, still blasted by locomotive noise, and the contrasting muffled nooks and crannies of the suburban side. The diesels still followed essentially steam practice, running out light to reverse

Most enthusiasts would agree that the Deltics were very impressive machines, as demonstrated by their sleek bulk when seen from the side. The 3,300hp Type 5s had two 18-cylinder Napier Deltic engines yet managed to weigh just 102 tons. Although the photograph is undated, it is probably early 1962 as D9016 is brand new and not yet named GORDON HIGHLANDER. Delivery to Haymarket was during December 1961 and after over seventeen years there, the loco moved to York in May 1979 by which time it had been 55 016 for five years. Preservation followed in December 1981 after twenty years working expresses into King's Cross. Photograph ColourRail

Birmingham RCW Sulzer Type 2 D5334 stands in the engine yard a on 12 August 1959. There is a puzzle concerning this loco as it was new in July 1959 and allocated to Haymarket. Maybe it was at the southern end of the GN for assessment or the like as it seems unlikely that it has worked a train all the way through from Edinburgh. A move north to Inverness took place during July 1960 and the diesel worked from there until May 1987. A transfer to Eastfield was effective from that month and withdrawal from there was in September 1989 after a creditable 30 years plus service. Nick Nicolson, transporttreasury

twice into the old servicing area. This was now equipped with diesel examination shed and refuelling tanks and every one of the frequent movements was accomplished to much shrieking and throbbing. The sudden plumes of exhaust, though a ghastly blue polluting oil mist, were a startling sight and now missed in their turn, despite 'green' considerations.

All this changed with electrification and the introduction of High Speed Trains. Many of the suburban trains were got rid of, diverted to the Northern City line to Moorgate, and overhead supports first appeared at Gasworks Tunnel around June 1976. The first stage of the £63M scheme, the inner suburban, was inaugurated in November 1976, despite shortages and a lack of experience with ultra-tight station stops and procedures, Of the eventual 64 class 313 units, 46 were to have been available for the inner suburban service and on the big day, but only 28 units, the operating minimum, were ready. Opprobrium followed, as surely as night comes after day, but it was nevertheless a remarkable staff effort – see in particular Ford's article in *Modern Railways* of

September 1977. The full electric timetable King's Cross-Royston came in February 1978 with the main line station energised in August the previous year. The new route to Moorgate had been commissioned with the earlier inner suburban schemes, so that the station could be remodelled, its principal effect the abandonment of the eastern Gasworks and Copenhagen bores and the Hotel and York Road curves. The track layout, known as 'the Throat' was remodelled and resignalled from January to April 1977, the final stage of a project involving over 80 route miles. The Up slow was taken across a renewed Holloway skew into the western Gasworks and Copenhagen tunnels and the eastern bores abandoned. All four remaining tracks in the Gasworks tunnels were put over to two way working. This was apparently influenced (in part at least) by an outstanding, though dropped, proposal to use the eastern Copenhagen bore for the erstwhile Third London Airport trains. These were to run from a new junction at Haringey, running up to the eastern tunnel and then swing over on a new bridge into a proper terminal in King's Cross goods yard. In the 1970s these

ideas were still borne in mind and years afterwards they had echoes in proposals for the Channel Tunnel. Five platforms were abandoned, the old ones on the 'local' side and various alterations made to those remaining.

HST sets (of class 254) began their upgraded work with the May 1978 timetable, allowing perhaps the greatest and most sustained impact on journey times ever. There were the usual delays, late deliveries and technical hitches, compounded by a Government decision to curtail the number of sets involved. The 1980s thereafter began the High Speed Train decade at The Cross, the snaking sets hurrying in and out with formidable efficiency. With them, the electrics and remodelling, the station lost its confused, rushing air; dereliction set in either side and the various abandoned tunnels gaped in rubbish-strewn reproof of modern development. With full main line electric working – in the early 1990s electrification was completed to Edinburgh and Glasgow – the station could then anticipate its newest incarnation, as 'International Passenger Terminal' developments.

This brings us into the present era in which King's Cross has entered into a

Brush D5614 alongside King's Cross signal cabin during July 1960. New in May 1960 and allocated to Finsbury Park its work ranged from piloting at the terminus to commuter and medium distance passenger traffic until a move to Immingham in May 1981 as 31 191. Renumbered 31 602 in June 1999, it went to work for British American Railway at Meldon in Devon. It is still operational, having been around for over 54 years! Photograph ColourRail

On 17 September 1966 Brush Type 2 D5625 stands in the North Engine Spur with York Road platform in the foreground and Gasworks Tunnel as a backdrop. This short stretch of track and two others like it had been the lairs of locos on shunt duties since the early days of the station and were very much the preserve of N2s from the 1920s to the 1950s. D5625 was new in June 1960 and worked from Ipswich, Stratford and March before a transfer to Finsbury Park in January 1965. It stayed until February 1980 and was withdrawn in February 1999. Photograph Peter Groom.

Brush Type 2 D5594 stands at Platform 5 one hot day in July 1960. Over at Platform 2 well-kept N2 69529 is engaged in empty stock duties, buffered up to a Gresley coach. The diesel was new in March 1960 and spent time at Hornsey then Finsbury Park before a transfer to Stratford in March 1961. There were subsequent periods at Finsbury Park prior to withdrawal in March 1999. Photograph ColourRail

English Electric Type 4 D207 backs down on to an express in Platform 8 during September 1958. The diesel was only a few weeks old, having been delivered new to Hornsey in July. There are looks of contemplation rather than euphoria from the driver of the N2 over at Platform 7 and the spotters on Platform 10. This was not inappropriate as despite looking impressive these were not the most reliable of machines. D207 was transferred to Finsbury Park in April 1960 and moved on to Stratford during July 1961. It was withdrawn in February 1983. Note the barrow load of corridor end doors on the left and another N2 further down Platform 10. RailOnline

Still carrying its Tees-Tyne Pullman headboard, D206 passes the loco yard at King's Cross on 3 September 1959. The loco is obscuring the diesel servicing facilities, but the mechanical plant, mineral wagons and tubs associated with steam are still prominent. RailOnline

Birmingham RC&W Type 2 D5308 draws empty coaching stock towards King's Cross Platform 6 on 3 September 1959. RailOnline

D5052 looks as if it had just been through a works visit when observed at King's Cross on 3 August 1962. The Derby Type 2 was new in November 1959 and worked from March shed until January 1961 when it moved to Finsbury Park. An A4 stands in Platform 4 on the left. RailOnline

transformed period. It is now part of a greater area providing the travelling public with access not only to the much of the British Isles, but also via High Speed One to large parts of Europe through the Channel Tunnel. Alongside the complete electrification of the East Coast main line came the opening of the link under the Channel in May 1994. The original terminus at Waterloo was soon seen as inadequate and the route of HS1 was quickly surveyed, approved and built from the existing tunnel entrance via Ashford, Stratford and into a renovated St Pancras brought into use in 2007. Its connection with King's Cross was both as its neighbour, in walking distance for passengers making the transfer, but also in that it carried HS1 over the main line from King's Cross. This was done in the area between Gasworks and Copenhagen tunnels, and using the site of the former 'Top Shed' as the final approach under the towering arch of the St Pancras train shed.

When we look at the transformation of King's Cross over the years to meet the needs of contemporary passengers we can recognise, looking back, how engineering and technical skills have been driven by the social and cultural needs of the time. When we entered the period of radical change from 1955, the industry found itself moving from an age of apparent immutability as a vital service with the public called *passengers*, to consumers *having* expectations of a reliable and continually improving experience at a competitive price! Trains are modern and sealed, gliding to and fro and the circulation area is as anonymous as a motorway service station (if a bit more upmarket) but walk outwards to the well of light at the end of Cubitt's screen; in the yellow bricks, the shadows and archways, the curves and still-oddly deserted corners, the Great station, of Atlantics, Pacifics and Deltics, waits still …

Below. There were still L1s working at King's Cross as the diesels moved in, like 67749 on 28 May 1960, about to take empty stock out of the terminus. This had been one of the L1s moved to Hornsey at the end of 1951 for similar work, the idea being to avoid double heading on heavier trains being returned to the carriage sidings. Unfortunately the 2-6-4Ts were not an immediate success and two of them had to work together on occasions. In March 1952 67749 went back to Neasden but returned to the GN in July 1956 and was allocated to King's Cross and Hitchin until banished to Colwick in September 1961. This loco was one of the 21 victims of a cull in December 1962 which finished off the class. Nick Nicolson, transporttreasury

Right. Some of the newer J50 tanks also remained in service alongside diesel locos, as in the case of 68981, at Platform 1 on 3 May 1960. This engine had been at Leicester Central then Colwick until September 1952 when it was moved to Hornsey so that loads could be increased on trip workings and transfer freights to the Southern Region via Snow Hill. Built at Gorton Works in December 1938 as LNER 605, 68981 was withdrawn during April 1961 while still at Hornsey. Nick Nicolson, transporttreasury

Bottom right. It is early 1960 and A5 69814 is quite an unusual sight on empty stock at Platform 12 in the Suburban Station. This particular 4-6-2T was only at King's Cross shed from December 1959 to June 1960, although it had been based there for a short time in the distant past. It was one of four A5s sent to Top Shed in 1928 for outer suburban services to Hitchin and Baldock with the aim of preventing tender-first running with the 4-4-0s then employed, though it returned home to Neasden in 1929. In the background a Cravens 2-car DMU with car E51270 leading is at Platform 16 forming a service from Moorgate to Welwyn Garden City.

60013 DOMINION OF NEW ZEALAND leaving Platform 8 with the Flying Scotsman on 5 March 1960. Built as 4492 in June 1957 for the Coronation train it almost immediately set up a remarkable record, working the Flying Scotsman and ordinary Sunday expresses to Waverley to the extent that 62 turns were made between King's Cross and Edinburgh, 52 of them consecutively. Only a week after this marathon, 4492 did the first three trips of the West Riding Limited. Photograph ColourRail

BR announced that steam traction would not be used on the non-stop Elizabethan after the summer 1960 season, which was from 13 June to 10 September, but in the event the diesels were not ready and steam had another fling the following year. Haymarket A4 60027 MERLIN was a regular performer during 1960, doing 74 runs altogether, 46 of them between 21 August and 10 September. In this view the engine backs out of The Cross towards Top Shed on 20 August 1960, brilliantly maintained in Edinburgh as usual. The badges of HMS Merlin, an Admiralty Shore Establishment, were applied to the cab sides in May 1946 and later moved to the streamlined boiler casing. MERLIN was withdrawn from St Margarets in September 1965. Photograph Brian Stephenson.

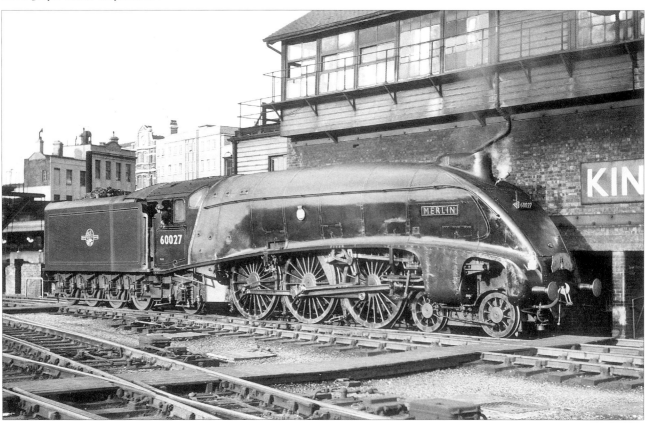

In morning sunshine on 5 March 1960, Copley Hill A1 60133 POMMERN eases past King's Cross signal box with a train most probably originating at Leeds Central. Photograph ColourRail

Doncaster A1 60125 SCOTTISH UNION arrives with an express on 5 March 1960, the weather having clouded over. This Pacific had been allocated to Doncaster when new in April 1949 but left for Copley Hill just over a year later. After periods at Grantham, Copley Hill again and Grantham again it became a King's Cross loco in June 1957, but not for long. During January 1958 it returned to Doncaster and stayed there until withdrawn in July 1964. SCOTTISH UNION may seem to have some sort of political connection, but it was actually the horse that won the St Leger in 1938. Photograph ColourRail

60130 KESTREL, another Copley Hill A1, passes the engine yard on 27 February 1960. This was one of the Darlington-built A1s and spent most of its time at Ardsley and Copley Hill until withdrawn in October 1965. Photograph D M Alexander, transporttreasury

A3 60039 SANDWICH completes its journey in charge of a Leeds Central to King's Cross express on 19 March 1960. This engine had acquired its double chimney nine months earlier in July 1959 and would receive trough smoke deflectors just over a year later during June 1961. Its allocation to Top Shed from April 1957 to withdrawal in March 1963 was its third stay there, the others being in 1939-41 and 1950-51. Photograph transporttreasury

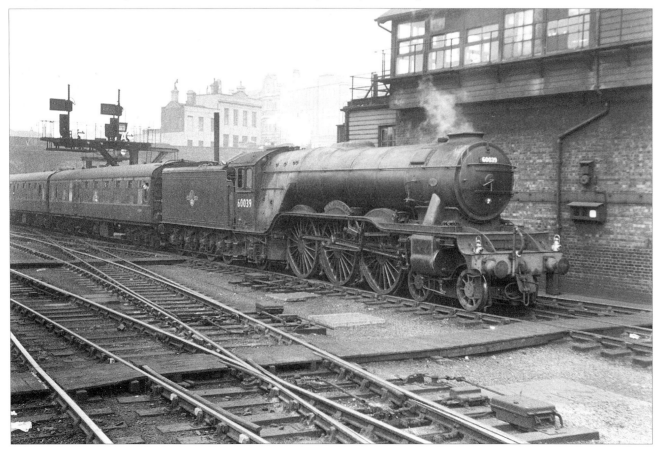

Of all the A3 racehorse names, surely this must have been the most appropriate! 60076 GALOPIN backs out of Platform 4 on a sunny day in 1961. It was actually named after the winner of the 1875 Derby and the owner with the sense of humour as well as an interesting name was Prince Batthyany. The loco spent its entire 38 year existence at three sheds in the North East, moving no less than ten times between Gateshead and Darlington before finishing up at Heaton for a year prior to withdrawal in October 1962. Nick Nicolson, transporttreasury

60113 GREAT NORTHERN in the engine yard on 3 May 1961 with D5609 standing near the specially constructed examination shed. The Brush Type 2 was new to Finsbury Park in April 1960 and remained there until May 1980, apart from a couple of years at Gateshead. Like D5614, this loco was withdrawn by EWS in April 1998 but is still operated by British American Railway and based at Meldon in Devon. Nick Nicolson, transporttreasury

Brush Type 2 D5635 leaves Copenhagen Tunnel in morning sunshine on 17 May 1961 with a semi-fast to Grantham. The allotments behind the loco are clearly flourishing and the semaphore signals remain in full bloom. The grand central tower of Caledonian Road Cattle Market is on the extreme right while one of the four ornate pubs found at each corner of the market site is prominent above the second and third coaches. Photograph Brian Morrison.

The English Electric Type 4 1Co-Co1 diesels certainly had bulk, weighing in at 133 tons, but they did not prove to be an outstanding success on the Great Northern line. D248 stands at the head of an express in Platform 4 on 4 August 1961. This particular machine was new to Gateshead in November 1957, moved to Hornsey during December 1959 and was at Finsbury Park from April 1960 to July 1961 when it returned to Gateshead for just under six years. It was withdrawn from Haymarket in October 1977. Nick Nicolson, transporttreasury

The Sheffield Pullman hauled by an English Electric Type 4 makes its way past Belle Isle between Gasworks and Copenhagen Tunnels on 31 August 1961 as an English Electric Type 1 crosses the North London viaduct with a modest goods train. Tracks leading to Top Shed and King's Cross Goods are on the left beyond the retaining wall while the half viaduct half retaining wall further up the slope marks the beginning of a branch to Caledonian Road Goods. This climbs behind Goods and Mineral Signal Box, reverses in the distance then passes above the southern portal of Copenhagen Tunnel to reach the depot. The Ebonite tower announces its ownership at the top whilst the Caledonian Road Market tower above the D8000 diesel. Photograph Peter Groom.

Sleeper trains were once a regular feature of King's Cross and there were four weekday departures during summer 1961, about the time this photograph was taken. The Aberdonian left at 7.30pm and called at Grantham, York, Darlington and Newcastle before reaching Edinburgh at 3.0am. The train then went on to Dundee, Arbroath, Montrose and Stonehaven, reaching Aberdeen at 6.27am. Next came the 'Car Sleeper' which departed from King's Cross at 8.5pm and arrived in Perth at 5.40am, although passengers were allowed to stay in their berths until 6.30am. The cost for a car and driver was £21-0s-0d. The Night Scotsman left King's Cross at 11.35pm and arrived in Waverley at 7.20am with no intermediate calls. Finally, the Tynesider departed from London at 1.0am and called at Darlington and Durham before arriving in Newcastle at 6.31am.

On 16 June 1961 60103 FLYING SCOTSMAN still looks superb at the head of the White Rose in Platform 6. The Pacific was just over four years into its fourth and final period at Top Shed and still a year and a half away from withdrawal and preservation. Another A3 is at Platform 5, probably with an express. Nick Nicolson, transporttreasury

There were still shunt duties for L1s during the early 1960s despite the diesels and 67745 in quite presentable condition is making a good effort as it passes King's Cross box on 19 February 1961. Photograph L Rowe, ColourRail

A last look at one of the N2s which were so much a part of the King's Cross scene for so long. 69568 has featured earlier and was the very last one to leave King's Cross shed for storage at New England. On 10 June 1961 the engine is a bit grime-laden, although it was certainly cleaned up later. Nick Nicolson, transporttreasury

It was rather murky over London on 19 May 1961 and King's Cross A4 60003 ANDREW K MCCOSH was not quite as sparkling as it might have been, but whatever the situation the streamlined Pacifics always looked impressive. With York Road station and the buildings of York Road in the background, the engine backs out of Platform 2 and still has a good supply of coal in the tender. Photograph J Robertson, transporttreasury

60010 DOMINION OF CANADA reverses out of Platform 4 past a Brush Type 2 in Platform 5 on 2 March 1961. The Top Shed cleaning gang have made a very good job of this loco and sunshine helps to show it off. Not only was a revolution in motive power taking place but the landscape around King's Cross was changing as well. There were still plenty of bomb sites around London and redevelopment was taking place at an increasing pace by the 1960s, but not all of it involved open spaces resulting from the war. The block on York Road in the middle distance replaced existing buildings and unfortunately had a blandness typical of the time. Nick Nicolson, transporttreasury

The A4 which started it all, 60014 SILVER LINK, backs down to its train in Platform 8 on 1 April 1961. With the door open, some detail of the inside of the corridor tender can be seen, notably the 2ft step up to the corridor itself. A small circular window helped shed a modicum of light on this corner of the narrow passage. This historic loco was twenty months away from its withdrawal along with five others from King's Cross on 29 December 1962. To the intense regret of numerous enthusiasts, there was no attempt to preserve the celebrity and it was cut up at Doncaster Works where it was built. Photograph Alec Swain, transporttreasury

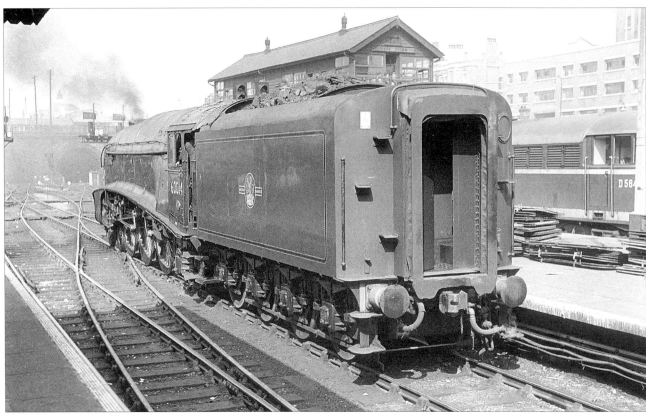

Another fine example of Top Shed cleaning was 60028 WALTER K WHIGHAM, backing down to its train at Platform 8 on 8 May 1961. The A4s had hauled Royal trains on many occasions over the lifetime of the class but 60028 was about to participate in the last truly Royal occasion for a streamlined Pacific. For the wedding of the Duke of York on 8 June 1961, three specials were run from King's Cross to York and WALTER K WHIGHAM was in charge of the Royal train itself. The other two carrying guests were headed by 60003 ANDREW K MCCOSH and 60015 QUICKSILVER. All were spotlessly clean, as was the standby engine 60014 SILVER LINK. Photograph Alec Swain, transporttreasury

WALTER K WHIGHAM on 23 June 1961, just less than a fortnight after hauling the Duke of York's wedding train from King's Cross to York and back. The engine still looks absolutely immaculate in the afternoon sunshine, although the white painted cab roof which it had for the occasion is no longer an embellishment. The A4 has just brought the Elizabethan from Edinburgh and is making its way to Top Shed. Nick Nicolson, transporttreasury

On a cold misty day in January 1962 the frontage of King's Cross did not look that different from a decade or so earlier. Fay Harris is still selling lingerie, Jamet the Chemist is still trading and the Covent Garden flower shop is much the same. On the extreme left the snack bar seems to be emphasising that Melbray ice cream is on sale there rather than the same company's pies. Nevertheless that will all change before long. More modern versions of the black cab are apparent and the number of vehicles has increased. In fact traffic lights have been erected near the café and in front of the Underground station. Photograph **T J Edgington.**

Inside, the western train shed not much has altered either, certainly as far as the structure is concerned. There are some new suspended lamps and the advertisements above the concourse are larger, one being for Head Wrightson, 'Engineering for World Industry' and another for Booth's Gin. There have though been developments as far as the trains are concerned. All the coaches are now painted maroon and they are BR Standard Mk.1s, with the exception of the Gresley catering vehicle nearest the camera. Most significant of all is the motive power, the only steam-hauled service being that which has arrived behind an A4 at Platform 7. A Brush Type 2 heads the train which is standing at Platform 6 and an English Electric Type 4 is near the buffer stops at platform 10. The stock at Platform 8 has been propelled in.

Two large locomotives of very different types were photographed together at Top Shed on 19 August 1962. Taking up most of the view is Deltic D9001 ST PADDY which was a year and a half old at the time. It was allocated to Finsbury Park from the outset and remained at that depot until withdrawn in January 1980. On the right there is a glimpse of 9F 2-10-0 92180; a few freight engines had always been diagrammed to come on to the shed during the day and the New England 9Fs were the last of a long line. Photograph Peter Groom.

Deltic D9012 CREPELLO in the engine yard in the 1960s. This loco was new from English Electric Vulcan Foundry in September 1961 and spent its whole existence working from Finsbury Park, withdrawal coming in May 1981. The first Brush Type 4 D1500 is on the left, the curious roofline of the District Road Motor Repair Depot forms the familiar backdrop and diesel fuel tanks are on the right. Photograph ColourRail

The background is familiar enough, comprising the tall brick building overlooking the goods bays and Widened Lines platform, together with the inevitable gasometers, but the locos are now all diesels. On the extreme left a Brush Type 2 lurks in one of the docks while the side of an English Electric Type 4 can be seen on the right. The subject of this photograph is Derby Sulzer Type 2 D5063 which was built by Crewe Works in January 1960 and was based at March then Willesden before coming to Finsbury Park in February 1961. The loco stayed until October 1966 when it departed for Haymarket. Photograph ColourRail

The last full year of scheduled steam traction at King's Cross was 1962 and some engines were still looking very smart while others became very grubby; 60061 PRETTY POLLY occupies a place somewhere in between. It had gone to the shops to have its smoke deflectors fitted in February 1962, the double chimney having been acquired in October 1958.

In steam's protracted final fling the presence of a Pacific, particularly a King's Cross one in smart condition, was almost hypnotic. On 31 March 1962 A3 60061 PRETTY POLLY is ready to leave Platform 10 with an express, possibly a relief to the Heart of Midlothian, as Brush Type 2 diesels occupy the adjacent tracks. The loco had been fitted with its trough smoke deflectors the previous month. PRETTY POLLY had only spent three short sessions at Top Shed during the 1950s, but it was back again in November 1959 and stayed almost until withdrawn in September 1963. Photograph Les Perrin.

Grantham A3 60056 CENTENARY gets underway from Platform 6 with the Down Heart of Midlothian on 31 March 1962 as the fireman trims coal in the tender of 60512 STEADY AIM over at Platform 4. As 2555 was the first Pacific built at Doncaster Works in the year when celebrations took place for the opening of the Stockton & Darlington Railway a hundred years earlier, it was given the appropriate name CENTENARY. Along with 2553 PRINCE OF WALES, 2555 was allocated to Copley Hill in October 1936 for the Queen of Scots Pullman. This followed strengthening of Calder Viaduct at Wakefield, thus enabling Pacifics access to Leeds over the Great Northern route, although it also spelled the end of the long and distinguished career of Ivatt Atlantics on this train. Photograph Les Perrin.

60141 ABBOTSFORD began life as a York engine in December 1948 and was withdrawn from there during October 1964. In between it was at King's Cross from October 1949 to May 1950 and Copley Hill from then until September 1963. On this occasion it is easing a Leeds express into the terminus watched by a couple of railwaymen and two youngsters who had managed to get permission to visit the signal box. Photograph ColourRail

At the end of its long career, which started back in April 1923 at King's Cross, Grantham's 60106 FLYING FOX leaves with an express one day in 1962. Towards the end of 1964 there were only three A3s left on the Great Northern section, 60062, 60106 and 60112, and they frequently took over the 9.0am parcels train from March to Doncaster at Peterborough. 60106 was officially withdrawn on Boxing Day 1964, but was noted in charge of the 4.50pm Leeds-Doncaster stopping passenger train on 5 January 1965! To quote the RCTS Guide, this was 'the last recorded working of this grand old engine'. Photograph ColourRail

60022 MALLARD backing out of King's Cross towards Top Shed some time during 1962. Different generations pay homage as another A4 passes a Brush Type 2 in the North Engine Spur next to Gasworks Tunnel. Photograph ColourRail

60113 GREAT NORTHERN in charge of the 1.15pm to Leeds Central on 20 August 1962. When it first appeared after the 1945 rebuilding, the loco had quite a different appearance. It did not have any smoke deflectors, the double chimney was without a lip and the straight nameplate extended the full length of the smokebox. Photograph Peter Groom.

A little later GREAT NORTHERN gets underway with the train, 1.15pm King's Cross-Leeds. It has just left Gasworks Tunnel on the climb up Holloway Bank, passing a Cravens DMU. In the background York Road viaduct crosses the fan of tracks leading to King's Cross goods depot. Photograph Peter Groom.

York's 60516 HYCILLA waits at the head of an express at Platform 7. It is a grey wet day in 1962 and to the casual observer everything is a bit grim. This engine was new from Doncaster Works in November 1946 and was allocated to Heaton until July 1952. It then had a long stay at Gateshead and after a very brief return to Heaton in May 1960 went to York the following month. That shed had regular turns to London and HYCILLA worked into the capital until withdrawn during November 1962. Photograph N Lester, transporttreasury

It is 9 April 1963, just a couple of months from the end of steam at Top Shed and, in theory, on the Great Northern main line south of Peterborough. A4 60013 DOMINION OF NEW ZEALAND backs out of Platform 1 having brought in a train, maybe parcels on this occasion. In the distance on the left there are Brush Type 2 diesels in both the North and Centre Engine Spurs, while immediately to the right of the Pacific the entrance to the Moorgate line tunnel is visible. Nick Nicolson, transporttreasury

On 17 May 1963 A4 60026 MILES BEEVOR backs down towards Platform 8 in very bright evening sunshine. Even at this late stage, with closure of Top Shed just days away, an effort was still being made to keep some of the streamlined Pacifics reasonably clean. Photograph Alec Swain, transporttreasury

MILES BEEVOR continues to back down to the 6.12pm for Leeds on 17 May 1963; a Brush Type 2 is at Platform 6. This was one of the A4s which went to New England but later enjoyed further service in Scotland. Firstly it went into store at Galashiels then Bathgate with 60034 but was soon transferred to St Margarets. Then Aberdeen beckoned in April 1964 and 60026 stayed there for the Glasgow expresses until December 1965. Photograph Alec Swain, transporttreasury

60010 DOMINION OF CANADA was not exactly in pristine condition towards the end, yet was obviously mechanically sound as it was another one chosen to go to Scotland. Withdrawal from Aberdeen was in May 1965, although the engine had actually been sent to Darlington for repair. Its boiler was found to be in very bad condition so it was condemned, but instead of being scrapped it languished in Bank Top shed for a while. Eventually it was put into good external condition at Crewe and presented to the Canadian Railroad Historical Association, complete with its bell, during 1967. The last recorded normal working of an A4 out of King's Cross was on 29 October 1963 when 60017, then at New England, headed the 6.40 pm express to Leeds. Steam had actually been banned south of Peterborough four months previously. Photograph transporttreasury

Although the ban on steam over the Great Northern main line south of Peterborough was concurrent with the closure of Top Shed in June 1963, Control further north was forced in numerous instances to send steam locomotives through. One has to be a bit careful about telescoping 50-year memories but it was exciting how a vigil, hour after hour at New Southgate, could produce nothing but diesels, then a couple of Pacifics in rapid succession. York A1 60140 BALMORAL has arrived at Platform 7 with an express on 7 December 1963. It also looks in clean condition. Withdrawal was in January 1965. Photograph L Rowe, ColourRail

Having been dispatched north to Grantham when Top Shed closed, A3 60063 ISINGLASS is back at King's Cross on 13 August 1963. The ER obviously knew that 'the ban' might prove a little porous; these were early days in the planned elimination of steam and coaling and turning arrangements were left in place at the London end. A couple of year later attitudes had changed; nothing could be allowed to slow the pace of change and coalers, turntables and water columns would be simply ripped up. The familiar goods depot buildings form the skyline as ever. The last instance of an A3 working south of Peterborough on the GN main line is believed to have been 12 November 1964 when 60112 ST SIMON worked empty coaching stock bound for Hornsey from New England. Photograph ColourRail

The steam ban flouted on 31 July 1963, by Doncaster's A1 60119 PATRICK STIRLING with the Up Norseman. The engine is backing out of Platform 6 after the stock had been removed and there looks like enough coal in the tender to get it back home. New from Doncaster Works in November 1948, the loco was at Copley Hill until December 1955, Grantham until September 1957, King's Cross until August 1958 then Doncaster until withdrawal in May 1964.

It is 24 December 1963 and at long last a start has been made on demolishing the 'native village'. The Art Deco shops have already gone so the lingerie business which greeted those arriving at King's Cross for so long has finally faded into history. A sad loss. There is a demolition company sign on the former Great Northern Piccadilly & Brompton Underground building so that will soon be going as well. Road traffic is still relatively light and there is plenty of space for the Rover and Ford Zephyr to park in the Station Approach. Try doing that now. Photograph T J Edgington.

The western train shed, probably during the mid to late 1960s. when a start had been made on replacing the green and maroon loco and rolling stock livery of British Railways with the blue and grey corporate image of British Rail. Scaffolding has been erected on Platforms 5 and 6 where it looks as if a start has been made removing soot from the roof boarding ready for some fresh paint. One of the best developments has been the removal of that dreadful cladding from the lower part of the end screens, thus allowing more light in. Whatever the date, Platforms 6, 7, 8 and 10 are remarkably quiet. Photograph ColourRail

On 3 May 1965 the booking office still featured the rather bleak structure put up after the bomb wrecked the old place, although it looks quite smart after a recent lick of paint. Ticket windows still differentiate between stations before or beyond Peterborough, but the one noted earlier catering for those who wish to convey motors and horses now dispenses tickets for trains from other London termini. These were very negative times and those boards at the far end have chalked notices concerning the withdrawal of Hatfield-Luton-Dunstable passenger services and the replacement of Pullman cars on the Talisman with standard First Class coaches. Although the booking hall is much improved today, the balcony is still there.

York Road platform on 5 March 1965. The rather neglected canopy has finally gone beyond economic repair and has simply been cut back, the station being treated to a coat of paint at the same time. There is still a reasonable amount of shelter, not that many people actually boarded trains here. The ramp down to the entrance is behind the wall on the right and is still there today. A Brush Type 2 waits in the North Engine Spur in the distance.

Close to York Road platform, two contrasting diesels stand in the Centre Engine Spur on 17 September 1966; 400hp 0-6-0 shunter D3308, new to King's Cross shed in May 1956 and after that Finsbury Park when it opened, and a BTH D8200 Type 1, of which Finsbury Park had half a dozen or so. This is in fact is a most unusual photograph; diesel shunters were effectively barred from the confines of the terminus, for they were too short for the track circuits. The suspicion is, it's somehow got to the station only to be retrieved by the Type 1. Photograph Peter Groom.

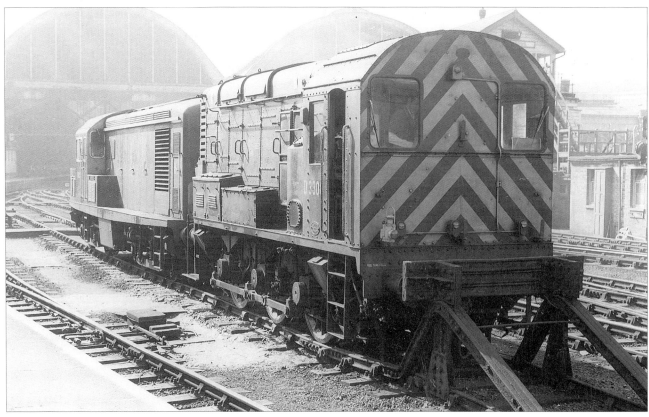

The 'station loco' on 7 April 1978; by now the corporate blue is all-encompassing. Fuel tankers have long taken over from loco coal wagons as well. Two Brush Type 4s and three Deltics await their next duties in the foreground, although only 55 007 PINZA can be identified. At the top right, beyond the overhead electrification equipment, a trio of Class 47s and the remains of York Road station can be seen. In the top right a loco and an electric multiple unit are barely visible through the copious emissions from two of the Deltics. Photograph Peter Groom.

Another change of policy led to the creation of sectors, including Intercity which was identified by a pleasant cream, grey and red livery. Since then, two types of train have dominated long distance services out of King's Cross and they are illustrated here on 24 November 1989. Power Car 43077 is at the front of the 19.00 HST to Newcastle at Platform 2 while 91 009 heads the 19.30 to Leeds at Platform 4. The former entered service in January 1978 when corporate blue still reigned and was based at Neville Hill. At the time of writing it still works on the East Coast main line. The electric locomotive was new in September 1988 and has been based at Bounds Green ever since. Photograph Brian Morrison.

On the rainy evening of 17 February 1989, the unique Brush electric loco 89 001 AVOCET with charter stock rather than the usual Mk.3s and DVT awaits departure time at Platform 1 with the 17.36 to Peterborough. High Speed Trains soon established themselves as very worthy successors to the Deltics and in this view they are providing services to Hull, Glasgow and Bradford from Platforms 2, 3 and 4 respectively. The Glasgow train is just departing and leading Power Car 43074 was maintained at Bounds Green at the time. On the right, 43121 had Neville Hill as its base, although it had been a Western Region unit at Old Oak Common and Laira prior to 1981. Photograph Brian Morrison.

Privatisation was the next fundamental development and in August 2000 a GNER HST in the distinctive dark blue and red livery stands at Platform 6 as a similarly adorned Class 91 arrives in Platform 5. In addition to electrification, a substantial clean up took place and the platforms were renumbered in a logical way for the first time. Furthermore, both roofs were re-glazed in the original way resulting in much more daylight reaching the platforms. One feature has not reverted to its previous state however, but only a few of those passing through the station will know where to look. The three roof supports of a different pattern are still there on the left, a reminder of much darker days for the terminus. Photograph Brian Bailey.

A lunchtime line-up of departures between 12.45 and 13.30 occupy Platforms 3 to 6 one day in August 2000, three powered by Class 91 electric locos, the other an HST. The outside of the train sheds have been tidied up, the brickwork has been cleaned and there is a friendly sign saying 'Welcome to King's Cross'. Photograph Brian Bailey.

For a while there was even a Eurostar service from King's Cross to York branded the 'White Rose' and deploying borrowed sets painted in GNER blue, this view showing one of them on arrival in London during August 2000. Unfortunately they made rather too many demands on the overhead. Eventually it was the Gothic edifice next door which became the true Eurostar terminus and was able to add 'International' to its name. Nevertheless, there is plenty of international business at The Cross in the form of Platform 9¾, the Harry Potter shop where fans from all over the world often have to queue to get in. Yet another page in the story of this remarkable station has unfolded. It is interesting to reflect that at time of writing (April 2016) the Harry Potter author's oak chair has sold for more than the cost of Cubitt's original station – relatively, it was 'very cheap' after all! Photograph Brian Bailey.

Platforms 14 to 16 on a sunny afternoon in the mid-1970s, with the deserted air which always descended on this corner outside the rush hours. The platform beyond plays host to a variety of parcels vans while the train shed and spiky towers of St Pancras form the skyline as always. RailOnline

Around 9.30 on the evening of 25 September 1971 Deltic 9003 MELD waits at Platform 10 with an overnight train for Scotland. RailOnline

It is 10 July 1971 and a couple of Deltics have retired to King's Cross loco yard between duties. Nearest the camera is 9015 TULYAR, another of those with racehorse names which were based at Finsbury Park. The new power box is taking shape in the background and the little tower belongs to York Road School. RailOnline

Deltic 9006 THE FIFE AND FORFAR YEOMANRY has come from Edinburgh with an express and stands in King's Cross loco yard on 1 December 1971. Also present are three Brush Type 4s, that buffered up to the Deltic being 1511. RailOnline

Probably the worst phase experienced by regular travellers from the suburbs to King's Cross was when Cravens diesel multiple units were employed in considerable numbers from the late 1950s to the mid-1970s. N2s and Gresley quad-arts looked the part, tough and up to the job. The Cravens units were unsuitable, but it was not their fault as they were designed for light rural duties, not lifting a full complement of rush hour travellers up Hotel Curve and getting going again from Platform 16. A solitary 2-car set was deemed adequate for this afternoon service from Platform 12 in the Suburban Station around 1975. RailOnline

A Cravens 2-car set arrives at Platform 13 in the Suburban Station one afternoon in 1975 as a Brush Type 4 sits in the loco yard, which was still a useful asset for diesel traction over a decade after the end of steam at King's Cross. There are still a few enthusiasts at the end of Platform 10, but it is clear that the fascination had waned by this time. RailOnline

A total of 402 railcar vehicles were built by Cravens of Sheffield for BR, 275 of them power cars. Some of their serious drawbacks for intensive suburban work are apparent in this view of a late afternoon peak service at Platform 11 in King's Cross, again around 1975. Up to four 2-car sets could be coupled together meaning that seven driving cabs were wasted space and four lots of unnecessary parcels accommodation were crammed with standing passengers. Just two doors per side in each coach hindered unloading and the bus-type seats were hardly popular either. RailOnline

There had been some relief for commuters when twenty sets of true high-density 3-car Derby suburban dmus with hydraulic transmission were cascaded on to King's Cross duties as a result of the Great Eastern Lea Valley electrification. One such train is leaving the Suburban Station on an early afternoon working for Welwyn Garden City around 1970. By this time Moorgate services were almost always operated by Brush Type 2s and five BR Standard non-corridor coaches, the Cravens sets having proved very unreliable on the Widened Lines gradients long before. The loco fuel tanks are evident again on the left while a Brush Type 2 waits in the North Engine Spur. RailOnline

This remote corner of King's Cross between Platform 17 and the loading docks was livened up when locos reversed here on their way between the main platform roads and the loco yard. On day in 1976 Gateshead Deltic 55014 THE DUKE OF WELLINGTON'S REGIMENT is undertaking this manoeuvre as a Class 31 Brush Type 2 stands at Platform 17. By this time passenger services had long ceased to depart from here. The distinctive outline of St Pancras and the German Gymnasium dominate the left background. RailOnline

Seen from the erstwhile Platform 17, 9015 TULYAR transfers between the main station and the loco yard on 3 March 1971. RailOnline

Some time in the mid-1970s, BR/Sulzer Type 4 46046 has arrived on a train from the North East. New out of Derby Works as D183 in October 1962, the loco was delivered to Gateshead and remained there for many years. It stayed in service until May 1994. RailOnline

On 3 June 1977 Brush Type 2 31405 brings the empty stock for a main line departure. The new signalling centre can be seen on the right. RailOnline

With the track layout changes associated with electrification in the mid-1970s a couple of roads were created at the outer end of Platform 1 to stable locomotives. In September 1977 55016 GORDON HIGHLANDER stands in one of them with the cleaned and tidied-up train sheds in the background. RailOnline

Despite faster expresses and electrification of local services, King's Cross was the same old gloomy place under the train sheds in the mid-1970s. The roofs still had far more boarding than glazing, which was the configuration dating from just before World War Two, although this arrangement would soon change. This view probably dates from 1977 and two Deltics have arrived on passenger trains at the east side of the station. On the left is Haymarket based 55016 GORDON HIGHLANDER while on the right is 55012 CREPELLO of Finsbury Park. RailOnline

The stock brought in by 55012 is being removed, quite possibly by a Class 31. This particular Deltic was new to Finsbury Park in September 1961 and remained in service there until withdrawn during May 1981. Air-conditioned coaches made up the train which arrived behind 55016, as can be seen in the distance. RailOnline

In October 1978 Deltic 55003 MELD stands near the buffer stops at Platform 1 with inner suburban electric unit 313002 behind it. The barrow loads of mail sacks were just as much of a feature as in steam days. Occupying the adjacent road is an Intercity 125, the latest manifestation of that quest for speed which had characterised the Great Northern main line for well over a century. Power car 254 025 had just been completed at Crewe Works and was allocated to Neville Hill. Electrification only extended out to Royston and High Speed Trains, HSTs in common parlance of course, dominated the East Coast route after the demise of the Deltics. By the time of the photograph the terminus had been cleaned and the proportion of roof glazing increased substantially. RailOnline

Above. Here is another contrast between successive generations of express motive power on the east side of King's Cross, this time early in 1979. The uncharacteristically scruffy Deltic is 55013 THE BLACK WATCH which was allocated to Haymarket when new in September 1961. It was withdrawn in December 1981. HST Power Car 254 029 was new to Neville Hill from Crewe Works in February 1979 and as with all the others illustrated here remains operational. It later became 43112 then 43312. RailOnline

Left. On an unknown date, probably in 1979, Deltic 55017 THE DURHAM LIGHT INFANTRY stands in the Suburban Station with a parcels train, the leading vehicle being a Siphon G. With the influx of HSTs the Deltics tended to be found on secondary duties, although they sounded just as impressive and ready for any job. Towards the end they had a following and even adoration similar to that seen in the last days of the Gresley Pacifics. As D9017, this particular one was new from English Electric in November 1961 and allocated to Gateshead. It was taken out of service during November 1981. RailOnline

By the early 1970s BR decided that something had to be done about the state of Great Northern suburban services. They were among the most uneconomic operations on the entire network and bizarrely inner suburban trains went to four destinations in the capital, King's Cross Suburban Station, Moorgate, Broad Street and even Finsbury Park. Electrification was agreed in August 1971, but only as far as Royston. Part of the project was to provide access to Moorgate via the Great Northern & City tube and that meant the end of services over the Widened Lines in November 1976. Inner and outer suburban electric trains are in the Suburban Station on 13 January 1979 RailOnline

Outer suburban electric units on the Great Northern were designated Class 312 which was a variant of Class 310 employed on services out of Euston. These 26 four-car sets were built by British Rail Engineering Ltd at York from 1977 and were the last electric trains with slam doors but the first capable of 90mph. They also had a small amount of 1st Class accommodation and toilets. Set 312710 leaves King's Cross for Royston some time in 1977 as a Class 31 occupies the North Engine Spur in time honoured fashion. By now the outer reaches of the loco yard on the left were rather unkempt. RailOnline

Inner Suburban set 313013 with Moorgate erroneously displayed at the rear departs from King's Cross on 28 June 1984. A total of 64 of these three-car sets were built by BREL at York and were equipped for both 25kv overhead and 750v third-rail current collection, the latter for the Great Northern & City tube from Drayton Park through Highbury & Islington, Essex Road and Old Street to Moorgate. RailOnline

Away from its regular haunts, 313045 has arrived at Platform 1 on a special working some time during 1979. Alongside is one of the early Intercity 125s headed by Power Car 254 006 which was completed at Crewe Works in October 1977. One advantage of electric traction was the acceleration and a Class 313 would be able to reach 60mph from standstill in about 1½ minutes whereas a Cravens dmu would need up to six minutes with passengers only too aware that the effort was being made. RailOnline

Considering their patchy performance when first introduced on the East Coast main line, some of the English Electric Type 4s managed to stay the course well. On 20 June 1984, 40058 arrives at King's Cross with what is probably a seasonal extra or excursion. RailOnline

On 20 June 1984 40058 stands at Platform 1 with what is probably the return working of the additional train. The tidied up end screen looks very smart with the glazing arranged to show off decorative work in the girders. Increasing the area of roof glass has brightened the interior considerably. Parcel are being moved about in the usual way on the left and an HST waits for departure time in the western train shed to the right.

For decades hardly any improvements were made to King's Cross but in recent years upgrading seems to have been an almost continuous process. By 12 November 2008 it was the turn of the old office block alongside Platform 1 to receive some attention. Platform 0 is now below this. In this view electric trains stand at Platforms 1 and 2 while HSTs occupy Platforms 4 and 6. The logical renumbering of the platforms was to the benefit of all. This is just after the franchise changed from Sea Containers to National Express and the dark blue livery was giving way to silver and white. The missing panes of glass in the end screens spoil the overall impression to a certain extent. RailOnline

Two Class 91 electric locomotives in Platforms 1 and 2, 91103 on the left and 91114 on the right. The former was new as 91003 in April 1988 and renumbered in September 2001 while the latter entered service as 91014 during May 1990, acquiring its new identity in May 2002. RailOnline

The history of the East Coast franchise has been varied, to say the least. Sea Containers under the guise of GNER had it from 1996 until it was taken away in 2007. Then it was the turn of National Express which was encountering serious financial problems by 2009 so the operation was renationalised. Despite contributing £1 billion to the Treasury over the next six years, East Coast was put out to tender again in 2015 and a Stagecoach-Virgin bid was successful. On 4 September 2016 82231 will leave shortly with the 12.20pm service to Newcastle.

On 13 November 2008 one of the Class 67 Bo-Bo diesels originally intended for express parcels traffic stands in one of the spurs at the end of Platform 1. 67024 was completed by General Motors/Alstom in Spain during May 2000 and is probably acting as a 'Thunderbird' in case of a serious train breakdown at King's Cross. One of the newer electric multiple units can be seen in the distance. Note that the loco yard has come to the end of its long and useful life and new buildings have appeared on part of the site. In fact much of the railway scene featured in this book is undergoing a massive change and has been described as the largest redevelopment project in Europe. RailOnline

Until recently blackened by soot and certainly not enhanced by the nether reaches of King's Cross, the German Gymnasium off Pancras Road has now been beautifully restored as a restaurant. It was designed by Edward Gruning for the German Gymnastics Society, a sporting association founded in London during 1861. It was the first purpose-built gymnasium in England and opened in 1865, funding coming from Germans living in London. It pioneered women's athletics and hosted Indian club swinging, but the latter has long been forgotten. The building, which ceased to be a gymnasium in the 1930s, is seen in its renovated glory on 24 February 2016.

Unfortunately, not all of the railway fabric in the King's Cross area is in pristine condition. The bricks and stonework at the southern end of Copenhagen Tunnel look as if they were cleaned at some time in the past, but on 24 February 2016 vegetation had gained a good hold on the portal. This was where several scenes from *The Ladykillers* were filmed, including the one where The Professor and Louis met their end. New flats in the background mark the site of Frederick Street and Mrs Wilberforce's rickety house.

The revitalisation of the King's Cross-St Pancras area has to be seen to be believed because it is truly spectacular and there is enough of interest to occupy most of a day. One of the fine edifices which stood derelict for many years and looked as if it might be demolished is the Great Northern Hotel, opened a couple of years after King's Cross and a very fine building in its own right. Here it is on 24 February 2016, now physically linked to the terminus by the spacious covered forecourt which gives access to the booking office as well as the Harry Potter emporium for youngsters from around the world.

Near the booking office at King's Cross is this fitting tribute to the man who created the express passenger locomotives which gave the East Coast main line its charisma for so many years. Herbert Nigel Gresley was born in Edinburgh in 1876 and joined the Great Northern Railway in 1905. After the first of the famous Gresley Pacifics entered service in 1922, he was well fitted to take up the post of Chief Mechanical Engineer of the newly formed LNER the following year. The results of his brilliant mind can be seen throughout this book. He was knighted in 1936 and died in office on 5 April 1941.